THE FRAYNE BROTHERS

Welcome to the terrifying world of the notorious Frayne Brothers

Leighton Frayne

JOHN BLAKE

Published by John Blake Publishing Ltd,
3, Bramber Court, 2 Bramber Road,
London W14 9PB, England

First published in hardback in 2003

ISBN 1 904034 64 0

British Library Cataloguing-in-Publication Data:

A catalogue record for this book is available from the British Library.

Design by ENVY

Printed in Great Britain by Creative Print and Design, Wales

1 3 5 7 9 10 8 6 4 2

Papers used by John Blake Publishing are natural, recyclable products made from wood grown in sustainable forests. The manufacturing processes conform to the environmental regulations of the country of origin.

This book is dedicated to Merryl Hayes

1953 - 2003

ACKNOWLEDGEMENTS

My love and thanks to Merryl who made this book possible, her love and inspiration her patience, and belief in me. And most of all, thank you Merryl, for the happiness in such the short time we both had together.

My thanks to Lauren, Merryl s Daughter who spent many long hours working on this book.

A big thank you to my parents for their unfailing support throughout the adversity and strife, my thanks to my children Zoe Leigh, Leah Jane, Shaileigh Katie and my son Leighton Ray Frayne Jnr, to which through troubled times gave me strength to survive my ordeals.

Respect to my brother, Lindsay who watched my back so many times.

We have a bond only close brothers understand.

And thank you to everyone else who stood by our sides, never to falter, giving support and friendship with loyalty and trust of a family.

YOU KNOW WHO YOU ARE!

CONTENTS

FOREWORD

> When laws are unjust, monstrous, ridiculous.
> That same average man, willy nilly, then becomes the criminal.
> And the law requires a Tcheka or Gestapo with dictatorial powers and no safeguards to maintain the farce.
> Also, corruption in all fields becomes normal in official circles and is excused!

I have been asked time and time again to write about my involvement with Reggie and Ronnie Kray. Many times I have declined through lack of interest. 'What would such a book achieve?' I often asked myself. Such a book would take the reader on a journey of treachery, corruption, highs and lows, and brutal violence.

When I think about the process of becoming a criminal, I'm taken back to when I was 16 years old, when a dozen or so of us lads went on a spree, breaking into shops and schools and stealing cars. It was the summer of 1977 and I was the youngest in our gang. As we all stood in front of the magistrates, the other lads were given probation and I alone was given three months detention. It was as a result of that experience that I learned there is no such thing as honour amongst thieves, and for the first time I fully understood the meaning of the word 'grass'.

Many people say the birth of the criminal is down to the family background. I beg to differ. My brother and I come from a very good and loving family. My father was, at the time, a union leader of thousands of men at the Alcan factory, and a local councillor of Plaid Cymru, the Welsh National Party. My mother was a dinner lady at a local school.

As I sat in the detention cell, suffering many beatings off the warders – which in effect is grown men beating children – then being locked up in a cell all alone, I had plenty of time to reflect. I wondered whether the system was supposed to reform and rehabilitate offenders. Of course it wasn't: it was barbaric, and as I faced the lies, corruption and brutality, the resentment festered and I knew in my heart a criminal was born.

Out of the twelve boys I stood with in court that day, a number went on to become police officers. Others walked around frowning at the path I was to take, but of course they were given another chance that day in court. They were looked upon as 'young men in the making' and in that summer of madness they were described as 'boisterous', their thefts put down to 'their last bit of devilment as they moved into manhood'.

I boxed for Newbridge ABC, coached by my trainers Mr Fred Taylor and Paul Williams, but my boxing skills spilled out onto the streets as I dealt with the bullies, unfortunately leaving many in hospital. My prison terms began as a result of the lies that were fabricated by the bullies due to their embarrassment at being beaten.

It was during those prison terms, in the universities of crime, that I found I could sift through who were the tossers and who were the real men. I was soon to learn that there was an 'us' and a 'them'. I detested the grass, or informer; those who run with the hare and the hounds, so to speak. When they were found, they suffered the consequences.

I am not on a mission to discredit the police, because I am sure there are men who put on that uniform and wear it with pride and are honest and fair in their profession. Once the criminal has hung up his swag bag and the copper his uniform, both can get on in a civilised manner. Yet the criminal could later be on a job and get caught by that very same copper and with his code of conduct will say to the copper, 'Fair cop'. And the copper will go through his nicking in a fair manner, as the law states.

It is codes of conduct I speak of here: the criminal who lives strictly detests the child molester, the rapist, the women beater and those who rob or upset the elderly. Such people are called nonces. As barbaric as it sounds, I have taken great pleasure in beating those slags to a pulp.

Then there are the corrupt police officers, to use a polite term. We look on them as the vilest. The ones who hide behind a system called law. They have no guts or principles and exist in a no-man's-land. However, I must be careful here because there is a difference between this and a fair copper having a hunch that a criminal has committed a crime. It is then that the battle of wills begins.

Corrupt police officers are the ones who lie in statements and in court in order to secure a conviction. It is those slags that I and others detest. Nevertheless, they get the backing of prosecution solicitors, barristers and judges. I have even seen defence solicitors in cahoots with corrupt officers in order to solve a crime.

Where do the Kray twins come into the equation? My brother and I lived by the strict code of conduct and it was through the prison grapevine that we came to the attention of the Kray twins. Am I to be honoured? There is no honour in sitting in jail as a result of people and their bullshit. I won't spoil it for you: take the journey and make your own judgement. Be the criminal, police officer, barrister, solicitor, the judge.

By the last page, you'll be exhausted.

Leighton Frayne, 2003

1

NATURAL LAW

A member of my family had been severely attacked. Even though the police had been called, they seemed more interested in the fact that my brother and I would become involved than in going after the attacker.

I looked at Lindsay and he gave me a look that said it was up to me. Neither of us had any faith in the police to bring justice to the man who had committed the offence. The only law I knew was natural law, but Christmas was only two weeks away so I put any revenge attack on hold until the New Year. The police seemed satisfied that we wouldn't get involved and, as usual, they gave me the bullshit of how they would nail the bastard.

The days passed and I went to my sister's to meet up with Lindsay for a Christmas drink. When I walked through her door she put her hands to her face, but when I asked what was wrong no one gave any answers. So I asked again, 'What the fuck is wrong?'

My sister began crying, then the whole room seemed to erupt, with friends of hers who were there caring for her screaming that the attacker's brother had set upon my sister and her friend the night before. Her friend was in hospital suffering from concussion after being knocked out cold by him, and when I looked more closely at my sister, I could see her ears were bleeding. She was still crying, so I told her she should go to the hospital in case any permanent damage had been done.

We found out that the attack on the two girls took place at a local pub. Lindsay and I were well aware of what a shitpit the place was, and we knew that the two brothers would more than likely be there with all their shithouse friends. Lindsay and I got into the car; there was no need to discuss where we were heading.

I picked up and loaded a .44 magnum and put it in my jacket.

'What the fuck do you want that for?' Lindsay asked.

'Because, Linds, if they are in there they are having some. I've had a gut full of these fucking maggots taking the piss.'

I could see Lindsay wasn't happy about the gun but I wouldn't back down. 'Look,' I said. 'I'll pull the gun if anyone else gets involved, which I know they will. You have the one who beat up our sister, and I will deal with the other fucker, ok?'

We parked the car up ready for our getaway and walked towards the pub. I found a pencil in my jacket pocket and decided I would ram it straight through the fucker's ear. When we reached the front door, we could see the man who had beaten our sister and her friend the previous night sitting on a bar-stool. I told Lindsay to go straight for him while I looked for his brother.

Then we were through the door and Lindsay threw a punch, hitting him off his stool. Then, holding him up by his head, he started punching him big time. His friends came towards us, smashing their beer glasses on the way, but I pulled out the gun, which stopped them in their tracks.

'Fucking move and you are having some,' I shouted.

They all put their hands in the air and Lindsay by then was kicking the fuck out of the brother, splattering blood all over the barman. As we backed out of the door, Lindsay gave one final boot to the top of the brother's head.

There was no sign of the other brother, but I knew where he lived, so we dumped the car and ran the mountain road to his house. I wanted the bastard and I knew full well what I was going to do, but as we got close to the house we realised the police had beaten us to it. Not only were the police there, the armed response unit was also waiting for us.

It was time for us to back off, so we ran back down the mountain and by jumping on a bus we managed to avoid all the police roadblocks. We headed for Newport to give ourselves time to think. We still had the gun, and so we knew if we were caught we wouldn't be asked any questions. With the armed response men in pursuit, we'd just have been shot!

We bought a replica .44 magnum and lost the real firearm, then decided our only option was to get to my house and give ourselves up. I rang my father to tell him what had happened and he pleaded with us to hand ourselves in. We arranged to meet him at my home, and on getting there I placed the replica gun on top of the fireplace.

The police were soon there and we were cuffed up and taken to the police station. I knew there was no chance of bail but felt there was no harm in asking. The police, as usual, gave us the bollocks that although what we had done was wrong they understood why we did it. Rubbish! If they had done their jobs properly in the beginning, we wouldn't have had to take the law into our own hands.

The CID deals with the more serious cases, and who should come along, sticking his arrogant face into mine? It was Gareth Edwards – now an inspector. I used to like him at one time, thinking he was a fair copper.

After going through interviews, and everything else they throw at you, we were remanded, as we expected, and taken to Cardiff prison, five days before Christmas - gutting for anyone going into a shithouse jail. We got onto our solicitors to ask for judge and chambers, still thinking there might be a chance as Christmas was just days away.

Lindsay and I were 'two'd up and we arranged for a visit from our family as soon as possible. We also asked for some cans of beer to be brought in, which – as we were on remand – was allowed. In the meantime, we wasted no time arranging some deals to buy cans of beer from other prisoners. After all, one can of beer wasn't enough to have a piss-up.

After having a good drink on the first night, we were woken by the cell door swinging open and a screw shouting that it was breakfast time. Hung-over, we dragged ourselves out of bed, picked up our piss-pots and headed for the recess to empty them.

As can be imagined, with three to four hundred men all emptying their piss-pots, the smell is disgusting: it is a stench beyond description. In fact, the whole place stank of every bodily odour that God gave man. It is at the recess that the men air their grievances and where confrontations often take place. It is never a surprise to see a man go in to empty his pot and have a wash, and see him come out with his face smashed in.

Having washed, it was down for breakfast.

After picking up the metal tray, which makes a wonderful weapon, the men line up to inch along for a piece of bacon the size of my thumb, and pieces of bread that are like cardboard. Then they get to the end of the queue to have a dollop of lumpy porridge slapped on their trays. Looking at what they call breakfast is enough to turn anyone's stomach.

'Frayne and Frayne, you are to move to a three-man cell,' a screw shouted through the cell door.

'Bollocks,' I shouted back, but the screw was too busy to hear what I had said.

I looked at Lindsay and said, 'That's all we need. Being 'three'd up with a fucking prat.'

We grabbed our few belongings and were standing outside the cell waiting for the screw to tell us where to go, when a lad walked up to us saying, 'You two are in with me.'

The screw came along and confirmed what the lad had said. The advantage of moving was that the lad, who introduced himself as Robert, had been there for some time, so he was well sorted – he even had a radio!

Then came the inevitable question: 'What are you two in for?'

'We have been charged with attempted murder,' I said.

'Oh, I'm in for murder,' Robert said with a smile on his face.

I knew what the smile was about: he was happy to be with someone who was in the same boat. There is nothing worse than looking at a long sentence to then be put in a cell with someone who is only serving a few weeks.

'Well, Robert, I hope I'm not sleeping with one eye open tonight mate,' I said.

'What do you mean?' he asked.

'I hope you haven't got that killing feeling still in your blood,' I replied.

He laughed, so that was good enough for me. Then the door banged shut and we chatted until it was opened for exercise.

'Coming out on exercise, lads?' Robert asked, putting on his coat.

We both shook our heads. We'd had enough exercise running around mountains two days before. A screw poked his head around the door. 'Come on, out you go,' he shouted, but I shook my head. He walked back in and I could see we'd got a nasty one. 'You've got to go on exercise, so fucking shift,' he shouted.

'I haven't got to do fuck all, mate. Now fuck off,' I shouted back.

He stepped back onto the landing and looked up and down. Then, seeing us both on our feet, he pointed his finger and said, 'I will be watching you two.'

Then he slammed the door shut and we could hear him screaming at some other prisoner as he walked up the landing.

Lindsay and I were preparing for our afternoon visit. Being on remand we were entitled to 15 minutes every day, plus we wanted our cans of beer.

After the visit we were told that our solicitors had been successful in applying for judge and chambers with a view to getting bail, but just in case we were refused I pulled some more deals to get extra beer. Robert had sorted himself out with a few cans too, so it was on for the three of us to get pissed and listen to the radio.

'Are we all done?' I asked Lindsay and Robert after we had brought our tea trays up. When they both nodded I kicked the door shut so we could have some peace eating our tea. Our cans of beer were in the window, chilling nicely.

Suddenly the door opened and we saw a few screws standing there.

'Frayne and Frayne,' one shouted.

I immediately got to my feet as I noticed the shithead screw from the morning. Lindsay also stood up, wondering what was about to happen.

'Get your kit, both of you,' the screw said with a smile on his face.

'What's going on, boss?' Robert chirped in.

I could see that even though we had only known him for a short time, he was up for it with Lindsay and me.

'You've got bail, so shift your arses. You are going home,' the screw said, still smiling.

I could see the disappointment on Roberts's face as Lindsay and I gathered our kit together as fast as we could.

'Don't look so disappointed, Robert. You can have all the cans and get rat-arsed tonight,' I said, shaking his hand. Then we were off down the landing, heading towards reception, and before we knew it we were outside the prison in the freezing cold.

As we walked around the corner from Knox Road, we found ourselves in amongst the hustle and bustle of Christmas shoppers. Getting out had been so fast that there hadn't been time to arrange a lift, so we headed to the bus stop. What a buzz we got to think that only a few hours before, we were looking at spending Christmas in jail. Now we were at the bus station waiting to go home.

We arrived home to a big welcome from the family. We were told we had strict bail conditions, which stated that we were to sign on at the police station every day, and were not allowed to enter any public house in our location for a drink. Our solicitor told us that we were lucky to have been in front of a lady judge, but if we breached our conditions of bail we would be back on remand.

We enjoyed Christmas and New Year, and throughout January we kept to our conditions, although we did drink in pubs outside our area.

One night, after a few drinks too many, we decided to go to one of our locals to finish off. The pub was quite full and for a while everything was okay. Then I went to the toilet, where I found Lindsay arguing with two blokes. I tried to calm the situation, knowing that we were on strict bail conditions, but it was getting out of hand and the argument soon came to blows. Lindsay started fighting with one bloke who he said had pissed on his shoes, and I saw the other one pull out a lump hammer.

I grabbed hold of the bloke's hand and told him to let it go, but he wasn't having any of it, so I slammed the head into him, which slowed him down. Then the toilet door opened and more men were coming in, fighting and punching each other. It seemed we had got ourselves caught between two gangs wanting to have a go at each other. It was time for us to leave, but Lindsay hadn't finished with the bloke he was fighting. It was a case of the drink being in and the senses out.

Lindsay went off chasing the two blokes. Although I knew that one had a lump hammer, Lindsay was unaware of it so I had to catch up with him to warn him. As I ran, I was looking for a house brick, or any other object that would stand up to the hammer. I turned a corner to see Lindsay beating the fuck out of one bloke, yet at the same time the other was behind him, smashing the hammer into his head. I ran at the one with the hammer and he caught me across the side of the head with it as I threw a right into him. He turned to run away so I turned my attention to Lindsay, who had keeled over. I could see it was bad: the blood was oozing from his head.

'Are you okay, Linds?' I asked, knowing it was a stupid question. Lindsay just groaned. I looked at his head, which had opened up like a smashed orange. I shook him and he groaned again, so at least I knew he was alive, but then he started mumbling that he couldn't see. I asked him if he wanted me to put him out of his misery – it seemed a fair enough question in my drunken state!

Coppers seemed to come from everywhere. Lindsay was groaning and mumbling as a copper looked at the damage. I was amazed that, as injured as he was, all they could say was, 'You pair are going back on remand.'

An ambulance arrived fairly quickly, so I jumped in while I waited for the medics to tend to my brother's injuries and strap him onto the trolley. While I was waiting, a huge copper came to me asking, 'Is your name Frayne? As soon as I replied that it was, he dragged me out of the ambulance, giving me a few digs as he did so. I couldn't believe he could be so callous, but before he could do anything else people from the pub surrounded us.

It seems a huge fight had broken out and then spilled out onto the street. The gangs then started kicking the shit out of the copper that had grabbed me. I turned him around, which left me taking the brunt of the blows, even though I knew that, whatever injuries he got, I would get the blame. The fight was soon brought under control by other coppers, but even though I was shielding him, the copper began laying into me again. I knew I couldn't chin him so I was shouting like fuck at him.

The next thing I knew was that Lindsay had grabbed him by the head, bitten a massive chunk out of it and spat it on the floor. Then, after ripping his coat in half, he started driving his fists into the copper's ribs. The copper shit himself. I could see he was in shock and blood was pouring from his head. My feelings were mixed: I was glad that Lindsay seemed to be okay after his beating, but I also realised the shit we were in. Lindsay must have had half a dozen coppers piled on him but he was still going hell for leather.

I helped the injured copper back to his car – he was shaking like fuck – then I went to see if Lindsay had calmed down. The medics just stood there not quite knowing what to do about Lindsay, who was still bleeding from his head wound but charging around with the straps he had ripped from the trolley still hanging off him. When I managed to calm him down, the coppers began the friendly approach, so I told them I would go to the hospital with Lindsay. But one of them told me I was arrested because I had breached my bail conditions.

I knew we had blown it and that we would more than likely have further charges brought against us considering a few of the policemen had been slapped. I was put into the car with the injured copper, who was still shaking. The other coppers told him to go in the ambulance to have treatment to his wounds but he refused, saying, 'I am not getting in the ambulance with him,' even though Lindsay had calmed down.

Lindsay was taken to the hospital to see what damage had been done, while I was taken to Risca police station and put in a cell. I could still hear the police trying to persuade the injured copper to go to the hospital and he finally agreed. I called a copper to the cell and showed him a mark on my head, telling him I too had been hit and that the copper had done it. I also told him that I was entitled to go to the hospital under PACE rules (1984 Criminal Evidence Act, sect 28(3), ensuring all detainees receive any necessary medical treatment).

The copper left and I could hear him discussing what I had told him. Soon he came back and agreed to my request and told me that Lindsay was acting up at the hospital. Transport was arranged and we were soon off to the hospital, along with the injured copper.

When we arrived we saw that Lindsay was refusing to let the nurses stitch his head because the police wouldn't take the cuffs off him. I was cuffed to the injured policeman who, although he was still in shock, agreed to take my cuffs off so that I could try to calm Lindsay down. But he wouldn't listen, so I let him get on with pissing them all off.

The injured copper was having a bollocking for taking my cuffs off, but he defended his actions by saying that he wanted to stay as far away from Lindsay as possible. I took the opportunity to tell him that there had been no need for him to drag me out of the ambulance, and I reminded him that even after he had done that I had still shielded him from the punches during the fight. I could sense his remorse and he told me that they had all been told to treat us badly because we had breached our bail conditions.

Lindsay decided he didn't want treatment, so the police took us back to the station in separate cars. The injured copper stayed behind for further treatment – it appeared that Lindsay had bitten away a chunk of his scalp.

Almost as soon as we arrived back at the police station, Lindsay decided he wanted to go back to be stitched and pointed out PACE rules. He said that he was suffering from concussion and that he now realised where he was, so they went back to the hospital.

I was put in a cell, and after an hour or so my door was opened by a policeman telling me that I was being charged for hitting the copper. I pointed out that he had waded into me, which caused the injury to the side of my head, and that the people from the pub had witnessed it. The policeman went away for a while then told me that the officer in question wanted to take it no further, so there would be no further charges.

When Lindsay came back from the hospital with his head stitched, they told us that they were moving us to Blackwood police station for a hearing the next day. We had to travel in separate cars, with extra cars as an escort. I heard them radio through to Blackwood, saying, 'We are bringing in the Fraynes.'

I smiled to myself. They must have thought they were in the Wild West.

When we arrived and were waiting for a cell to be arranged for us, I heard shouting coming from one of the cells. I went over and asked the bloke if he could keep it down, as I had just spent a long night with the filth and needed some shut-eye. Before he could respond, I told him that if he didn't keep quiet I would rip his eye out in the morning. As the desk sergeant locked my cell door, he wondered why the noisy bastard had gone quiet.

We went in front of the magistrates the next morning and, as we expected, were remanded back to jail, this time with no chance of bail.

It was only a matter of weeks since we had walked out through the gates and now we were back: same faces, same landing, same wing.

For the first couple of weeks Lindsay and I played cards – which I hated, but it helped pass the time. We didn't play cards the traditional way, simply because Lindsay and I could remember the order of the cards, so we would know which card was coming next. We found from an early age that we could look at books and remember every page in detail, so for a number of weeks we would each read a book then ask each other questions, like what chapter, page or even paragraph could such and such a word be found in?

We would blank out our cell window so that it was completely dark. One day, we were having an afternoon sleep after the muck they call dinner, when the cell door opened, which was unusual as all the screws were usually on their dinner break. However, when our eyes adjusted to the light we saw a vicar standing there. My heart sank and I looked at Lindsay. His face said it all. I couldn't speak. I wanted the vicar to go away and not say anything. We both knew that vicars never open a door to bring good tidings.

'Leighton,' he said.

I could only look at him.

Then he spoke again. 'Leighton Frayne, can I have a word with you?'

I had no option, so, trying to find some sort of voice, I blurted out, 'Yes.'

'Can you come and see the insurance man dealing with the car crash you and your friend had last year?'

'What?' I said 'What of it?'

He explained that the insurance man was a good friend of his and asked if I would go and make a statement about the crash.

Feeling a sense of relief, and coming round from my sleep, I understood what the vicar was talking about. I'd had a serious road accident involving an idiot who wanted to drive while I was driving, and we had hit a wall, cutting the car in half. With petrol spraying over me I went back into the car and got my friend out. He was well out of it and suffered terrible injuries.

I looked at the vicar and, without showing him any disrespect, told him to tell his friend the insurance man to fuck right off.

Being on remand is horrible because everyone is in the same boat. You don't know where you are going, and sometimes we tended to envy the 3s and 4s because they had already been sentenced and were settled. Yet they would look down at our landing and envy those on remand because of the cans of beer, visits, etc.

We moved across the landing to cell No. 26, which had a big window. Spring had arrived but there was still no sign of a date for Crown Court. Because of overcrowding in prisons, everyone was three to a cell and we were in with a chap called Ray. We had progressed from playing cards to playing Pop Trivial Pursuit, which was another game I hated.

We were having visits from our solicitor and, more often than not, he would bring us fags and we would talk about who was going to be our defence in Crown Court.

It was coming up to Easter, which meant long bang-ups over the bank holiday weekend, and, of all the times for it to happen, I had terrible toothache. The screws just gave me a few painkillers, which did no good at all. The dentist wasn't due in until the Thursday, so I had some serious pain to contend with.

When Thursday came I couldn't wait to get to the dentist and have the tooth out. The bloke next door had a problem with a loose tooth, so we were both taken to the hospital wing where a few others were waiting. We were taken in and given an injection, and what a relief it was. I watched the others go in one at a time and they seemed to take forever; so long, in fact, that the bloke from next door pulled his tooth out himself while he was waiting.

All I could think was, 'Thank Christ for that,' as I knew I didn't have to wait for him to be treated. But I'd waited so long that the injection began to wear off and the pain was coming back with a vengeance by the time they called me in. The dentist told me to take a seat and I thought he was going to have a browse around in my mouth first, but before I knew it he had snapped my tooth. I started tapping him, shouting that the injection had worn off, and I saw the face of the screw sitting opposite me crumple up as he realised the pain I was going through.

The dentist then stuck a spiky thing in and said, 'Oh look, an abscess,' as brown blood squirted all over him. He then stuck something else in, ripped out the rest of the tooth, shoved in a cotton swab and sent me out. I started walking up the corridor towards the nutters. I didn't have a clue where I was going, then two screws came along, picked me up by my arms and dragged me back to my cell. Lindsay and Ray were laughing as the screws threw me on the bed, where I stayed for a few days.

Then we had a visit from our solicitor to tell us who we were having as our barristers. Lindsay had Gregory Bull and I had Patrick Harrington. Bull had represented me in the past and I was not happy. However, in my opinion, they were the best available. I don't find any of the defence barristers to be any good.

Our solicitor began to question us about Lindsay's age, as he had worked out that Lindsay was only 19. I told him that Lindsay would be 21 that coming June, and that if we were to get a sentence we would prefer to be together, but he wasn't convinced and said he would check with my father. I knew I had to persuade Dad to tell him that Lindsay was nearly 21, because if the screws found out the truth Lindsay would be sent to the YPs (Young Prisoners).

I was soon on the phone to my father who wasn't too keen on the idea, but when I explained about us wanting to be together so that we could watch out for each other, and in doing so make it less of a worry for the family, he reluctantly agreed.

We decided to go to the classes that were on offer to all prisoners, mainly because it gave us an hour or two out of our cells. Lindsay and I would take our case papers with us and discuss our case, but one day I forgot to take them back to the cell. A screw came to return them and told us that he understood why we had done what we did, and that the fuckers who had committed the offences should be the ones locked up. It didn't make us feel any better, but at least we knew the screw was honest and fair. We got to know him as Mr GL Davies or GL as we called him.

With the weather breaking, Lindsay and I would go on exercise to get some air and it was during one of the breaks that a screw called our names. He told us that we had a visit from the filth and escorted us to a classroom. We couldn't understand why he was taking us to a classroom because all visits should be held in the legal visiting rooms.

When we went in, we saw two plain clothed coppers sitting by the window. They told us in no uncertain terms to stay out of Wales and never come back. I couldn't believe their cheek. We told them to piss off and were quickly taken back to our cells.

The next day we were taken to Cardiff Crown Court for direction, where the judge offered us a deal of two years.

'Bollocks to that,' I thought. 'I would rather take a chance with a jury.'

We were very close to a date for our trial, and Lindsay and I would often wonder whether luck would be on our side and we'd just get probation.

When the day finally arrived, we were taken to the reception area of the prison, along with others whose cases were to be heard the same day. We were all wondering what fate had in store for us, when we saw a bus pull in at the gatehouse. We were paired up and cuffed, and as usual I was cuffed to Lindsay.

We were the first ones to be escorted to the bus, with a few of the other lads following behind, then the screws jumped on and the bus was on the move. I was a bit confused at that point because there were quite a few lads still in reception, but with the courts at Cardiff being within walking distance of the prison, I thought that maybe the same bus would go back for them later.

'Oh well,' I said to Lindsay. 'We must be straight up with our trial.'

But as the courts came into view I could see the bus driver had no intention of pulling in and we drove straight past.

I shouted over to a screw, 'What the fuck is going on? We are at Cardiff.'

The screw, looking at his paperwork, replied, 'You are all at Penarth Crown Court, mate.

A few of the lads seemed to think it was a good sign for us all, and said that it was very rare that people were sent back to jail from there, so I settled back in my seat thinking that maybe the day would have a good end.

When we arrived at Penarth Court it seemed more like a club than a court. We were taken to the cells, but the strange thing was that the cells were upstairs. A couple of the lads laughed and joked, saying that if we got sentenced the judge would be saying, 'Take them up.'

As usual, we were taken from our cells to have a briefing with our barristers. Our solicitor wasn't there and I wondered if he knew that we were at Penarth. I also wondered whether our family had been told. On walking into the room where our barristers were, I recognised Lindsay's. I also recognised my barrister, Patrick Harrington. I told them that we were not going to plead guilty to attempted murder.

Then we were told that the trial was held up, as the witnesses, and our family, were still at Cardiff. In the meantime, one of the lads came back from his trial with a sentence and I began to doubt what he and his friend had said earlier. We were finally called down to the court, escorted by two screws, and when I looked around I was glad to see that my family and solicitor had arrived.

Judge Martin Stevens took his seat, the jury was sworn in and the trial began.

The first witness was the one brother who was hammered in the pub and Lindsay and I were shocked by what he was saying. He said that what his brother had done was very wrong, and he realised that beating up my sister and her friend was also very wrong indeed. He then went into great detail, describing what his brother had done.

Lindsay and I could see the jury looking at us with sympathy and understanding, and I could see the judge sensed it too.

Obviously, the prosecution barrister wasn't happy with his witness, so he was soon out of the box. Even our defence barrister tried to salvage him for the prosecution, but he was talking away with no one advising him on anything.

The trial was folding quickly and the judge ordered the jury to leave, which they did, still showing sympathy to my brother and me. My father had seen the jury's reaction and arranged, through our solicitor, to speak to the judge from the witness box. When the screws sitting either side of us gave the thumbs up, we were sure it was all over.

My father pleaded with the judge, saying that the family had been through enough, and pointed out that he knew what we had done in the pub that night was very wrong indeed, but the time spent on remand was more than enough punishment for us.

I could see the judge was deliberately ignoring my father and felt like jumping to my feet and shouting, 'Leave the fucker, Dad. He doesn't want to know.'

The judge looked up after my father finished speaking and blurted out, 'That's enough. We will adjourn until after lunch.'

The two screws looked at Lindsay and me as if to say, 'What the fuck is this?'

I must admit I was a bit bewildered as we were escorted up the stairs to the cells.

The screw who brought our lunch asked what was going on. I just shrugged my shoulders. I didn't have a clue. We ate our lunch in silence, then the door opened and a screw was telling us that our briefs wanted to see us.

Patrick Harrington, being the main spokesman of the two, explained the likely sentence if we pleaded guilty to assault occasioning actual bodily harm. The two screws who were standing by us began shaking our hands. Then, as they took us back to the cell, they were tapping us both on the back and telling us we were going home.

Five minutes later we were on our way back to the court. The jury was no longer there but everyone else was in place. We were asked what our plea was and I, along with Lindsay, pleaded guilty to assault occasioning actual bodily harm.

As soon as it was said the judge said, 'Right, two years nine months. Take them away.'

I stood there in disbelief and I think the two screws were even more shocked than us. I looked at my father and could see the strain on his face. Turning, I looked the judge in the eyes, and if I could have made my mouth work I would have told him he was damned.

We turned to walk up the stairs knowing we had a sentence to do, and I knew from that day, I would never have any looks on their system.

Patrick Harrington and The Bull were soon there, giving us all the bollocks, saying that we could appeal. Appeal, my arse. We won that trial.

We were put in the cells where one of the lads asked what had gone wrong, but I couldn't speak. The screw had to tell him. All was silent until we were being cuffed up to go back to prison. Then, as we walked to the bus, the screw indicated that he was willing to give us the chance to run. I looked at Lindsay and his face gave me his answer: Lets do our time and get it over with. On the bus, having had time to think, I realised that the reason our trial had been moved to Penarth was because it was such an emotive subject. They wanted to avoid the publicity that we would have had at Cardiff.

When we arrived at Cardiff prison, we knew we were in blues, which meant we had to wear prison clothes as we had been convicted. As we waited in the reception cells before going to the allocation cells on A wing, I was aware that Lindsay would have had a shorter sentence if they had known he was only 19 but, although I felt a little guilty, I was sure that being together would help our sentence pass more easily.

Then I noticed Lindsay's driving licence on the table. If the screws saw it they would know his real age. I quickly picked it up and handed it to one of the screws and told him that it was mine and should be put into my property bag. I looked at Lindsay and we breathed a sigh of relief as the screw threw it into my bag without looking at it.

We changed into prison blues and grabbed what we needed – blankets, toothbrushes, big plastic mugs – and were taken to the allocation cells where we were put in together. Just outside our door was the television and all the lads were watching it on association – the time when prisoners could do their own thing.

Then who should come to the door but Graham, a good friend from my school days who was in and out of prison as often as me. We both laughed, as Graham was there on my last two sentences too.

Most of the lads who had just been sentenced didn't take long to get off to sleep, and as we, too, prepared ourselves for bed I told Lindsay that we would try to get onto A wing and go for jobs as cleaners.

I closed my eyes and dropped off to sleep, glad to escape the reality of prison life.

2

TWO YEARS NINE MONTHS

It is bad enough waking up on the first morning of a sentence, but it must be even worse to be weighed off, straight from the street.

A screw came to the allocation cell to tell us all to go down to the servery to see the Governor. I just wanted to get to a more permanent cell so that I could settle in and get it over with as quickly as possible.

After we had gone through all the bollocks of the Governor asking us daft questions, we were taken to our permanent cells, which in our case was No18 on A2, right down in the corner by the tea urn, so that wasn't too bad.

Graham, being the cleaner on our wing, knew where we could get a mop and bucket so that we could give the cell a clean, so while he and Lindsay went off to get them I began unpacking my belongings. We had quite a large amount of tobacco with which to do business on the wings, and I had already been warned that a few bullies were on the wander.

I had just finished making up my bed when three lads walked into my cell. The one with the loudest mouth was quite a large bloke who held out his hand and growled, 'Give me your burn.'

There was no point in telling him to fuck off, so I drove a right into his head, hitting him so hard that when he fell he took his two mates down with him. He should have known not to fuck with someone who had just been weighed off. I had so much aggression built up inside that even though I could see he'd had enough I opened up, punching the fuck into his head.

His two mates backed off down the landing then, dragging the fucker back into my cell out of the way of the screws, I hammered him some more until I was out of breath. I kneeled over him and laid down the law. He didn't move, so I picked him up and told him to piss off and that I would be up later to see what tobacco he had for me. With that he staggered off up the landing in a hell of a mess and his two mates, if that's what you could call them, helped him back to his cell.

Lindsay came back to the landing with a mop and bucket and on seeing traces of blood asked me what had happened. I told him the score then we cleaned the landing and our cell, eliminating all traces of blood. When I took the mop and bucket back to the recess, I saw the bloke I had just hammered being taken off by a couple of screws, so I went straight to his two friends and said, 'Let me tell you little fuckers, if you say anything to the screws other than he fell, you will have worse.' They both looked at me with sorry heads. I didn't need to say any more.

Lindsay and I strolled down to Graham's cell for a cup of tea. I knew we needed to get cleaning jobs, as the cleaners were never banged up, but I found out that there was a waiting list, so we added our names to it.

Our solicitor soon came down to see us and said what a terrible deal we'd had in court. He didn't need to remind me of what a terrible deal it was; I only had to look at the '2 years 9' on my cell door. We agreed that the solicitors should go for an appeal. We didn't think we had much of a chance, but it keeps them in jobs, I suppose.

We started a job in the tailors. The bloke running it was a civilian screw and a decent bloke. It passed the time and Lindsay and I found that, if needed, we could make a suit. The weather was getting warmer and it was extremely hot in our cell. Then we found out that the screw from the tailors was going on holiday for a month, meaning that we'd have to do a fair bit of bang-up.

Being locked in a cell in the sweltering heat was no joke, so Lindsay and I developed a way of easing the problem. We got a few extra blankets and made, as best we could, a shower curtain, and by making holes in a washing bowl we had an ideal shower. Lindsay would stand outside the curtain with a mop and bucket, mopping up the water as it ran from our temporary shower.

Being banged up throughout the day in the heatwave was getting us down, and it didn't help that we were down to one visit a month, which was a big difference from being on remand. I found myself looking down at the remands thinking how lucky they were having visits every day.

Our names were soon at the top of the list for cleaners jobs, but the lads who were cleaners on the 3s and 4s had quite a bit of their sentence left to do, so it was a case of waiting. It wasn't as though we were going anywhere!

Both of us needed haircuts but there was no one to cut our hair, so we asked if we could have a razor-blade out of the box. None of the screws would hear of it.

We hadn't bothered to shave and were told that we must make an application to grow a beard, but we replied that we were not prepared to use the razors in the box. We pointed out that, even though each razor-blade was in a particular slot for each individual person, one of them could easily be put in the wrong slot and if that person had AIDS then we would have every chance of catching it. Therefore, we felt we had the right to refuse to use the razors. The screw, GL, took my concerns seriously and presented my case to the No. 1 Governor. The next day the box was ditched and we were all given disposable Bic razors.

Having no excuses, we shaved off our beards and decided to cut our hair with the razors. While Lindsay was cutting mine, I could hear him laughing and when I asked him what was so funny he told me that he had shaved the sides of my head, leaving a clump of hair on the top. I looked like a monk with the hole filled in. We ended up laughing our heads off.

We learned how to duck and dive the screws, and would sit in Graham's cell chatting. Some of the fairer screws would turn a blind eye, but others would march us back to our cell, and we'd be back on the bell. Being on the bell meant having to press a button in your cell if you need to go to the toilet or anything. When the bell was pressed, a box at the end of the landing would display the number of the cell that was calling for assistance. Of course, if one screw put you back in your cell, you'd then look out for a different one to open the door again, with the same excuse! A different screw would open the door and we'd be off on our wanders again.

One of the screws pulled me one day and said there was to be a big release in a week or two, and that everyone with 12 months or under would be given half remission. It was the first time in the British prison system and it wasn't long before I found out that all the cleaners on the 4s were included in the release.

Sure enough it was soon announced on the board in the servery, so I checked to see if Lindsay and I were to be the next cleaners and was given the nod. The civilian screw was due back from his holiday and we needed to go through the proper channels in order to have the new jobs, but when we saw him he told us that he wouldn't let us go. I thought what a bastard he was. If we had shown him any disrespect he would have thrown us out.

GL, being one of the fairer screws, came to me asking whether we had the cleaning jobs, so I explained what the civilian screw had said, and said that we were pissed off with it. He told me to leave it to him, and within the hour he came back to tell us that we were out of the tailors and, as soon as the two cleaners were released, we had the jobs. Lindsay and I knew it would make our lives a little better as the cleaning cell was much bigger, plus it had two single beds instead of bunk beds.

The release date came as we were moving our gear onto the 4s and into the cleaning cell. We looked out of our window and watched as nearly a hundred men walked to freedom under the new half-remission rule.

We soon got our cell the way we wanted it and the cleaning job was a piece of cake. We could have a shower whenever we wanted one and could wander over to B wing anytime we liked. Being cleaners, we found that all the lads who were stuck behind their doors on bang-up would ask us to get them deals regarding their weed. The stuff had never appealed to me, but I saw it as part of my job for the lads. Even though we used to lend out half-ounce of tobacco for threequarters back, we would never see an old boy pick up nips from the floor and would slip him a few ounces and some fag papers.

Another perk of the job was having extra access to the gym. Our sport had always been boxing – we had boxed for Newbridge for a number of years – so we began using the gym regularly and made a makeshift bag in order to keep up our fitness.

We would often look over the railings outside our cell, and by looking through the wire we could see right down through 3s and 2s and both stairs to 43s and the block. '43s' was the term used for where vulnerable prisoners were kept, such as sex offenders or child molesters. They were, obviously, kept separate from the rest of the prisoners for fear that they would be harmed by other inmates. The term came from 'Rule 43', which was the prison system's rule for a vulnerable prisoner. 'The block' refers to the area where normal prisoners were kept for punishment.

One day we saw a lot of activity going on down the block, so I pulled one of the passing screws and asked him what was happening. As he rushed past me he said that they were bringing in a bloke from a top security prison who was to spend a few weeks on a lay-down. This meant that he had gone off big time, so they sent him to the blocks until he cooled down. The bloke walked through A2 with muftis either side of him and screws lining the route all the way to the block.

Graham had his landing going well on the 3s and we soon got our landing running smoothly. We made sure all the blokes on our landing had the best, such as clean sheets or extra blankets if it got too cold, and we found that, because we gave the best weed deals to the kitchen boys by not taxing them, they would arrange for us to have more or less any food we wanted.

Each evening we would go to the kitchens to bring up the tea buckets ready to pour into the tea urn and, more often than not, I would bring up lumps of cheese almost the size of pillowcases. Then Lindsay would run down and bring up onions and tomatoes. As we slid the tea urn up onto the rail, Lindsay would cut the cheese and put it in the sinks in the recess. The lads would then ask to use the toilets and go and pick up their suppers. Some days it would be beef, some days chicken or whatever else we fancied.

The bloke from the top security prison was due a visit and we could see that the screws weren't taking any chances as they lined the corridors, escorting him to the visiting rooms. He looked up at Lindsay and me, stopped and stared but said nothing. I wondered what his problem was as I had never met him before.

Lindsay was down on the 2s doing a bit of business when the bloke came back with the full escort taking him back to his cell, but he stopped by Lindsay and said, 'You remind me of someone I knew some time ago.' Then he smiled and was led down the block.

Lindsay asked one of the screws who he was and was told that his name was Joey Martin. The screw added, 'He's a friend of the Krays. It's reputed that he dug the hole through which John McVicar escaped.'

It soon went around the jail who was on the block and Lindsay arranged to send a parcel down for him.

We were out on exercise one day when Joey called us to his window to thank us for the lump of weed, tobacco and foodstuff. I left Lindsay chatting by his window as I had a few deals to put together, but when he got back he told me that Joey Martin thought we looked like the Kray twins, and that we should really consider auditioning for the main parts in a film that was being made about their lives.

I didn't know who the Kray twins were, let alone want to play their parts in a film, but Joey Martin suggested that Lindsay should write to Reg and gave him the address, and promised that he would write to Reg telling him to expect a letter from Lindsay.

One of the lads on our landing had a book on the Krays called *The Profession of Violence*, and after I read it I felt a little sorry for them for being kept in prison for such a long time. I was surrounded by murderers, some down on visits from Ley Hill, and they were due for release after spending only eight or ten years.

The screws had a bloke transferred from Dartmoor prison who was doing life, and they placed him on our landing when one of the boys was released. I went to see if he needed anything, such as a piss-pot, bowls, etc., but he seemed to have a problem with me. He started demanding this and that, but when I tried to reason with him, he had the attitude that he was a lifer so I had to do as he said. He wasn't willing to listen to me, so rather than give him everything brand new, which I did for all the boys, I went down to B wing where there was a cell for dumping beds, smelly buckets and anything else that had come to the end of its life.

I grabbed every item that the bloke had requested, but the shabbiest I could find, and took them back to him. He took one look at them and, in temper, threw them out onto the wires on A2, then he started shouting at me, but I just smiled and walked away. When the screws heard him shouting they went down to see him, then came to ask me why he had been given such terrible items. I told them that I didn't like his attitude and that I'd only given him what I could find at B wing stores. The screws just shrugged their shoulders and left it at that – after all, I did my job as a cleaner well.

The screws very rarely banged up a lifer, so he came up to my cell, still with a bad attitude. I could have hammered him but I knew he was all mouth and no threat to me, so I asked him to calm down and invited him into my cell for a cup of tea and a sandwich after his long journey from Dartmoor. He was quite taken aback and seemed to lose the attitude straight away, so I went under my bed and pulled out everything he needed, but this time it was all brand new. He looked puzzled, so I pointed out that although I understood his anger at being sentenced to life, he must realise that I, too, was doing a sentence. He was no mug and could see my point, so we shook hands, sat down to a cup of tea and a doorstep of a cheese and onion sandwich and chatted away.

We began to find that we had too much tobacco and that it wasn't being turned into money quickly enough. The only ploy we could think of was to see if the civilian screw would change it for us, but we were well aware that if we asked him straight out to change it, he would tell us where to go. So I went to him and asked him to change our tobacco into other items as I had got it wrong, and he was dealing with so many prisoners that he simply forgot that I did not buy tobacco at all.

We sold everything on a book, from shampoo to chocolate. We

would even have the screws' toilet rolls in bulk from the stores – no one on our landing used the Izal paper, which was pretty bad stuff.

Every Thursday was sheet day, when all the lads would hang their sheets over the rail for collection. The prison only allowed one sheet per man, but we allowed two each as we had deals going with the store boys.

One day in particular there was a new lad in the stores and I told him that we wanted 150 sheets. I was allowed far less but I had to keep the tally with A4 landing numbers. He wasn't having any of it. I even tried to bribe him with tobacco, but he didn't want to know. I told him that he wasn't a screw and I wasn't asking him to do it for nothing, but he had come in with quite a few ounces of weed, so of course he thought he was the big man.

When I got back to the wing, I found he had given us the rubbish sheets. It was no great problem as far as the landing went, as I had hundreds of sheets all over the wing with other cleaners, but the battle was on!

I shut down all lending of tobacco and everything else, such as the potheads' munchies. I waited a day or two, then the lads from the kitchens were up asking for burn to go and buy their weed, but I refused. Then the other cleaners started asking me what was bothering me.

When I explained what had happened with the sheets, the kitchen boys decided to boycott the stores lad and when he went down for his food he found he had only the standard rations. When he gave a questioning look towards the screws they could only shrug their shoulders. He found that anything illegal he wanted was out of reach.

One day, after about a week, he came to my door looking very sheepish and holding a big bag of brand new pants, vests and T-shirts. I had proved the point that tobacco was the currency at that time, and very soon all the lads on the landing were walking around in their nice new T-shirts, vests and pants.

We took an interest in the art classes and found that the teacher, Mr Walters, was a very quiet and patient man. I didn't have much interest in the classes as such. I was more interested in the deals we could pull and whatever gear we could nick, so the art classes were a stopping point for me to have a fag and a general chat.

Mr Walters was the sort of teacher who believed he could do some good with us prisoners, and even though some of us would mess around he would still encourage us to have a go at drawing. I knew I could draw from my schooldays, where coming first in the art class bored me.

At one of the classes, Mr Walters challenged me, along with a few others. He showed us a book full of pictures and said that if we could draw any of them, we would prove to him we had talent and shouldn't be in prison. The pictures were a piece of cake and, of course, Mr Walters was using a form of psychology on us, but I knew I could draw them.

The challenge was on! He supplied me with all the equipment I needed, including the best graded paper, then I was off to my cell. I drew the picture overnight and left it on the side. Drawing from memory was something I'd always found easy, and the next morning some of the lads came in and asked whether they could buy it. Even the screws commented on the professional finish.

When I took it to show Mr Walters I could see he was pleased, and impressed by my ability to draw it down to the finest detail from memory. Not taking much notice of his praise, I gave it to him.

The following week Mr Walters brought in my picture, which he had taken to be framed, and I was impressed with how the frame made it look – so much more professional. Mr Walters said that his wife had told him to give it back to me, and although I didn't want it, he insisted I keep it, but asked me to draw him another one exactly the same, which I agreed to do. The screws wouldn't let me take the picture back to my cell because of the glass in the frame, which I thought sounded ridiculous as we had glass windows and razors everywhere.

Lindsay could also draw and, as well as drawing many pictures which he sold, he would regularly draw portraits of some of the lads' families, charging an ounce or two, depending on how many and what size they wanted.

I was fast becoming the prison's agony uncle and began to compose poems. which the lads would send to their loved ones, claiming they had written them. I often wondered how many marriages I saved by advising what should be written to a wife or girlfriend.

When we looked through our window, we could see work being undertaken on a new gatehouse and, from our position on A4, we could see right over the wall and noticed that even out there changes were going on with the building of a courthouse. Like everyone in prison, we tended to forget about what was going on in the outside world. Those thoughts are enough to get the mind going into overdrive.

Before long, we realised that there was nothing we did not know about the jail. We even had connections with the YPs over on the next block. We communicated with them by shouting over, or sending messages via the lads who worked with the electricians.

One of the nicer screws came to see us one day and asked if we could get an original prison chess set for him. I told him that for a price I could get one and that I knew where one was. I told him that there was one over on the YPs wing, when, in fact, I had one in my drawer, but I knew if I showed it to him then he could well have taken it off me. I told him to come back in a few days and my sources would arrange to get it delivered to me, and he went away as happy as Larry.

Lindsay sometimes wandered over to B wing to smoke the weed with a few friends. One of the lads from B wing cleaners came to my cell asking me to go over and have a puff with them, but I have never been one for taking tablets if I have a headache, let alone smoking weed. But this lad decided to have a few spots, as they call them, and coaxed me into having a go, so I thought that breathing in a few spots off the top of a fag wouldn't do any harm.

After a few spots, he and I began laughing at any old crap, then suddenly the cell door opened and in walked two screws. I tried to keep a straight face, but I couldn't hold it and burst out laughing. The two screws could see we were stoned and the cell must have stunk of weed. The other lad was laughing at me and I was laughing at how serious the screws were looking. Luckily they saw the funny side of it, but if they had been bastards I could have lost my job as a cleaner. That was the end of my weed-smoking days. I like to be in control, not have the weed controlling me.

3

DOING BIRD

We would often have some of the lads skiving in our cell, and one lad in particular hated the screws so much that he would slag them off all the time. He was a big bloke, about 6ft 8in, and 22 stone, and the decision had been made to send him up to Dartmoor prison, mainly I think because the screws found his size too intimidating. I have seen many big blokes return from Dartmoor half their weight, because they weren't given enough to eat. He didn't want to go, but it was too late – he had upset too many screws. I tried to explain to him that it wasn't the screws who had put us in jail, it was the police. It was fair to say that there were a few bastard screws but we tended to stay out of their way.

Lindsay and I were on our beds one day reading the papers, when one of the bastard screws walked in and made a comment about one of Lindsay's photos on the wall. I was straight up off the bed and told him to fuck right off. He was stunned by my reaction and walked out onto the landing, shouting at me as he went. I grabbed him by his collar and told him that if he ever did that to us again I would throw him over the rail. A few of the screws could see what was going on but they just walked away, so it appears that even the bastard screws are disliked by their own, just as bastard cons are disliked by decent ones.

Most blokes in prison just want to get their sentences done as best as they can. It's the bullies I can't stand. Cleaning job or no cleaning job, I give it back tenfold – block or not. One bloke from B wing came to

Lindsay and me asking to borrow a fair amount of tobacco, but when I pressed him on why he wanted so much, as I knew he smoked neither tobacco nor weed, he broke down crying. It's terrible seeing a bloke cry in jail, and believe me it happens many times, but we all know it's a cry for help.

I managed to calm him down and he told me that he had broken into a bloke's house and that the same bloke was on his wing, also doing time for burglary. He said that he was being forced to smuggle money in through his wife to pay the bloke and his mates, which was difficult and, as they had small children to bring up, it left her short of money. He looked at me pitifully, knowing that we were the only ones able to help him, but I told him that I wouldn't lend him the tobacco because he would only be back in a day or two for more. On hearing what I had to say, the colour drained from his face.

When I turned to the drawer, Lindsay thought I was going to give him the tobacco, but instead I pulled out a brand new pair of socks and in one I placed a PP9 battery. I didn't need to tell Lindsay what to do next – he flushed the other sock down the toilet. I made the bloke tell me what cell they were in, then told Lindsay to stay at the end of B wing and give me the all clear when I could go in.

I marched into the cell and hit one of them full in the face with the sock, then I swung around hitting another one. The last one just dropped to the floor, screaming, 'No!' I could see the first one I'd hit was in a bad way and was bleeding pretty bad. The one on the floor was still screaming, so I told him to get up and give me all their burn and he was soon on his feet. As he opened the drawer I saw him try to hide the money, so I gave him a punch to the side of the jaw. He was out of it. I grabbed what I could and on leaving their cell I told them to fuck off down the block as I was going to send others in to turn them over. When I came out I passed the sock, still containing the battery, to Lindsay which he passed to a friend to get rid of, then I went straight to the shower and dumped my clothes – just in case.

When I got back to my cell, the bloke was still there and still upset, so I gave him the money and kept the burn for my troubles. Before long, the screws were running around and taking one of the men I'd hit to an outside hospital, while one of the others came to my cell asking us not to go down the block and promising that they wouldn't say anything. I told him that I would leave it up to the one they had been bullying. The screws seemed to have an idea that I had done them all but, as none of the blokes were talking, they had no proof. They didn't go down the block and they all sorted out their differences.

I was mooching through B wing stores for some old bed bits to put some beds in an empty cell, when I came across a pile of hacksaw blades. I put them back, thinking that someone was plotting an escape – there's not much worse than when one of your own fucks off with your blades when an escape is being planned. Lindsay and I had sussed out Cardiff prison for an escape but we weren't doing long enough to worry about going over the wall. Anyway, the prison was changing: rules were being relaxed and we were allowed to have Walkmans with booster speakers.

As I wasn't a weed smoker, I decided to find out how to brew hooch. The brewing seemed easy enough, so I got some yeast and oranges from the kitchen boys. I soon had a gallon on the go under my bed, but keeping it hidden and stopping the screws smelling it was a problem. So, to disguise the smell, I used furniture polish and metal cleaner, which didn't draw anyone's attention because such items were allocated to us for landing cleaning.

The brew was bubbling away nicely, but we realised it was beginning to stink on the landing, so we decided to put an 'Out of Order' sign on one of the toilet doors and brass up the pipes with plenty of metal polish all around the recess. The idea seemed to work, but it was dodgy moving from the cell to the toilet and back. Once back down in B wings stores, I checked to see if the blades were still there. Nothing had moved, so I took one out and snapped off a piece the size of my finger, knowing that if I got caught with it I would be in stripes or down the block. When I got back to A4, I covered it in dust and placed it on top of the casing which held the electrical wiring.

Just around the corner from our cell was the probation office and the PO's (Principal Officer) office. The PO had the nickname Buttons and he was of the old fold: chest out, hat brim to his nose and, of course, shining buttons on his uniform. I knocked on his door and was told to enter. I stood there and asked if there was any chance I could have an extra visiting order. 'No chance,' he replied. I knew others were getting extra ones from other SOs (Senior Officer) and POs, but no one dared to ask Buttons. I asked again but he wouldn't budge, so off I went.

I then got a chair and ran a brush over the top of the electrical casing as fast as I could. I swept a stone off and watched as it dropped from the 4s to the 3s and hit a screw on the head on the 2s. He looked up and shouted, 'You're nicked.' I had a job to keep a straight face. When he came storming up, I put my plan into action, telling the screw it was an accident and that I had just found a hacksaw blade and was on my way to take it to Buttons. The screw took my word for it, thinking I was a good little chap to declare the blade.

Knocking on Buttons's door again, I entered, held up the hacksaw blade and told him I had found it while working hard cleaning the landing. He couldn't take it off me fast enough. I turned to leave but expected him to call me back, and he did, saying, 'Frayne, I will arrange a couple of visiting orders because of your honesty in handing in the blade.'

'Thank you,' I said, smiling, adding as I left his office, 'I dread to think what would happen if such an implement got into the wrong hands.'

The old gatehouse was finally closed due to the completion of the new one and the new visiting room. I often wondered how the prison managed with the old billet room, as it was so small, and even visits with solicitors were held there, as well as family visits.

Lindsay and I, along with other cleaners, were asked to go over to the new building to clean up after the builders and carpenters. It was very impressive compared with the old one. Everything was modern and even the legal visiting area was separate from the main one, with extra rooms so that each legal visit could be held in private.

The only thing we didn't like about it was that there was panelling in front of each table, so basically we were the other side of a counter from family and friends. However, the screws said that we would get longer visits because of the size of the place.

Buttons kept his word and I had four extra VOs. We thought that if we had a visit from our parents, Lindsay and I could both sit on the same visit. So I asked a screw if it was possible, but was told, 'One visit per man.' I pointed out that there was no point in having a table each if we were chatting to the same parents and friends, but the answer was still no. I had one more idea and that was to ask a PO. Buttons was out of the question as he had given the VOs to me and would just think I was taking advantage.

The only other PO was the one in the centre, and he was a right bastard. When anyone approached him he would look down his nose, with a face like a sack of chisels and his hands behind his back. I asked him if it was possible for my brother and me to sit at the same table with a visiting order, and went on to say that the screw in question had told me that he, as a PO, didn't have the authority to grant my request.

The PO's face went redder and redder, which made me think I was going to get the big, 'Fuck right off', but he put his hands on my shoulders and said, 'You go on a visit with your brother and share a table. And if anyone asks, send them to me.'

I had just conned him and was away to tell Lindsay the good news.

My booze project was a success, and Lindsay and I got rat-arsed for a night or two. The only problem we had was that, because we had the recess so clean, the screws began using our showers after using the gym. So I put the booze making on hold for a while.

Lindsay and I were called to the probation office to begin filling in our parole forms. Having two years nine, or 33 months, we were entitled to apply for parole in the eleventh month. The first thing I was asked was whether I regretted what I had done. I replied that I had no regrets. Then it was pointed out to me that we had beat up the wrong man, but I said that we hadn't, and that we'd had every intention of doing what we did, it was just fortunate for the other brother that we didn't get to him as well. The probation officer seemed surprised. However, being a woman, she understood why we had done it. I filled in the forms with no real hope of getting parole.

Some nights, some of the blokes would have their girlfriends outside, shouting over the wall to them. It amused me, as they would be talking intimately, then half the wing would join in the conversation.

Many nights, Lindsay and I, having the tea urn in our cell, would have a line passing all over the place, sending bottles of tea here and there and, knowing the tea boy was below us, we would often drop him a line and he would send up toasted cheese for our supper.

Very often Lindsay and I would lean over the bars on the 4s, chatting in general, and for a laugh we would whistle 'Don't Cry For Me Argentina'. By the end of the day we would hear about a dozen people whistling the same song, and we would be doubled up to hear that even the night watchman was whistling it. The next day we would whistle something else.

One day, when a new lot of prisoners and remands were coming in, I looked on to the centre to see if I knew anyone, and spotted an old friend called Nipplo. I knew he would be in the allocation cells for the night, so there was no chance of seeing him until the next day. So the next day, when he came up for a cup of tea and a skive, I introduced him to Lindsay. He wasn't happy to be doing bird again: he had done Long Lartin in the seventies with John McVicar.

He got a job cleaning on the centre, so we saw him quite often and, when he wasn't stoned, he was running around doing deals with weed. One day he was asked to go to another landing and do a deal for some of the lads. He pushed the envelope through the door and, taking the weed, he was gone. But when the lads opened up the envelope, they found that the ten-pound note was Monopoly money so, of course, they were none too pleased.

They called him back to the cell door and told him they were going to break his neck, but when he went back to the lads who had given him the envelope, they were stoned and just laughed at him. He didn't know what to do, so I had a word with the lads who had given him the weed, and told them that he'd been had, good and proper. The ones who had given him the Monopoly money weren't prepared to accept they were in the wrong, and as they were from Cardiff they began to mass all their friends, tooling themselves up.

What they didn't realise was that it had became a town and valley dispute, with all the lads from the valleys up for it, and they, too, began tooling themselves up. The screws could sense something was going on, so I headed down to the centre, but the screws must have decided to let us get on with it and went off into the tea room.

The Cardiff lads began to realise that all the valley lads were amassing for a major punch-up. Nipplo was well known throughout the valleys, reaching as far as the Rhondda. The Cardiff crowd knew they were outnumbered and promptly dealt with the matter amongst themselves. The dispute with Nipplo was very short-lived. A valuable lesson for Nipplo, but even after that he got himself into more bother.

He became good friends with the Cardiff lads, and a couple of them were pestering a bloke who was in stripes and also in an E-man's cell, a holding cell for potential escapees – or Category A. The bloke must have been a martial arts fighter and, to relieve the boredom in his cell, kept up his training. Nipplo and a few others were very impressed with his dedication and would lift up the door flap and spy on him, but the bloke was annoyed at being watched and would run to his door, kicking fuck out of it. However, one day Nipplo forgot to put the flap down as he ran away, resulting in the man seeing him.

As he was in an E-man's cell, he was only let out if he was accompanied by a screw at all times, including when he went to get his meals. He soon bumped into Nipplo and told him that he was going to rip his head off at the first opportunity. A decade previously, Nipplo would have dealt with him with ease and more than likely have chopped him up, but now he was older and had calmed down a lot, so he would come to our cell to hide. I tried to persuade him to go and see the bloke to explain that it was out of admiration he was watching him, not malice. But Nipplo felt it was better to lie low and hope the bloke would be shipped out fairly soon.

My business down at the canteen was thriving and I needed other cleaners to exchange their tobacco for such items as toiletries. One day

Nipplo came along with me to exchange some, but what he didn't realise was that, when he was queuing up, screws were bringing in the E-men to get their food, and the bloke he was hiding from walked in with them. By the time Nipplo spotted him he knew there was nowhere to run and the bloke turned around, giving him a nasty stare. Nipplo bowed his head in shame at spying through the bloke's gaff and stood there like a naughty schoolboy. I couldn't help smiling and felt that Nipplo had been put in his place with just one glare.

Then I noticed that the bloke started giving me the eye, so I called him over and told him to forget about the screws and let's get on with it. He was taken aback, but still I told him, 'Either let's have it out, or fuck off and stop giving me the eye.'

He backed down and turned to get his food. Nipplo came back to life like a wilting flower that had just been given water.

Of course, I knew that having it out in front of everyone would have been pretty stupid, so after I took my canteen back I went to his cell on B wing and asked if he would prefer to have it out in the recess when he was due to have a shower.

With respect, he admitted he was in the wrong, and that was the end of the matter for me, but Nipplo became exclusive to him, running around sorting out his deals and taking messages to his mates in other E cells.

I was writing to Phil Regnard, a mate of mine who was due down from Dartmoor prison, and I had a cell prepared for him on the 3s on our wing. I had met him on my last sentence when he was doing seven years for arson. He was a true firebug, always blowing up buildings. As the sentence went on, I could see it was kicking the shit out of him. He was on a visit for a month, and for the time he was there it was nice to see him and chat about the past and, more often than not, about the future. I introduced him to Lindsay and was pleased when they got on well.

Lindsay began getting letters from Reggie Kray, by way of the lads coming to Cardiff prison for visits, but he found the letters very hard to read. After working out what he had written, it was clear that he wanted us to audition for the parts in the film about him and Ron. He also asked if we could send photographs of ourselves to various people.

Not being familiar with the acting profession, I though it was a pretty daft idea, but being in jail we all tended to grasp at anything that could lead to us bettering ourselves when we got out. We went to photography classes, and the screw who dedicated his time to the evenings was a very nice chap named Mr Miller, who was more than happy to help, but pointed out that we had to take a genuine interest in the class. We found that we actually enjoyed the class and Mr Miller had a lot of patience with us. We were even able to take and develop our own photos, as requested by Reggie.

We each had a Walkman strapped to our waistbands, and Lindsay and I would find a kind of solace buffing the landing with the electric buffers. We also found that the more polish we put on, the more the floor would come up like glass after buffing. So all the cleaners got it into their heads to buff the floors outside the cells, then we would wait for the female probation officers to come along, stop them for a chat and have a good look up their skirts.

It amazed us cleaners that as the prison was so strict on cleanliness. Every night, when we went down to pick up the tea buckets, the 1s on B wing would be infested with cockroaches: not just one or two but thousands. We were glad to be high up on the 4s of A wing, where most of the lads would use their green top blankets as rugs on the floor, just to make it that little bit more homely.

Two lads from Scotland, who had been doing a bit of pick-pocketing at the football games in Cardiff, were moved onto our wing and I watched one of them lift a screw's wallet and, as he walked back around the other side of the wing, he put it back. He knew there was no way he could keep it, as he would have been the prime suspect.

Graham came running from the office one day, telling me that he had seen that one of the lads had got parole but the other hadn't. I asked him if he was sure and he explained that, if the letter was small it was a knock-back, but a big letter indicated that parole was being given. I decided to go and tell the one that he had parole and, as sad as it was, the other hadn't.

Their cell door was locked, so lifting up the flap I called the one to the door and told him that we had seen proof that he had parole. He began dancing around with joy. The other lad asked whether I had any information about his application, but I could only give him the bad news. The one was dancing like an idiot and I couldn't blame him, but he was ramming it down his mate's throat that he was off home to Scotland.

The screws came around opening the doors for exercise, and the lad who'd got parole danced his way down the steps. I couldn't help feeling sorry for his friend, so I invited him up for a cup of tea. He was so upset that he hadn't got it I thought he was going to cry, but I told him that he shouldn't feel alone as we were all there for him.

When exercise was over, his mate was still dancing, and by that time had arranged to give his shampoo and other items – what we call a drop

– to his friends. This upset the lad even more because he felt that his mate should have left all his gear to him.

The screw was soon around with the mail and, just as Graham had said, a small letter went to one and a large letter to the other. But the lad stopped dancing as he read his parole answer – while his mate was jumping up and down waving his parole paper in the other's face.

Graham was soon at my cell telling me he had got it wrong. I felt terrible and, even though I tried to tell the lad who was expecting parole that I was sorry for the mix-up, he must have been in shock because he didn't move. The worst news for him was that his mate was out the next day. After that, I made sure that he wanted for nothing. I had learned a very valuable lesson: as much as we all like to see someone get parole, never get involved. Leave it to the screws.

Lindsay and I became friendly with two lads named Tom and Steve, who were serving a short sentence for fraud. They were a little out of their depth in the prison system, although they were clever little bastards and there was nothing they didn't know about electronics.

They could convert an ordinary radio to one that picked up all sorts, even the screws' radio messages. We would sit and chat over a cup of tea and they would tell us how they had bugged businesses, playing one businessman off against another. But they weren't very criminally minded and had been caught for getting credit card numbers electronically, and trying to take the money out of the cashpoint machines.

Tom was the specialist on computers, which were way above my head, while Steve was the expert on radios. They were a likeable pair but always seemed to be in bother with electrical items, and alarm bells on the wing would go off at random as the pair of them giggled away. Lindsay and I could only smile, but we kept an eye on them from a distance, knowing they were easy targets for bullies.

Christmas was soon upon us, and we were all given small Christmas cakes from the kitchen, but most of the lads didn't want theirs, so, rather than throw them away, Lindsay and I stored them in our cupboards.

The church held a Christmas service and two presenters from Radio Wales, Roy Noble and Frank Hennessey, did a live broadcast and interviewed a number of the lads. Word had gone around about how I wrote poems (a talent I've no doubt I inherited from my father, who wrote wonderful poems) for the lads to send to their wives and girlfriends, so I was invited along.

I had just written a poem, which I called 'Peace at Christmas', and was asked to read it for the live radio programme. All the lads had tuned in on their radios and when I finished reading it, I heard a loud roar of approval coming from the wings.

The next day, a number of screws turned up with orders from their wives to bring tobacco in for me. They said that their wives had listened to me reading the poem on their radios and it had brought tears to their eyes.

With Christmas and New Year out of the way, we were waiting to hear about our applications for parole, but we weren't very hopeful. However, when the letters came we were shocked but very pleased to read that we were both given six months' parole. This gave us a summer release.

4

BUSINESS AS USUAL

As any man or woman who has spent time in prison knows, the day of release brings a buzz that can only be understood by the prisoners themselves – however long or short the sentence – and is indescribable to those who have never experienced it.

Lindsay and I had spent a sleepless night talking about what we were going to do, where we would go, what beer we wanted to drink and so on. With our bed packs all wrapped up and our belongings packed in our prison-issue bags, we sat and waited for the door to open. I looked through our cell window to see if my father was in the car park and saw the screws arriving ready to start their shift.

Turning around to Lindsay, I said, 'I can't see our dad's car out there.'

'Don't worry, he'll be here,' Lindsay replied.

As I heard the screws coming onto the landing, my mind began to race. What if he'd forgotten, got the date wrong? I felt a shiver run down my spine; this was our day, our release. In my mind I was screaming, 'For fuck's sake, open the bastard door.' Then I heard a screw outside our door. His keys clanked and the door swung open. Standing there was GL and, with a big smile on his face, he said, 'Well, lads, this is it. Got everything ready?'

We nodded.

As we walked up to the recess to have our final wash, GL told Lindsay that he could now celebrate his 21st birthday in style. Lindsay and I looked at each other. We both knew GL was a very fair man and we shook his hand as a man, not a screw.

We were soon in reception, where we dumped all of our prison kit, stripped off and put on our own clothes, which had been boxed up for so long. Everyone was chatting happily and as soon as we gave the screws our names and numbers they handed us money to get us by.

As we waited by the reception gate with our own clothes on and money in our pockets, we began to feel the full effect of the buzz. We were on our way to freedom. We went through the new electronic gates and entered the gatehouse to give our names and numbers, as another screw checked our photographs. Then came the nod to release us.

We stood in silence as we watched the big door slide open, giving us our first glimpse of freedom, and some of the lads were through the door when the gap was barely big enough for them to squeeze through. Then, finally, the door was fully open and I could see my father on the other side waiting to greet us. I took a final look at the bleak building that had been my home for well over a year. We were on our way back to the valleys.

Lindsay and I knew we had problems ahead after the threat we'd had from the two coppers while we were on remand, but for the time being I put it to the back of my mind. As we travelled up through the valleys, I'd forgotten how beautiful the area was: how green the trees were, how high the mountains towered up to the sky. As I breathed in the fresh air, the stench of prison was quickly erased from my mind.

Our family and friends welcomed us home and, although it was only nine o'clock in the morning, the beer was flowing.

Like most prisoners on their release, I wanted to believe that my life of crime was at an end and that this was a fresh start, but I knew deep down it was only the beginning as I watched a police car pass by – their way of letting us know they knew we were out. However, I wasn't going to let them spoil my day, so it was drinks all round.

Lindsay had given Reggie his address and they were writing to each other regularly. The audition date for the Kray film passed, but deep in the back of my mind I wondered if it could have been us playing Reg and Ron.

We had a friend in prison who had promised to sort out cars for us on our release, but Lindsay and I felt that he was all talk, we had heard it all before. However, we were proved wrong and cars were soon ready to be picked up.

The days passed with such speed that it was soon time for Lindsay and me to decide what we were going to do in the future. We both knew we had no chance of ever getting jobs, so we decided to set up our own business.

As we were good at art, we advertised in local papers offering our services for things such as personal drawings, paintings, etc., and, to our amazement, we began selling.

We approached the Welsh Development Agency (WDA), which gave financial advice as well as advising on selling techniques abroad. Soon we were being invited to seminars in the city.

We met a lot of businessmen at the seminars and the conversation would usually begin with how interested they were in our business. However, most people would then go on to say, '*If* I get back some money I'm owed, *then* I would be happy to buy your artwork.'

This sounded more like my cup of tea. Even though Lindsay and I had a talent for drawing, we considered it a pastime while in prison, but to sit down when we were free and draw a picture pissed us right off.

Soon we were huddled in corners, with other businessmen giving details of who owed what and to whom, but we made it clear that on no account would we chase after money at people's homes. The host of the seminars would approach us at the end of each one and ask whether it had been beneficial. We would simply smile and say, 'Nice.'

We soon got the hang of going to business premises and telling debtors we had come to collect the money they owed, and if they didn't pay up I would give them a few slaps. Shaken up, they were only too pleased to drive to the bank and pay, just to get us off their backs. We would then return to the businessmen with their money, take our percentage and sell them one of our pictures. Word soon got around and more and more businessmen approached us, wanting us to recover their debts, and the amount of money involved became greater.

On one occasion we took a job where a business rival, who owed a considerable amount of money, had a number of men around him for protection. Of course, we knew that for him to need protection he couldn't be on the straight and narrow. We also knew that if we approached the bloke and asked for the cash, there was no telling what tools or weapons his minders would have. But we had an advantage over them: they didn't know us and they weren't expecting a visit.

We arranged a meeting, fooling him into thinking it was about a business deal, and when we arrived at his office the main man was surrounded by three of his people, which we expected. With no ifs or buts, I went for one, chinning him out cold. Lindsay wasn't far behind, knocking the other out. The other bloke gave us a look which said, 'It's fuck all to do with me.'

The businessman didn't flinch. He smiled and said that he liked our style, then asked what the problem was. We told him that we had come on behalf of his old friend and asked for the money. He replied, 'No sweat. Cash or cheque?

'Cash,' I said. As he got up from his chair, Lindsay and I moved forward. I knew that if I saw him going for anything he was going to have one hell of a hook, but he explained that he was getting the key to the safe to give us the money. When he opened the safe, we could see it was full to the brim with cash, and even after he had taken out the cash we had come to collect, there was still a hell of a lot left.

As we picked up the money, the two blokes were coming round and the businessman looked at them, then at us, and asked us whether we would consider working for him full time. I looked at Lindsay, then back at the bloke, and together we said, 'Na.' And with that we were through the door and away.

A few of the lads we had met in prison were due out, so we arranged to go to Cardiff to pick them up. You know when you've met a good bloke, because they don't bullshit you. Lindsay and I knew we needed to bring in a few good blokes and found they were all up for it.

Lindsay had mentioned our art business to Reggie in letters. Reg suggested that a friend of his, who was on the out, may be able to help. This friend was Pete Gillett. We knew from seeing press reports and a TV programme that he called himself Reggie's adopted son and I remember thinking, 'God, the lengths some people go to in order to become adopted at that age.'

Using the telephone number Reg had given, I rang Pete, who immediately asked what I wanted and what I could do, then started going on about how art wouldn't get me anywhere. I wondered whether this bloke would talk to me the same way if we were face to face. I very much doubted it, as I knew he would have been minus one eye, with it being rammed down the back of his throat. 'Oh my,' I thought, 'I am speaking to Reggie Kray's adopted son – fucking tosser.' And that was the end of that conversation.

Lindsay sent a letter to Reg telling him about Gillett's attitude. Reggie's reply was that Gillett was okay really, he just got carried away with himself from time to time.

People began to show an interest in our drawings. Lindsay and I would draw in the style of Boris Vallejo and we did a number of copies of his work in pencil, but decided we needed to develop our own ideas. Most of Boris Vallejo's work was of nudes in the fantasy art theme, so we decided to book our own model and take photographs, directing the model in the poses we felt we could elaborate on in a similar setting. We arranged the photo shoot; we knew how to operate the camera and lighting equipment, as we had been taught in the photography class in prison.

We had a chat with the model, who introduced herself as Lisa, told her our ideas and soon had the photographs we needed to start work. Our aim was to produce the pictures in a futuristic theme. We would then run off copies in bulk to sell to Athena International.

Businesses in the South Wales valleys were expanding as a result of new small units and factories being built, so we made enquiries with a view to renting a number of factories. Of course, we needed silkscreen printers and major equipment, but we knew that once all that was organised, avenues would be open to us throughout the world.

Lindsay and I would often drop in to our local boxing gym at Newbridge, where we had boxed for years and, apart from doing a bit of bag work to keep ourselves in trim, we enjoyed chatting with our trainers: Paul Williams, Ted Price and Dennis Rogers. Paul was the main trainer and had always been there for us, even when we were in jail. He was there for all the lads, irrespective of their ages, and gave them lifts to various boxing venues throughout the country.

Newbridge Amateur Boxing Club had a number of British and Welsh champions, ranging in age from 11 upwards. The gym must have been one of the roughest in the country, the sparring gloves were from the year dot, and when sparring we all used to hate the one who had grabbed the old gloves, which had been made in the 1950s and were filled with straw.

Sitting in the corner, never missing a day, was Fred Taylor. He had started the boxing club in 1940 and was well into his eighties. He never said a lot, but if any of the lads had problems with stiffness or knots, it was as though Fred's hands could enter the skin and relieve all the pain.

Sometimes we would ask Paul about giving the place a coat of paint, but he would reply, 'You have come here to box, not to watch paint dry, now get on with your training.'

We became friendly with a bloke named Paul Chamberlain, who was from the next valley and whose two brothers I had met in Cardiff prison – one of them was starting a four year sentence just before I got out. I got on with Paul from the start. He had a problem with one of his own standing against him in court, so rather than send his own people to deal with the matter, which would have looked too obvious, we visited the grass ourselves. We booted his door in and dragged him outside his flat where we gave him a few digs, then hung him over the stairs, telling him to lose himself for some time. Hanging upside down, with piss running down his legs to his face, he was more than eager to oblige.

We began to move over each valley, meeting up with others who had the same sort of problem, and it was agreed by all that if we dealt with their shit they would come and deal with ours – an arrangement that worked to everyone's advantage.

Meetings – sometimes involving 50 or so people – became very frequent, so we found a number of pub managers who were more than happy for us to take over rooms at their pubs. However, with such a large number attending, we felt we were becoming a bit conspicuous, so we decided to reduce the meetings down to a more practical number.

We began to find out who the police informers were and would arrange to buy a shipment of goods, which was all legal and above board, then tip off who we suspected the informers were, telling them that we had a truck load of hot gear coming in. They would then run back to their handlers, who would fund them to buy goods which they thought were stolen, and we would double our profits.

A few of the lads would play cat and mouse with them over the goods and where they could be picked up, knowing full well the informers were being followed in order for the police to build up a case against us. But, of course, we had receipts for everything, and we must have sold off thousands of pounds worth of goods to them. We would laugh like hell wondering what they were going to do with it all after they realised it was all bought legally. When the informers' handlers did the bust, they found that everything was in order and they could only watch in disbelief as we produced the receipts, before going on to receive a massive bollocking from their superiors.

I was in a meeting when one of the lads came over to me saying that two strange-looking blokes wanted a word with me. When I looked through the door I could see Tom and Steve, looking like two professors. I asked them what they were doing in our neck of the woods and they said that they wanted to work for us, telling us that one of the lads working with us was under surveillance by the police. I called Lindsay over and told him to end the meeting a bit sharpish, then I invited Tom and Steve for a drink at another place so that they could tell me in more detail what was going on. They happily agreed, so we headed back to a friend's house.

When we arrived, Tom and Steve went to the boot of their car, where they took out silver-coloured cases and asked to talk inside. They explained that they had picked up police messages regarding one of the lads, who, it seemed, had been under surveillance for some time. When they opened the cases it was as though the FBI were about to set up an observation post. They had taped police conversations with a machine they called a scanner, which was very new to me – we had the simple method of tuning into the police on an ordinary radio. The two of them laughed, telling us how out of touch we were and that technology had moved on considerably.

Lindsay and I, on a more serious note, asked them how they could justify working for us. Tuning into police messages was all very well, but it was something we could do ourselves on a radio. They told us that, for a fee, they would monitor information and relay it directly back to us. I had to give them ten out of ten for asking, and I could see that it would be extremely useful to us. I knew I could trust them: they were good blokes, so I felt we had nothing to lose.

I gave them a drink while I talked to Lindsay in another room, but he didn't seem very impressed. I explained the advantages, not just for us but others within our circle, and he nodded hesitantly. When we returned to Tom and Steve they asked us to listen, then Steve turned on one of the machines. The cheeky bastard had taped the conversation Lindsay and I had just had in the next room.

When Tom explained that they had up-to-date bugging equipment I was even more impressed, then Steve took the telephone apart and I watched in amazement as he checked to see if it was bugged. They were pulling wires here, there and everywhere. It was like being with two Inspector Gadgets. I sat down and asked what their fee was.

'A couple of grand,' one chirped up.

'A couple of grand for listening in to the police? You are having a fucking laugh,' I said, laughing myself. But they were serious and pointed out that their equipment would get more sophisticated as time went on. I told them we would think about it, and after a drink and a chat we bade them goodnight.

Immediately I telephoned the lad that Tom and Steve had said was under surveillance. I knew he was involved in selling weed, although I didn't have a clue how much was involved. I was beginning to get paranoid, and decided to set up a meeting that night. There were areas throughout South Wales where we were able to have confidential meetings, safe in the knowledge we hadn't been followed. So, agreeing on a venue, we met up and relayed the conversation we'd had with Tom and Steve.

It was agreed that it would be wise to have Tom and Steve on side, as they were able to check if any more of our boys were under surveillance. As we were grateful for the information they had given us, a token payment of £500 was given, with a further meeting arranged to put them on the payroll on a temporary basis.

Within a week or two, Tom and Steve proved without a doubt what great assets they were. It was quite an eye-opener seeing them bugging everyone and tapping the phone lines of businessmen.

Lindsay and I, and many others within our circle of friends, despised hard drugs, and although smoking cannabis wasn't my cup of tea, I didn't see it as a hard drug. Of course, some people would disagree, but I can only say that I would prefer to be in a room full of potheads than a room full of pissheads.

It was well known amongst police and solicitors alike that hard drugs were given a wide berth by us. One establishment figure in particular came to Lindsay and me asking for help as a relative was being supplied with drugs and was developing a very bad addiction. He went on to explain that the police would do nothing about this major supplier, and it was felt he was an informer for higher-ranking officers.

A meeting was set up with all our friends and contacts, including contacts from what we termed the prison university, to find out the identity of the supplier. With the solicitor present, and all relevant information compiled on this particular drug dealer, it was decided to hit him – along with others – big time. We knew that his minders and users surrounded him, but we were prepared to deal with them all.

Our sources came back with the information that the dealer was doing quite well in his trade of selling heroin. The main priority, as far as we were concerned, was to find out if any children were living at the place we were to hit. This code of conduct, which we followed strictly, ensured that, regardless of who we were to grab or slap, we would not be taking any grievance to a man's family home.

We placed the drug dealer's house under a 24-hour watch to monitor his comings and goings. In the meantime, our surveillance chaps found no evidence that this person was under surveillance from the police, which assured us that he was a police informer.

With everyone and everything in place we made our move, but we must have been spotted going down the drive as they were all piling out of the back door, leaving the dealer and one minder in the building. The dealer came out and challenged Lindsay as I went through the building after the others. One of the minders had no intention of running and, as he smoked his fag, let me know that he was up for it. Grabbing his hand, I pushed the fag into his eye while at the same time driving a few good hooks into his ribs. Then, screaming in pain, he too was heading for the door.

Lindsay had done the damage on the drug dealer by busting his nose with a split from eye to eye. Then he laid the law down to him about shoving his shit onto youngsters. He seemed to get the message.

It wasn't long before the police were on our case, which added more weight to our theory about him being an informer. He had obviously run to his handler looking a right mess. To my surprise, it was Lindsay who was charged, with no mention of me, and the case was thrown out of court. The job had been successful.

A few of our lads who were still in jails throughout the country, such as Cardiff and Dartmoor, would suffer problems, and I vowed when I was in jail that I would never let them be forgotten. If I said that things were going to be sent in I kept to my word. I have heard it so many times when people promise to keep in touch and you never hear from them again. After all, you never know when you could end up back in jail and be glad of help from them.

One of the lads, Carl, was serving a few years and had come down to Cardiff prison for visits. He was troubled by some prick going to his home, pestering his wife and coming onto her. She was petrified but knew that the police would do nothing about it. I was enraged. I detested people like that and knew what it could do to a man when he was stuck in a cell all day not being able to protect his family. There has been many a good bloke who has put himself upon the bars because of arseholes trying it on with his girlfriend or wife when she is vulnerable with her bloke in jail.

Of course, some women don't give a fuck and put it about, hoping their blokes won't find out. But this particular case was different: the wife wanted nothing to do with the bloke, proving that there are some who stand by their men.

I got the address, and Lindsay and I made our way to the house. The door was opened by a meek-looking woman with a baby in her arms, and I could see the strain on her face. We introduced ourselves as friends of her husband and said that he had explained the situation about her being pestered. She looked quite surprised. I asked her the name of the person who was giving her grief and if she wanted it to stop. She gave me his name. I had heard of him. She then said that he was a right nutcase and everyone in the village was afraid of him.

When we asked where we could find him, she looked at her clock and said that he would be calling by very soon, as he did regularly. She went on to say that he had a bad reputation in the area and thought nothing of putting blokes in hospital. I checked with her one more time that what she wanted was for him to leave her alone, but she seemed more concerned that if we said anything to him, he would cause her more grief. It was obvious she was terrified.

I told her not to worry and asked if she could go to a friend's for a few hours. Without hesitation she grabbed her coat, but before she left I asked what he looked like. 'Bald head and mad eyes,' was her reply, as she quickly disappeared through the door.

We didn't have to wait long before there was banging on the door; the prick didn't even knock, he just kicked the door. When I opened it I could see he was surprised.

'Who the fuck are you?' he asked, with an attitude.

In my mind I was saying, 'Your worst fucking nightmare,' but I replied, 'Carl's cousin. Me and my brother are down to visit him at Cardiff.'

He walked straight past me with a tray of 24 cans and went into the living room, where Lindsay just sat looking at him. I have come across many blokes who put the mad act on, displaying psycho eyes, such as this bloke.

I asked him if he was going to give us a can of beer, and the cheeky bastard wanted us to pay £1 for one! I gave Lindsay the nod to keep him talking and said I was off to the toilet. Then I went upstairs, tied a length of flex to the banister, and hung it down the stairs before walking back into the room.

He asked Lindsay about being in prison and said that the prison wouldn't have him as he got into fights, so he was sent to a nuthouse. I knew what he was talking about: it was a Regional Secure Unit (RSU), where most of the lads go when they have mental-health problems. But there are some who pretend they have problems in order to avoid prison – the ones who can't handle their bird. Swilling his can down and farting, he was getting right up my nose. I thought I would give him one last chance to fuck off, so I told him he was frightening Carl's wife and asked if he thought it was about time he fucked off.

He didn't have to say anything. His eyes said it all. As he jumped up I threw a cracking right hand and pole-axed him over the chair. Lindsay was on his feet and we grabbed him and dragged him into the hall. We lifted him up, and I shoved his head into the electrical flex, at the same time as grabbing his feet.

He began to splutter and gasp for air but Lindsay had hold of his hands. Then, with his eyes looking as if they were about to pop, we lifted him up, took the flex away from his neck and dragged him back into the room. If I'd had my way I would have kicked ten tons of shit out of him, but it would have messed up the woman's house.

While he was still reeling from his ordeal, I jammed his hand in the gas fire and switched it on. I had no pity for tossers like him, and I knew what he had put Carl through. He deserved what he was getting, and while he was screaming like fuck, I slammed another bastard of a punch in for good measure.

Lindsay helped himself to the cans of lager and took a seat. I knew the bloke had had enough so I told him that if he ever came back, or bothered Carl's wife again, I was going to strap breeze blocks to his feet and hang him. Then, slinging him onto a chair, I asked him whether he wanted a can of my lager to help him with his pain.

His hand had popped open like a burnt sausage, and as he came round, his psycho eyes looked more like puppy eyes. Then I told him that I hoped he could grow wings in the next few seconds and, while he was still looking puzzled, Lindsay and I got to our feet, grabbed him – he wasn't on the small side – and threw him out through the door head first. He landed on the path with a hell of bump. Then, with his arse hanging out of his jeans, he was soon on his feet, bolting down the road and running out of sight.

A number of lads asked our advice on evading the police by installing cameras and tuning into police radios. I was tied up with boring matters to do with the legal aspect of our business, so Lindsay brought in Tom and Steve, who were specialists on the subject.

After spending a week away, Lindsay said that when he'd been with them, at a secret location, he could see why the lads wanted the cameras, as they were growing cannabis plants on a huge scale, and that he'd seen thousands of plants of dozens of different varieties. Tom and Steve had done a professional job and Lindsay had learned how to grow a plant from a cutting, through the various stages right up to the finished product.

Our business ventures had begun to separate, and sometimes Lindsay and I wouldn't see each other for a few days, sometimes a week. We later found out, when talking about what we'd been doing, that we were protecting both parties: Lindsay would be protecting the rivals of who I was looking after. The money was good and no one was complaining, so we couldn't see a problem and carried on going about our business.

5

TAKING CARE OF BUSINESS

Letters were coming thick and fast from Reggie. He wanted Lindsay and me to get involved with selling the new book which Fred Dinage had written about him. He also wanted our advice regarding picture posters of him and Ronnie. Reggie had asked Lindsay for his home phone number and they were soon chatting regularly. He wanted us to go to London to meet Tony Lambrianou and a lady friend named Liz, who arranged to meet us at Paddington station.

We found her in the station cafe, then went on to a nice little pub in the heart of London before our meeting with Tony that evening at a pub in the East End. We had an interesting chat with Liz and it was obvious that she was very close to Reg, and I was interested when she told us that she dealt with the publicity for the band Dire Straits, as I liked their music.

We booked into a plush hotel called The Great Eastern, and after we had freshened up with a shower and change of suits, we were soon on our way by taxi to the heart of the East End to meet Tony at a pub; a meeting which had been pre-arranged by Reg.

When we walked through the door, the place went from hustle and bustle to total silence. I asked the lady behind the bar if she could tell me if Tony Lambrianou was around but, with a look of horror on her face and shaking her head, she said that he wasn't there. Almost immediately, from the shadows, a figure emerged with his hand outstretched – it was Tony.

During the evening, Tony introduced us to his girlfriend, Wendy, and a number of his friends, including James Campbell and Adrian Bullen, who I got on very well with. Liz turned up with a friend who she introduced as Carol Clark. She was also in the music business, as editor of *Melody Maker*.

It was becoming a little embarrassing as Tony, along with others, kept repeating how much we resembled Reg and Ron and that we should have been the ones playing them in the new film, *The Krays: Bonded by Blood*. Nevertheless, we found the East End people to be very warm and friendly, and after our discussions we had a lovely evening.

Tony wanted to meet us the next day for further private discussions, so after checking out of our room we met him in the small hotel bar where we discussed various topics regarding Reggie and Ronnie. As Tony walked us back to the train station, he asked if we could lend him some money as his cashpoint card was broken.

After we returned home, Reggie telephoned Lindsay to ask how our trip to London had gone, and whether we had got on with Tony. He wanted Lindsay and me to go to a charity boxing show in aid of a little boy who'd had a nasty accident abroad, after which he wanted us to go to Broadmoor to visit Ronnie.

Reggie also wanted us to check out James Campbell who, with several others, was organiser of the event. Many famous people had been invited and were giving their support by raising funds for the little boy. The show was being held at a lavish hotel at Woodford Bridge, London, so we decided to book ourselves in the day before the event.

When we arrived, we contacted James Campbell and he was soon in our room joining us for refreshments. He told us that he was having problems with Pete Gillett and a bloke called Nicky Treeby, and that he was putting deals together only to be discredited by Gillett. I pointed out that I had spoken to Gillett some time before, as Reg had advised, concerning business proposals, and had found him to be very unprofessional. I also said that I found his adoption by Reg highly amusing.

Campbell asked if he could leave some of the items donated for an auction, to be held at the event, in our room overnight. One of the items was a platinum disc signed by all the members of Dire Straits. I liked Dire Straits' music, so to see the signed platinum disc gave me quite a buzz. There were other items from Tina Turner, David Bailey and many more celebrities who had kindly donated to this good cause.

We had a long chat with Campbell but I couldn't understand what Reg wanted checking out; he seemed genuine in his business dealings, and I well understood his dismay at having deals taken away from him.

The next day he came back with the bombshell that the little boy had died, and he was at a loss at what to do: whether to let the show go ahead or cancel. We suggested that he had a word with Reg, who told him to go ahead and give all the proceeds to the little boy's family.

A meeting was arranged in the bar before going into the main room where the boxing bouts were to take place. It was a smart event with all the men in dinner suits. When we met up with Tony he took us to meet Charlie Kray and, judging by the look on his face, he also thought we looked like his brothers. We bumped into Liz and Carol who introduced us to Kate, who was then Ronnie's wife and was a lovely person to chat with, and before she went to mingle with the other guests she wished us a good visit with Ron.

I also met up with Adrian Bullen who offered us the use of his flat on our next visit to London. I appreciated his kind gesture and we exchanged telephone numbers. We met many famous people at the show and, on sitting down to our meal, we found ourselves opposite Pat Fox, Samantha Fox's father.

After the meal had been cleared away the boxing bouts began. Lindsay and I had sponsored one of the bouts and subsequently presented the trophy. Tony introduced me to his brother Jimmy, who was accompanied by his wife, while Lindsay sat chatting to Gary Bushell about his support for Reg and Ron. We then retired to our room to have a meeting and discuss our visit with Ronnie, due to take place the next day.

Later, after changing out of our dinner suits into less formal suits and ties, we rejoined the boxing event for photographs with Tony and Charlie Kray. Tony went on to introduce us to others, including Ray Winstone, who asked if we wanted to hit the town for a late-night drink, but we declined, knowing we had an early visit with Ron the next day.

Unfortunately, we received a phone call the next morning to say the visit with Ronnie had been cancelled. Reggie telephoned Lindsay to ask about the boxing show, and told him that he had sent out a VO for us to visit him at Lewes prison, East Sussex. We arrived at Lewes in the evening in preparation for our visit the next day and booked into a nice little hotel opposite Lewes Crown Court.

We spent the morning visiting a few tourist attractions: Lindsay and I found Lewes Castle particularly fascinating. We checked out of the hotel at midday, then made our way to the prison, which was a short walk from the town centre. We met up with James Campbell as he was going to spend a short time on our visit with Reg.

Campbell pointed out that there were others also visiting Reg, and introduced us to Nicky Treeby, who was in partnership with Gillett. But realising that it was to be a shared visit pissed me right off, considering the distance we had travelled. It became clear that Reggie had arranged for us to visit him after he had talked to Treeby and that we were to go in with Campbell.

Lewes prison was an old Victorian building, and sitting in the waiting room was enough to depress anyone before seeing friends, family and loved ones. Our names were called, and walking in and seeing Reg I found pretty sad, but as we took our seats a big smile spread across his face. After the introductions, he asked for advice regarding limited-edition posters, which had been printed to coincide with the publication of Reg's book, *Our Story* by Fred Dinage.

I knew, through Campbell, that they weren't limited edition, as each poster wasn't individually numbered and there had been no certificate with any of them. Reggie instantly knew that he'd been had! He told Campbell to leave as he wanted to talk to Lindsay and me alone. As soon as Campbell left, I told Reg that I was pissed off at coming so far only to find that we shared the visit. Looking at me and going red in the face, he leaned over and said, 'You are just like Ron.'

I found Reg directing his conversation to me at all times, so Lindsay pulled him, asking him why, to which he replied that it was like talking to himself.

Reggie told us that he knew there was a grass in amongst his circle of so-called friends, and wanted Lindsay and me to find out who it was. On a less serious note, we chatted about things in general and soon the visit was at an end. After shaking hands with Reg, he helped us on with our coats and said that we reminded him of two blokes he once knew.

We moved into the development business and acquired land in Wales, and had plans drawn up which would help us to get our project under way. We needed to employ a building firm, planning to use the profit we made to set up an art business, which would give us access to the grants that were available at the time.

Lindsay and I knew we needed crooked builders – the sort that would cut a few corners and keep the costs down. We had a few friends who pointed us in the right direction. As soon as we met them, Lindsay and I could see they were a pair of crooks, which suited us fine.

They were quite happy to deal with us as they'd heard that other businessmen – in the same trade – wanted them done for ripping them off, so they agreed to take on the project and start as soon as possible.

Dave found he was having problems getting planning permission. We met the planning officer, and everything was sorted out.

With planning permission granted, builders were soon on site with their team and the development was under way.

We turned our attention back to the art business, and it was obvious that we needed a large factory to get the project up and running. Our enquiries for industrial equipment had been successful, so in order for us to man the machines and set up a design office, we decided to see what the Welsh Office had to offer and were pleased to find that a £250,000 grant was available to us. However, there was a clause in the contract which stated that a percentage of the workforce had to be made up of ex-miners and ex-steelworkers. That was fine by us: the more the merrier. The council was in the process of building a number of large factories, so we put our company forward for consideration.

When we were in London on business, we were often offered drinks so we decided to bring in drivers. One driver in particular was my former wife's cousin, Paul Edwards. I knew his father, who I'd grown to admire and ,although Paul was as thick as two short planks, we let him drive on a temporary basis as a favour to his father. Paul tried to impress us with tales of his time in the army, when, in fact, his father had told us that he'd had to buy him out of the Welsh Guards as he had cried to go home.

The police were still on our case on a lower level, and were becoming a pain in the arse. Certain police officers were getting quite personal.

At one of our regular meetings, a known gang which was bang at it clashed with us and it was about to get quite messy until the gang members realised they were faced with blokes who wouldn't bat an eyelid at doing them and spending a few years in prison. But there was no way they could back down and, of course, the police were called. We realised then that some of them must have been police informers as there were three divisions of police officers outside.

We began to control a number of pubs and clubs throughout South Wales, most of which Lindsay and I had never even visited. Businessmen still came to us with their problems, and one chap in particular, Bob, came to us about his ex-business partner, who had run off with his wife. Bob explained that he was getting threats from them.

On checking out his story we found out that Bob's ex-partner, a solicitor, had been in prison with us at Cardiff, having been sentenced for doing dodgy deals. It was funny because, when I was in prison, a bloke came to me asking what he should do regarding his case, so I told him to speak to his solicitor. Then, when we were outside on exercise, he pointed to a bloke and told us his solicitor was sitting a few feet away from us! We were all doubled up with laughter.

Bob was a nice bloke, and with him being in the estate agency business, he was a valuable contact to sell the properties we were having built. Also, Lindsay and I had talked about getting our own club to run, and so set Bob the task of finding one.

The ex-solicitor was sending threats to Bob, such as pictures of gravestones, and we knew we had to deal with the matter in a delicate way. It appeared that they'd had a few gripes with each other in the past, so we sent a team to the ex-solicitor, just to let him know Bob had people looking out for him.

Throughout the country a housing boom had taken off and house prices had doubled. Lindsay arranged a mortgage through Bob and bought a property from me, which resulted in a substantial profit. We then converted the house into a bed-and-breakfast establishment, which also made a nice profit.

My son had been knocked over by his schoolteacher and had suffered massive head injuries. Also, a fair bit of his back was ripped open. I was soon at the scene to comfort him while we waited for the ambulance. When it arrived, the ambulance-men requested a police escort to clear the traffic for a smooth run to the hospital, but after a long wait and no escort arriving, the ambulance raced to the hospital. My son was very lucky indeed, as he had no permanent injuries to the skull or spine, even though the car had run right over him. He was given quite a lot of stitches, and after spending some time in hospital he was sent home to heal.

A few days later, a police officer came to me blabbering on about how sorry he and his colleagues were, and that they felt enough was enough. I was rather perplexed by his confession and decided to tape the conversation without his knowledge. He told me that the reason the police escort did not turn up was because they were given instructions not to attend, and it was only later that they realised what they had done. My son was six years of age, with the same name as me!

I later learned that there was a split within the police. Not only did I have a grass in amongst them, I had a number of them prepared to give me information, but also, of course, I was well aware that there was the possibility of being set up, so we were extremely cautious.

We had a simple method of getting addresses, based on car number plates. We knew that an ordinary radio picked up the frequency of the police radios, so if we needed to find the address of a car owner, we would ring the police, reporting that we had seen the car being broken into and driven off at high speed, and give the car registration number.

Then tuning into the radio, we heard it being reported to all mobile police channels, and details of the owners' addresses were given to all police radios. We jotted down the information, then rang the police back, saying that it had been a mistake. But, of course, Tom and Steve could get both sides of the conversations, as opposed to an ordinary radio picking up the bleeps.

James Campbell needed me in London to finalise a number of deals. My friend, Phil Regnard, had recently been released from Dartmoor, so I invited him to join me, and made arrangements with Bullen to have the use of his flat in north London.

Lindsay had business to attend to in other parts of the country, leaving me to sound out what deals Campbell needed me to approve.

We met Campbell at a pub called The King's Oak in Epping Forest, a lovely place with a swimming pool and fountains at the back. Phil and I were given a tour of the building, after which we were served a beautiful meal. Campbell told me that we could conduct our business deals from the pub and have access to the living accommodation on the upper three floors.

We were then introduced to the head waiter, Jim O'Neill, a pleasant chap. He explained that The King's Oak was once known as The Dick Turpin, and was actually used by the man himself after his 'Stand and Delivers'. Knowing my history, I went on to further Jim's interpretation of Dick Turpin, telling them, 'Captain Tom King was one of the best highwaymen of his day, and was the swashbuckling, devil-may-care character who, legend says, would later influence Turpin. The two criminals teamed up, holed in a cave within the area of Epping Forest, but Dick Turpin shot Captain Tom King by mistake, as the plot went badly wrong when Turpin tried to free King from his captors.'

O'Neill and Campbell stood in silence as I asked, 'Was The King's Oak named after the true highwayman, Captain Tom King?'

They both stood there with a look of, 'Where the fuck did he get that from?'!

Even though Lindsay was receiving letters and telephone calls on a regular basis from Reggie, it was very unusual to receive a letter from Ronnie requesting a visit. I had been contacted by Kate, Ronnie's wife, with directions and visiting times. As Ronnie was in Broadmoor hospital for the criminally insane, the regime was very different from prison visits. We were to visit in the morning, as opposed to afternoon visits at prison.

We arrived at Broadmoor on a misty morning and went through the booking-in procedure. To sit in their comfortable waiting area was very different from prison waiting rooms and, even though the warders looked like screws with their keys on chains, they referred to themselves as nurses. All names were called for visits and we went through a number of gates before walking through the Victorian buildings.

When we arrived in the visiting room, Ronnie stood up with a big grin on his face. He was dressed in a smart suit and it was as though we were meeting him at his local pub. Lindsay and I were aware of his sexual proclivities, and both decided that if it was directed at us we would end the visit. I had nothing against gays, just as I had no prejudice against any race, religion, colour or creed. I had gone to school with Steven Harrington, now known as Steve Strange of Visage, and learned from a very early age to take a person for who they are, not what they are.

After we shook Ronnie's hand and sat at the table, we were approached by a bloke asking us what we wanted to drink. Ronnie jumped in with, 'My regular beers, please.' So, with alcohol-free lager, we sat down and chatted as if we had known each other for years. Sitting at the next table was Peter Sutcliffe. Ronnie told us not to take any notice of him.

I found Ronnie to be on the ball and he needed no time to think about decisions about business deals, which I liked. He asked why we hadn't visited him after the charity boxing event and when we explained that the visit had been cancelled, he went into deep thought, then looked at us, nodded and said, 'Right.'

What I found strange was that Ronnie seemed to talk directly to Lindsay and, like Lindsay had with Reggie, I pulled him, asking him why he didn't talk directly to me. He was more precise with his answer, explaining that he felt Lindsay was very much like Reg and I more like him, therefore, he need not explain things to me in such detail. Ronnie didn't mention anything about his sexual preferences and my respect for the man grew. We all had a good chat and some laughs. When the visit came to an end, Ronnie helped us on with our coats, as Reggie had done at Lewes prison.

Our building development with the two crooked builders was well under way. Through our contacts, and by mutual agreement, we were offered control of a number of fields that had come out of green belt into white belt. The transfer gave us a golden opportunity to prepare plans for the building of a hundred-plus properties.

Part of the agreement with having control of the land was for Lindsay and me to finance the project, and when we brought up the subject with Reg and Ron they advised us to meet a friend of theirs named Jeff Allen. Jeff had been a good friend of Reggie and Ronnie before their arrest and, through contact with Reg and Ron, he invited us to his country home.

When we met him, it became clear how big a developer he was: he had just sold a mansion to Bill Wyman of the Rolling Stones. We discussed business over a lovely lunch made by Jeff's wife, and we heard many tales of his encounters with Reggie and Ronnie in the sixties. We parted company with valuable information about the major development we had in mind.

After securing all our businesses in South Wales, we needed to spend a few days in London putting in place business proposals for Reg and Ron. We found they were both very generous with regard to their finances with friends, but we realised after meeting them that they did not conduct their business together. Each felt they should operate as a single unit, investing in successful business projects.

A substantial amount of money had gone missing from a number of charity events which Reggie had organised and, in view of the adverse press they were getting, it was agreed – after some discussion – to bring in a good PR man within the press.

However, we knew we had to get Reg and Ron in agreement to deal with one reporter, as opposed to the way information had been given to the press in the past. This was agreed fully by Reggie and Ronnie, and with their consent it was decided that James Campbell would be given the role of Mr Fix-it, being paid an agreed percentage at the end of each deal.

During discussions about which PR man was to be selected, Campbell suggested a freelance reporter named Jim Harding, who in the past had covered the Hungerford massacre. We held a meeting with him at The King's Oak and he agreed to take on the role of the Kray twins' PR man.

Of course, word soon got around and other reporters were eager to offer their services. We knew the Krays didn't have a very good name within the press and, with the view that the Kray film was soon to be released, it was important that Reggie and Ronnie were in agreement with which PR man was selected. We had their full co-operation for Lindsay and me to use our own judgement.

They were now doing something they hadn't done since being sentenced, i.e. dealing in the same business ventures. We had spoken to a number of reporters. I had even spoken to the editor of the *Daily Star*, Mr Brian Hutchins, seeking his advice on a number of issues.

After much deliberation as to who would take on the role, we met and chose Ted Hynds, who worked for the *Sunday People*. He was a well-spoken chap and we found him to be direct and straight to the point, and he was happy to take on the job.

Reggie was moved from Lewes prison, East Sussex, back to the top security prison, Gartree in Leicester; a backward step for him. Our contacts discovered that there was more to this than met the eye as, with Reg being at Gartree, it proved much more difficult to visit both him and Ronnie on the same day.

Tony Lambrianou was in negotiation regarding his book, *Inside the Firm*, so we went along with him and Carol Clark to meet Robert Smith, his publisher. It was inevitable that the book would be serialised in a national newspaper, but Ronnie became troubled about what was to be printed. Tony insisted that he would give a cut of his payment to Reggie and Ronnie, and although I felt he didn't really need to, Reg and Ron had already been told. Ronnie requested to see the final draft before publication, which was agreed by Tony, but when the serialisation went out in the *Sun*, Ronnie was livid.

Kate contacted Lindsay and me, asking us to get down to Broadmoor to see if we could calm him down. When we got there, Ronnie was in one hell of a temper, going on that he wanted something done about Tony as he had broken his promise of letting him see the final draft before publication. After I read the paper Ronnie had with him, I asked what he was so pissed off about. Still shouting, he said that it wasn't the story as such, it was the photograph that they had printed of him. Pointing to the paper, he said that his hair looked like he had just been though a wind tunnel. Lindsay and I couldn't help laughing. Ron looked at us, tears rolling down our cheeks, and soon started laughing with us.

After seeing the funny side of Ronnie's plight, I told him that he must not forget that Tony had a right to make a few bob – after all, he did do 15 years in prison. Ronnie, by then a lot calmer, nodded in agreement but said that Tony should not have suggested giving them a cut of the finance from serialisation.

The King's Oak was an ideal place for us to conduct our business meetings. Jim O'Neill became the manager.

One day, Jim requested that Lindsay and I had a meeting with him in the restaurant. He seemed amiable enough as he poured us each a glass of wine, but suddenly his mood changed and he told me that if I didn't play ball I would end up in the forest. I couldn't believe the prat had the gall to sit there and threaten me. So, in temper, I threw my wine glass at him, which bounced off his head. As the wine ran down his face, I told him that I would paint him on the walls with an Uzi. He just looked at me and burst into tears. I didn't know what had got into the man to warrant such an outburst. I told Lindsay to sort Jim out as he was becoming a little embarrassing, and then walked out of the room, giving him time to compose himself.

After Lindsay spoke to him and warned him about my temper, Jim apologised and we never had any more problems.

6

MORE TCB

We devised a way of smuggling in vodka for Reggie on our visits, and it seemed to relax him when discussing business propositions. I found that he would make a decision on a visit, yet within an hour or two of me leaving he would telephone me, changing his mind. After speaking to Ronnie we knew exactly what was happening. The people around Reg knew only too well that their meal ticket was coming to an end, and Ronnie decided that the best way to deal with it was by bringing in men we could trust, to pay those people a visit, in and out of jail.

We took Ted Hynds in to visit Ronnie and finalise the payment from the *Sunday People*. Ronnie, as usual, was on the ball. Ted was happy with the visit and arrangements were then made to visit Reg. We asked Reg to get his friends in prison to send visiting orders to various pre-arranged addresses, and travelling up in two cars we took a few friends, all of whom carried small bottles of vodka. We met Ted at Gartree prison, then went in to visit Reg.

Reggie and I went straight into a blazing row, as it was obvious to him that a few of his so-called friends had been slapped. I told him that he and Ron needed to know what deals were being pursued, and that if there were any outside influences, we would all be wasting our time. It was clear that neither Reggie nor I were going to budge, so I introduced Ted to him and moved to another table to visit a family member who was doing life.

Lindsay and Ted were in deep conversation while the lads kept the vodka flowing. There was no need for any of us visiting to drink as we could do that when we were back in London. Ted was happy with his visit and we all shook hands at the end of it. Reggie had calmed right down after his little tipple and shook my hand, but still gave me a stern look over the top of his glasses. Outside, we shook hands with Ted, who was very thankful for the visits we had arranged, and headed back to London to freshen up at Bullen's flat, ready to join Campbell, who had been working hard with a number of people we needed to meet.

We knew we needed Reggie and Ronnie's finances to go through the proper channels, so Campbell arranged for us to meet a financial expert, named David Ley, who we met at a north London pub. When we saw him sipping whisky, he looked the typical flash financial adviser, then Campbell introduced us and we got down to business. He was well up for dealing with Reggie and Ronnie's finances.

He told us he was in the insurance business and how he had most of the Tottenham Hotspur footballers on his books. We ended the meeting and headed down to The King's Oak, where Campbell had arranged another meeting. He had done his homework well and a meeting was held with David Ley's rival, although at one time they were very good friends. Campbell introduced us to Martin Mitchell, but he seemed a little on edge knowing we had just met his former business partner and, even though we hadn't made a decision, Martin was prepared to offer a better deal than David Ley.

Also at the meeting was Charlie Green, who had a holiday complex with a golfing range in Tenerife, and we all sat down to lunch to discuss future business ventures. We knew Reg and Ron's finances were looking rather shoddy, and realised that tracking down past business ventures and finances would take longer than building new ones. With Reg and Ron being involved in the same ventures, we had the task of tidying up their dealings. Having a picture disc in the making, under the guidance of Colin Fry, it became clear that Colin wanted to meet to discuss other ventures regarding Kray memorabilia.

Visits to Ronnie at Broadmoor several times a week were to become the norm, with much discussion regarding the story going in the *People* newspaper. Ronnie wanted us to arrange for the cheque from The Mirror Group to be sent directly to Kate, which we did. It didn't worry us too much as finances began to come in from various other avenues, so ten grand was peanuts compared with what we had on the go.

The Kray film was due out and Lindsay and I were invited to pick up a video of it and asked to give our views. Ronnie wasn't very pleased with it at all. He felt that improvements could have been made to the film. We were also given tickets for the premiere night, as well as Ronnie's password for Browns nightclub for an after-show party.

We began to notice that Paul Edwards was becoming too mouthy and big-headed around people we were meeting, and one night in particular he was wandering around the pub with a big knife. I was down the West End when I heard what Edwards was up to and, as I knew he wasn't very bright, I rang Lindsay to sort out the problem.

Lindsay approached him, telling him enough was enough, but Edwards made the mistake of holding the blade up to Lindsay, who took it out of his hand then head-butted him. I soon had a phone call saying he was asking for me. I was well pissed off and headed back to The King's Oak, where I found Edwards wandering down the road looking rather bruised. It was time for him to go back to Wales and take some time out.

Two men, who introduced themselves as Ian and Phil, sent a bottle of wine to us when we were in the back room of The King's Oak, and wanted to know if they could work for us; Lindsay and I were often approached by people asking to become part of our team. After having them checked, we decided to give them a task to prove themselves. They could look after The King's Oak when we weren't around.

Ronnie had been in touch, asking us to get down to Broadmoor for an urgent meeting, so we wasted no time and left early the next day.

Ron explained that he had two jobs for us to carry out on his behalf, the first being that we were to meet friends of his who were flying in to Heathrow Airport from America, and then escort them to a London hotel to discuss business. The second, Ronnie explained, concerned the fact that Samantha Fox's father was worried his daughter's ex-boyfriend was due in from Australia, and he believed that it could get a touch messy.

The difficulty we faced was that we couldn't be in two places at the same time, so we decided to call on Ian and Phil, as well as a trusted friend of Ronnie who had details of the Australian. The details were to be picked up from an address in London, so we sent Ian and Phil to collect them. When we arrived back at The King's Oak, Ian and Phil were waiting with the relevant information. Then, while we were freshening up before making our journey to Heathrow, a message came through that the Australian business was off, but we were still to meet the Americans. We left Ian and Phil at The King's Oak looking very disappointed.

As we had sent Edwards back to Wales to cool off, we headed off to Heathrow to pick up the Americans ourselves. The ice was broken when they thought Lindsay and I were Reggie and Ronnie Kray, and we all had a good laugh when we pointed out their mistake. After taking them to their hotel in London, we were soon in deep discussion about business deals we were setting up in the UK. We were under no illusions about the two Americans: they were obviously members of the Mafia. We'd had many a chat with Ronnie about his connection with the Mafia during the sixties.

One of the conversations centred around a ring that Ronnie was given by a Mafia Don when he was in America. Ronnie felt it was time to hand it back as a gift to the son of the Mafia Don in question. Of course, Ronnie knew that when a gift of such importance is given, another gift should be given in return, which would give us access to the American market with support from this organisation.

We ended the meeting and headed back to The King's Oak, and it wasn't long before Ronnie rang to see how things had gone. We told him that we were very happy with the meeting and of the prospect of future dealings, which pleased him considerably. As we pulled up at The King's Oak, we saw a police car pull away and were wondering what had happened when Phil and Ian met us at the door. They explained that a big fight had broken out when two rival gangs clashed, resulting in four people getting stabbed up pretty bad.

The next day we headed back to Wales as things needed to be dealt with there, but we stopped off on the way to visit Ron and inform him in detail of the meeting with the Americans.

Back in Wales we found we had quite a lot of business affairs to follow up. One in particular was the manager of a number of pubs who was having problems with a few bullies wrecking his pubs and causing mayhem within his businesses. He said that one of them was wandering around with a shotgun. Our priority was the man with the gun, so we decided to do him as he came out of his house. We knew that when he was with his mates the possibility of the gun being used was a cert.

We didn't have long to wait, and as soon as he was through the door we were on him and dragged him to one of the cars, punching fuck out of him on the way. We knew where his mates were hanging out so, driving in with a number of cars, we cut them off. They all stood still looking confused and, after taking their battered friend out of the car, we lined them all up against the wall. I knew then that it was finished as none of them had any fight left in them, so after each of them had been slapped, we warned them not to bother the man again.

But it wasn't long before the police tracked me down. The bloke we had grabbed was in hospital and, as usual, he had run to the police. However, I was surprised when the police praised me on the way we had dealt with the bullies. Then we found out that they had been bullying an old woman, amongst others. I told the copper I didn't have a clue what he was going on about and that was the end of that matter.

We had a job on in west Wales, where a number of businessmen were owed a substantial amount of money. They were prepared to pool their finances to employ us to recover what was owed, so we met them all individually and they each paid us a few thousand. We needed to send in a team to gather all the info we thought necessary, and although there was no shortage of men willing to take the job on, we chose a few close mates who had just been released from prison. I knew they would have the patience to lie in wait.

It worked better than we could have expected. One of the lads got in so close that he was drinking with the man we were after at his local club, and he found out that the bloke intended putting minders around himself for various reasons.

With all the information gathered in a few days, it was decided to make contact and make him pay what he owed. I made a phone call asking him to pay his debt. He replied by giving me quite a bit of abuse, but it was no more that I expected. The next day, Lindsay and I headed along with a few others to confront him.

When we arrived at his business premises, four of our team were with him. But he didn't realise that they were with us, he just thought he had found four nasty pieces of work to protect his interests. After walking into his office, I told him that we had come to collect the money he owed. With a big smile on his face he told me to fuck off.

So, smiling back, I gave the nod to one of the men who he thought was protecting him and he was grabbed by the neck. I told him that on no account were we leaving without the money and asked him if he would like me to ring for an ambulance. After that, I couldn't have wished to meet a nicer man. We escorted him to the bank, picked up the cash and were soon heading back to South Wales. With everyone having been paid, we went to a pub and drank until the early hours.

We still didn't have our own pub, so the next day we chased up Bob, the estate agent, and spent the day looking around different pubs that were for sale. We took a fancy to one in particular, which was situated on top of a mountain and which had a fair bit of land with it. Bob was left to deal with the paperwork and make an offer on our behalf.

I was getting a bit pissed off with being asked to collect money from businessmen, so we decided to pass those jobs on to a few of the lads. I would make the phone calls and the lads would do the slappings if need be.

One day, when we were on our way to London, we dropped in to see Ronnie, who greeted us, as usual, with a smile and a handshake. He wanted us to give a letter to David Essex. Ronnie also spoke very highly of Peters and Lee and, after a general chat and an alcohol-free lager, Ron gave me the letter for David and we continued our journey to London.

We were at The King's Oak for a meeting with Charlie Green, when I mentioned the letter for David Essex and asked where we could find him. Charlie told us that he was playing at his friend's nightclub in Usk, South Wales, which was our neck of the woods. I had heard of the club, which was called Savvas. A member of our family had recently had a problem with a doorman there. Charlie went on to say that, as George Savvas was his friend, he would ring him and reserve a table for us.

At the meeting, Campbell said that even though the film *The Krays – Bonded by Blood* was due for release, there had already been talk of a sequel, which David Ley indicated he wanted to be involved with financially, as did his old rival, Martin Mitchell. Discussions were ongoing regarding a strategy for Reggie's release but, of course, we knew that a lot of thought needed to be put into the campaign.

We travelled back to Wales after dropping off supplies to Ronnie, and arranged to have a relaxing evening watching David Essex's show at Savvas. We weren't too bothered about the doorman, but we would make George aware of the incident. We arrived with a party of 12 and were escorted to our seats near the front. Then Lindsay and I went to meet George Savvas and found him to be a very nice chap. I explained that we needed to give David Essex a letter from Ron, so George said he would put it in his dressing room. That suited Lindsay and me. We knew that what Ronnie had to say was just between the two of them and not our affair.

The show started and, although I wasn't a fan of David Essex, I thoroughly enjoyed the evening. Later, I asked George whether David had picked up the letter from Ron, but he said he hadn't and that, even though he had arranged for us to go backstage for a chat, David hadn't hung around and left the club as soon as the show was over. George gave me the letter back so I could return it to Ron, and the night ended well, with the problem with the doorman sorted out amicably.

When we returned the letter he had given us for David Essex, he placed it in his pocket, smiled and said, 'They forget so easily.'

Meanwhile, Lindsay and I were beginning to know the layout of Broadmoor as well as the screws did, and we toyed with the idea of busting Ronnie out of there. Ronnie was well pleased with the idea of campaigning for Reggie's release, but asked us not to give Reggie too much information because he could be quite an impatient man. I asked Ronnie if he would like to get out some day, but he replied that he would like to see Reg get out first, as he had done some serious bird. Lindsay and I laughed as Ronnie had served the same amount of time, but we understood what he meant.

I was in touch regularly with Kate by telephone: we needed to know who was visiting Ronnie and when, as we didn't want visits to clash. (Reggie's visits were more straightforward, with either a visiting order arriving by post or, on some occasions, one waiting at the gate, depending on which prison he was in.)

Visits to Ronnie were more relaxed, and he would tell us stories of his and Reggie's time in the sixties. Ronnie would often say, 'Get the beers in, lads.' Then, settling down with our alcohol-free lager, Ronnie would light up one of his John Player Specials and go into great detail about their dealings with the villains of that time. He would speak highly of some of them, how they had both worked for Jack Spot and Billy Hill. He would say, 'Looking back on it, both Reg and I would be high-powered businessmen today, if it weren't for the fact that we did our own dirty work.'

On one visit we were all doubled up with laughter about an article which had gone in the paper showing one of Ronnie's drawings. A psychologist had done a profile on him, saying that Ronnie was a complete nutter because in the picture the sky was a dark purple. Ronnie, laughing, told us that the only reason the sky was purple was that he had run out of blue!

We could see that, even through the blur of heavy medication, Ronnie was as sharp as a razor. I could sense the same with Reg, but he could be very distant, which was more than likely the result of him being away from his supporting twin. Ronnie would sometimes complain that when they were allowed a visit together, they wouldn't be left to talk on their own, they always had two screws and two nurses in the same room.

When we visited Ronnie in the morning and Reg in the afternoon, Ronnie would give us personal messages to take to Reg, sometimes by letter and sometimes verbally. Usually, we would take a message back to Ron the next day and, even though the contact between them seemed inadequate, I could see a light within Reg ignite when he received his messages.

One day, Reg was troubled about photographs which had been taken in his cell and which he had given to Liz, who we met on our first visit to London. He asked us if we would pick them up and destroy them as he was due a parole review, and felt that if the photos got into the wrong hands, they could jeopardise the review. I wasn't too keen on getting involved in rows between Reg and his lady friends, but he was obviously extremely troubled by the matter.

I had met Liz on a number of occasions, so I telephoned her, explaining Reggie's worries and, although she was very good about it, I sensed that she and Reg may have fallen out. We collected the photos, some of which showed Reggie in his cell in boxing poses and others of him at his prison table writing letters.

Lindsay and I had given our word that we would destroy the photos, and we watched as each one curled up and turned to ashes. A few days later I looked into Reggie's eyes and told him that the photos had been destroyed. I was expecting some sense of relief from him, but he simply said, 'You both give me a sense of loyalty, and that is good.'

Reg always enjoyed talking about boxing and, as it was also our sport, we would exchange stories of how we had made very good friends in the boxing game. I often travelled to a Newport gym with a friend of mine, Andrew Gerrard, a heavyweight boxer who, at that time, was a sparring partner for Joe Bugner. I often did many rounds with Steve Sims, British Featherweight Champion, and on many occasions I would jump in the ring with David Pierce, who was British Champion in the heavyweight division.

Steve Sims was to fight a world title eliminator at St David's Hall, Cardiff, against a Canadian called Lores Stecca, but he had to lose a fair bit of weight to make the weigh-in. With a lot of skipping and me on the pads, Steve made the weight, although I remember wondering whether he had lost the weight too quickly.

At the fight I sat in the front row with David Pierce, but decided to move further back, where I got chatting to a chap who I assumed was Canadian and connected with Steve's opponent. Later, when I went back to the front row with David, he asked if I knew who I had been talking to. I told him I didn't have clue. Laughing, he told me that I had been chatting away with Angelo Dundee, Mohammed Ali's manager.

Reggie and Ronnie would love to hear stories about boxing, and Reggie in particular took notice when we spoke of our trainer from Newbridge, Paul Williams, who knew he had a world champion in the making. I explained how Joe Calzaghe was nine years old when he walked into the gym with his friend, Little Dai, and how Paul would make the youngsters jump onto our backs as we trained, running up and down the slag heaps. Joe went on to become Super Middleweight Champion of the World, and still holds the title today.

Taking a break from doing business for Reggie and Ronnie, we were invited to Jimmy Lambrianou's (Tony's brother) party in Oxford. Lindsay and I had met him at the boxing event in Woodford Bridge, and I found him to be a genuine bloke, so with our driver we travelled up to Oxford and booked into a hotel for the night.

We arrived at the party early and settled at a table, where Jimmy greeted us and thanked us for turning up. Crowds of people began to arrive and the club was soon full. Then, walking through the door with a beautiful woman on each arm, came a black bloke. The whole place came to a standstill for a few seconds, then came the words, 'Get rid of the coon.' I could see that the bloke was like a fish out of water, and the two ladies didn't know what to do.

My aunt had adopted a black child, so from an early age, growing up with my cousin, I had never been able to understand prejudice. I walked over to the bloke and told him that there were three spare seats at our table and pointed him in Lindsay's direction. By then a few of the doormen had come over to throw him out, so I told them that he was my driver. Jimmy hadn't been in the room at the time, but after I explained the situation to him he was more than happy for the bloke to stay with his lady friends.

Pink champagne was being delivered to our table and a lovely evening followed.

We left at around five in the morning as we were on an early morning visit to Ron. After showering and trying to bring myself round, we were on the road but we had to stop several times as I spewed up pure froth. Lindsay and our driver were doubled up, but I didn't find it so funny and felt I would have to sleep it off in the car while Lindsay visited Ron. But when we arrived at Broadmoor I felt a little better so I went in on the visit.

Ronnie could see I wasn't feeling too good and told me that he would sometimes get in the same shape, but that a good hearty breakfast would do the trick. That was me off again at the mention of breakfast, but not only did I have Lindsay finding it funny, Ron was also laughing as the mention of food resulted in me running to the toilets.

We were often invited to parties in the East End and always made to feel welcome. One night we were drinking and chatting with Tony in a pub called The Florist, when Tony decided he wanted to go on to another pub called The Dover Castle, which was a short walk away.

There were quite a few of us, including a few lads up with us from Wales as well as some of the Eastenders. After we had been walking for a few minutes, we could hear a hell of a racket and it was getting louder and louder. As we got closer, we could see dustbins being thrown over walls and heard the sound of glass smashing, then as we reached the end of the street and walked around the corner, we found that we had walked into a football riot.

We stopped in the middle of the street to get a better look, and at the same time the football hooligans stopped in their tracks, looking at us standing there in our dark suits and big black overcoats. It could only have been a few seconds but it seemed like an age of silence, then the leaders in the front turned into an alleyway and went on, still making a racket and with hundreds of people following them.

Tony just shrugged his shoulders and we continued our walk to The Dover Castle.

Ronnie, at times, would go through severe bouts of depression due to changes in the heavy medication prescribed to stabilise his illness. Kate would telephone me when he was having one of those bouts, knowing that Lindsay and I didn't find it a problem visiting him when he was depressed. Even though we could see that Ronnie was at a low ebb, we would simply sit and listen to him talking through his hurts, and I think he felt he was closer to Reg through us.

One day in particular, when Ronnie was feeling very low, his thoughts turned to his mother and he told us how he felt the need to visit her grave and talk about his feelings. We knew Ronnie and Reggie hadn't been to the grave since their mother's funeral, and they hadn't even attended their father's funeral as they felt the occasion had become a circus. I told Ron that we would go that afternoon to place flowers on the grave and, if necessary, tidy it up, and it was as though the life came back into him in an instant. It was no problem for us. After all, we were free to go where we pleased.

After buying flowers we had the task of finding the grave, but that proved not to be a problem as the grave-diggers gladly showed us the way, explaining how often they showed people to the Kray twins' parents graves. To the right of their mother and father's grave was the grave of Reggie's first wife, Frances. We could see that their parents' grave hadn't been very well maintained, so we set about tidying it up.

I had a camera with me and told Lindsay that I was going to take a number of photos, and although Lindsay didn't think it was a good idea, I could only do what I felt was right. If I had been in prison for the length of time Reg and Ron had, I knew that if all I could have was a photograph of my parents' gravestone, it would mean a lot to me. So, as Lindsay laid the flowers, I took photos from different angles and we had the film developed within the hour, then checked with Kate to make sure a visit was free the next day, which she confirmed.

Lindsay was still hesitant about giving Ronnie the photos, but the next day at Broadmoor, Ronnie was still looking very sad, so I explained that we had taken flowers and tidied up the grave, which seemed to lift his mood and he smiled. I could see Lindsay holding his breath as I took the photos from my pocket and said, 'Ronnie, if I am wrong here I will walk away from this visit and never return. I took a number of photos of your parents' grave. I know that if it were me I wouldn't be offended.' I then handed the photos to Ron.

There was silence and Lindsay was still holding his breath as Ronnie flicked through them one after the other. Then, taking off his glasses and placing them on the table, he rubbed his eyes and said, 'Thank you very much, my friends. May I keep these photos?' I nodded and pointed out that the negatives were in with them. Ronnie told us that he would be sending a few to Reg. Then, flicking through them again, he took out one which showed us laying the flowers and said, 'This is for you.'

We could both see that within a few minutes Ronnie was back to his usual sharp self, as if the dark cloud had moved on to some other distant land. Then, lighting up his John Player Special, he said, 'Get the beers in.'

Within a day or two of visiting Ron, we visited Reg and found that he instinctively knew Ron hadn't been too well, but we soon put him at ease by telling him that Ronnie was feeling much better.

Reg wanted us to travel to Doncaster to pick up 500 books of *Our Story*,written by Fred Dinage. The idea was for us to shift them in Wales. At Doncaster we were met by a lady named Kim and her son Brad. Soon after picking up the books we were on our way back to Wales. We knew that Reg and Ron wouldn't be able to sign so many books on one visit, so we came up with the idea of them signing 500 stickers, which we would stick into the books and sell as signed copies. When we went to pick up the stickers from Ronnie he laughed and said that he had spent all night signing each one and that he never wanted to sign his name again. Reggie sent his stickers by post.

On a few of our visits, Ronnie began to go into detail about what went on in the sixties leading up to their arrest. I pointed out that he needn't talk about such matters, but he said that when he and Reg were dead and gone, he knew people would crawl out of the woodwork, saying things that weren't true. The conversation sometimes became very serious indeed, with him telling us that he was giving us the deeds to his prime, and, of course, his prime was the time of their arrest.

Ronnie would go over certain details a number of times, then ask us questions on what he had said. It was as though he wanted to get a lot off his chest and we had no doubt that he was doing the same with Kate. It was as if he knew he wasn't going to get out of there.

I would ask him what he intended doing when he got out, but he always steered the conversation around to Reg, telling us we should work on getting him out first. He asked us if we would keep a close eye on Reg if a release did eventually come and, of course, we agreed, but pointed out that it would be easier if Reg could come to Wales. Ronnie nodded in agreement. He knew London had changed dramatically. I knew it would be difficult trying to persuade Reg that he was to live in Wales, but Ronnie said to leave it to him.

It wasn't long before I had Reg on the phone asking us to look around for a mansion in Wales for him, so we set about sending him brochures of various homes for his consideration. Ronnie asked us to look around for a flat or small house within walking distance of Broadmoor and I wondered if there was something he wasn't telling us.

Some of the businesses were beginning to come to fruition, and Robert Smith, who had just published Tony Lambrianou's book, was interested in publishing a book by Ronnie. As Robert pointed out, a few books had been published by Reg but none by Ron, and if he were to write one it would most certainly be a bestseller.

We met Robert at The King's Oak, along with David Ley and Charlie Green, and said that we would put the idea to Ron on our next visit. Lindsay and I had a lot on with other deals we were following up, so we thought that Kate would be the best person to arrange a book with Ronnie. She had a good business head on her, and if he was involved in writing a book with Kate helping him, it would be a good way of keeping him busy.

Ronnie wasn't too keen at first, but when we pointed out that Kate would write it with him, the idea began to grow on him and we knew Kate would be pleased to be involved.

Throughout the country, villains specialise in their various crimes, and different villains can drink or socialise in the same pubs and clubs, yet not know who does what. Most live by a code of conduct and it is those rules that make them stand out from the rest. It is that badge based on the code of conduct that is worn with pride and honour. They look upon the rapist as the beast, the child molester as the nonce and the informer as the grass.

Throughout London, as with many other parts of the country and no doubt the world, villains formed their own groups in their own areas. Within London those groups are known as manors. One group wouldn't interfere with another's manor unless there was good reason.

Ronnie used to say that if he knew in the sixties what he knew now after taking the criminal path, he would be a very powerful man indeed.

Meanwhile, I began to realise that there was an inner sanctum within the criminal circle, or underworld. You could say a wheel within a wheel. One of the key-holders to that inner circle was Ronnie, but when we broached the subject with him, the only response we would get was a smile and a tap on the shoulder, as if to say, 'Well done. Now you have ten brownie points.'

Ronnie wanted us to warn a few people from south London on a number of matters, but it would have been suicidal to take any Eastenders along, so Lindsay and I went along with a driver. The meeting had been arranged a few days earlier and was to take place in a south London pub.

We arrived early, and when we walked into the pub everyone went quiet. Lindsay got the drinks in while I used the toilet, and as I washed my hands a chap with a sawn-off shotgun came in, and in a strong Irish accent asked me what the fuck I was doing there. Drying my hands, and showing no concern about the shotgun pointing at me, I said that I was visiting friends in London and was about to have a drink with them. Looking at me rather puzzled, he went on to tell me that I was Welsh and asked again what was I doing in the south of London. Looking back at him, just as puzzled, I said that he must forgive my lack of knowledge with regard to the segregation of London, but I considered London to be inside the M25 and he too was a fair distance from his homeland. Then, placing the gun under his coat and smiling, he invited me to drink with him at his table.

When I returned to the bar I could see Lindsay was in conversation with the people we had come to meet and the pub was back to normal, with music playing and everyone chatting. The people in question were given the messages from Ron, the point was made, then our meeting turned in to a singalong and, as with most of the pubs we visited in London, we were invited back.

There wasn't anywhere we couldn't go in London, be it the south, east, west or north. We got on with everyone. If we went to a nightclub, the people we were with would say, 'Friends of the Krays,' and we would be taken straight through, and by the end of the night we were always invited back on our own merits.

We met friends of Reggie and Ronnie who they hadn't heard from for years and they would love to hear the stories of old friends sending their regards.

When visiting Reg, we found he always liked to give us a gift to show his appreciation. One day on a visit, he came out with some drawings for us, which he had signed. He asked me what I thought of them and, smiling at him, I asked, 'Do you really want to me to tell you, Reg?' He burst out laughing and said, 'Lowry wasn't much better.' I had to agree, but as Reg pointed out, it's the thought that counts and, like Lowry, I had no doubt Reggie's drawing would be much sought after when he was dead and gone. Reg agreed. It was nice to see him happy, but I knew I dare not show him one of our drawings.

And so it went on for some time: Reg sending us different pictures, versions of cowboys which he would label 'Cowboy with one gun', 'Cowboy with two guns', 'Cowboy with one gun drawn' and so on. Lindsay and I ended up with a full set of 26 of Reggie's drawings.

As we were spending so much time in London, we were getting phone calls telling us that liberties were being taken at a few of the pubs we had an interest in, so we decided to go back to Wales to sort it out. A gang had been threatening the landlady of one pub, demanding money. They were due to collect, so I told her not to worry as we would be down during the night.

We arranged for a few cars to stay hidden around the corner, all of which were tooled up, and it wasn't long before a big van pulled into the car park, packed with about a dozen blokes, none of which were on the small side. The landlady knew what was about to happen and screamed at us to take it outside, not to bash up her pub. So we decided to meet them at the door, where it went off big time, with Lindsay and me taking the brunt of the punches, which were coming from everywhere.

It wasn't long before our lot were there to even things up a bit. Lindsay and I were fighting like hell in the doorway, but with our lot behind the gang, they soon decided that things weren't going to plan, so they ran through the pub, trying to lock the door to stop us getting at them. A few were out cold on the floor, one was begging his mates to let him back in, but he was dragged outside where one of our lot set about him with a car jack. His mates could only look on in horror as he was rolled into the gutter in a hell of a shape. The pub window was put through with our lot going through it to have some more, but we could hear the police were on their way, so we got from there pretty sharpish.

We found out that the gang was operating under the instructions of another manager, who was after the pub we were protecting. So, wasting no time, we got a team together, masked them up and sent them off to retaliate. With all the doormen inside licking their wounds, our team set about putting their windows through and called them all out to where they were waiting with pickaxe handles to smash the first bastard through the door.

When the door opened there was a lot of shouting, and the manager was thrown out, begging them not to smash him, but there was no need to smash him – they were all finished. They knew the police were on their way, so, still masked up, our lads were away, leaving the manager whimpering.

Within an hour or two the police collared me as I was leaving my office. The manager had told them he'd seen me, but I knew that wasn't true. I hadn't been there and I knew the other lads had been masked up.

As the police cuffed me up, the manager pulled up in his car with plenty to say for himself, and began laying into me. The coppers turned their backs and let him give me some digs, but he couldn't punch his way out of a paper bag and he was beginning to piss me right off so I slammed the head into him, splitting open his nose. The police turned around to see the manager screaming on the floor and, putting me in the car, they said I would be charged. I laughed in their faces, asking them how they would explain me head butting the idiot when I had already been arrested by them, and a dumb look came over their faces.

The manager was adamant that it was me who bashed up his pub, but there was still no mention of men being masked and tooled up, so I admitted the charge of criminal damage. I knew I couldn't be done for head-butting. I had been cuffed in front of too many witnesses.

7

CONNECTIONS

It was becoming widely known that our business meetings were conducted at The King's Oak, where Jim would arrange evening meals for everyone after the meetings. Lindsay and I were approached about joining the Freemasons and, although it didn't appeal to us, we thought it was worth considering, especially after the shit we'd put up with in the past. Lindsay's application was successful but I was blackballed (knocked back), and for a number of days Lindsay was taken to several venues in connection with his initiation.

Ian and Phil had proved their loyalty to us, yet we could sense a bit of jealousy from Bullen and Edwards about the trust we put in Ian and Phil. Also, Edwards and Campbell didn't get on and I was forever pulling one or the other over the animosity between them. As long as Edwards was bullshitting with someone, we hardly heard anything out of him, yet we would always leave him in Wales when we had more serious business to deal with, as we knew that he and Bullen had big mouths.

I had spoken to Colin Fry on the telephone on a number of occasions before arranging to meet him at his home to discuss the picture disc featuring Reggie on a tape-recorded interview. We arranged to meet the film director Charles Rosenblatt, who had been in the motion picture industry for 40 years, making over 180 films including *Watership Down*, *Donovan's Reef* with John Wayne and Lee Marvin, and *Papillon* with Steve McQueen and Dustin Hoffman.

After meeting Colin at his home in the picturesque village of

Shrewton, we went to a local pub for lunch and to discuss our forthcoming meeting with Charles Rosenblatt. I told him about the problems we'd had obtaining the Kray film contract, which Charles had requested. Even though we had Reggie's consent to release the contract, their solicitor had no intention of letting us have it, but when we told Ronnie about the problem he promptly sorted it out and we received the document by courier that same afternoon.

Colin, pleased that we'd received the contract, said that although Charles was retired, he was willing to offer his services as a professional, putting us on the right path and – initially at least – there would be no charge.

When we met Charles at his home, he put us at ease by talking about the many photographs of him with Hollywood stars which surrounded him, and what films he had been involved with. He was a very quiet man but a very shrewd one. I asked him to take a look at the Kray film contract and when I handed it to him, he smiled and commented that the contract was very small indeed compared with the contracts of the great films he had produced, which were a considerable weight.

We sat in silence as Charles studied page after page, grinning to himself as he did so, obviously absorbing the contents.

Minutes of the meeting were taken by Colin, noting the advice given by Charles. They read as follows:

> The contract was in default since all monies mentioned in the contract had not been settled as pre-arranged.
> However, this could be rectified if Fugitive Films paid the full amount – Reggie and Ronnie's representatives would have to confirm in writing both acceptance of the monies, as yet unpaid, and the re-installment of the said contract.

Lindsay and I had made sure we had it in writing that we were given full and exclusive rights to deal with the next film based on Reggie and Ronnie's lives.

Charles' advice went further on quite a number of issues: 'There is nothing to stop anyone making a new Kray film – or any other film – concerning the Krays.'

That was all Lindsay and I wanted to hear: there were discrepancies in the contract, but Charles hadn't finished. He went on to say, 'Please understand that, in law, it is not necessary for Fugitive Films to make a deal with Reg and Ronnie Kray for the film rights, since they have already bought the rights to the book, *The Profession of Violence* by John Pearson. As I understand it, the money was paid to stop R & R Kray, over a three year period, from arranging for other films, documentaries, etc. to be made.'

What a pleasure it was to hear Charles go through the contract with such ease and finesse, and to top it all we were sitting in the master's home. What a feeling!

Charles would pause regularly, giving us time to take in his advice and the opportunity to ask any questions we might have. Then, moving on with such grace, he said, 'Problems could arise when dealing with distribution of a new film in the USA and other territories. Since Parkfield, through Fugitive Films, felt that they had a contract lasting three years or more, then they may have included in their deal, for example with Miramax in the USA, the option for a Kray II film.

'This may give problems in the USA, where Miramax could stop the film from going out on general release whilst the whole distribution position was going through litigation. This could cause considerable problems, and Miramax could ask for a pay-off/settlement and US $500,000 would not be out of the question.'

Charles said that more information was still needed on the Kray film, and suggested that all contracts concerning the Krays should be gathered together, along with all other available information on distribution, video rights, TV rights, soundtrack rights, etc. The contracts/papers were to be sent to Charles, through Colin, for close scrutiny.

He also said that if he had satisfactory answers and information on the Kray film, he would be more than happy to check out certain film companies, with which he was on excellent terms. Charles clearly indicated that he would advise us and point us in the right direction on the making of a new Kray motion picture.

We thanked him for his time and advice and left to go for further discussion at Colin's home. It was confirmed that there were too many inconsistencies within the contract, but we were pleased that Charles had given us full authority to work under his name. We knew that, as representatives of Charles Rosenblatt, we could sell the film before it had even been made. We left Colin to draw up the minutes of our meeting and headed back to Bullen's flat.

We had quite a lot to talk about regarding the film contract, but we knew that Reggie and Ronnie wouldn't be too pleased with the outcome of our meeting with Charles, so we decided to let them read the minutes.

Bullen was beginning to irritate me. He seemed to think he was taking on the role of our legal adviser. I liked Bullen as a friend but, even though he was an educated man, he wasn't streetwise and I knew that if things got rough Bullen was the type to crawl back under his stone.

Reggie was soon on the phone asking how the meeting had gone, but I could only answer that, up to that point, it had gone well and said that we were going to set in motion the second film. Reg seemed happy enough, but it wasn't long before he rang again after speaking to the doubting Thomases. We expected that and arranged to visit Ronnie.

We took the minutes with us and watched as he became increasingly annoyed with each page he read. We told him that the inconsistencies in the contract were nothing to do with us; it was something he needed to speak to his brother Charlie about. Our main priority was to get on with the second film.

We had already toyed with the idea of a joint American and British film, an idea which was backed by Charles Rosenblatt. Colin kept the ball rolling down his end. We knew we needed to build up a cast list of British actors and actresses. Ronnie wanted Barbara Windsor to play the part of their mother, which I felt was a good choice.

Ronnie said that Reggie had been talking to some of his friends regarding the validity of us meeting such a well-known director, and wanted us to have a meeting with a producer and his lawyer, but we had no problem with that. A meeting was arranged with his lawyer and Roy Baird. Roy, in partnership with Bill Curbishley – who was a friend of Reggie's – had produced the films, *McVicar* and *Quadraphenia*.

The meeting was held at The King's Oak, and after the introductions we sat down to a delicious meal arranged by O'Neill. During the course of the meeting, they were left in no doubt that we really were engaged in talks with the well-known film director. It was a successful meeting and they wanted to return the compliment by inviting Lindsay and me to see the making of *Alien III* at Pinewood Studios, followed by a meal in the West End. But to their surprise we declined the offer, knowing we had far too much of a workload with our own businesses.

Reggie was over the moon that the meeting was such a success, but he always wanted things done and dusted overnight and could be hard work, ringing regularly asking for updates. Ronnie was more laid back, so if Reg was giving us a hard time I would ask Ron to explain things to him.

We soon discovered who the mole was within Reggie's trusted circle of friends. It turned out to be an undercover copper and, not only was the copper within Reggie's circle of friends, he was also involved with known villains outside it.

When we visited Reg he told us – before we had a chance to tell him – that he knew who the mole was, and it was obvious that certain people were to be warned as soon as possible. Ronnie was owed a considerable amount of money by this person, so he asked us to go and see him, giving the message that he had to visit Ronnie. Campbell was only too pleased to give us directions to where we could find him.

When we arrived at our destination, the bloke was taken by surprise by our unannounced visit. Campbell went in first, asking him to come outside to where we were waiting. He came out holding a shotgun, but undeterred we passed on Ronnie's message requesting him to go and sort out his debt.

Ronnie showed he wasn't too worried about the discovery of the undercover copper because, and he quoted a saying by Winston Churchill, 'It's better to have your enemies pissing out of your tent than pissing in.'

We had no doubt we had come under surveillance ourselves, so decided to bring in our specialists to carry out surveillance on those watching us.

The film, *The Krays: Bonded by Blood*, was screened at the Odeon, Leicester Square, with the Kemp brothers playing the parts of Reg and Ron, and even though Lindsay and I had been given tickets, we decided to give it a miss as we had seen the film previously on video.

Ronnie wanted us to attend Browns nightclub where a party was arranged for after the premiere, so with a few friends of Ron and a few of our people brought up from Wales, we followed his instructions. He wanted them placed either side of Browns – at a distance – ensuring everything went smoothly. He felt that, in view of the film going out that night, it could be an opportunity for someone to try to make a name for themselves – in his words: 'Some nutter.'

Ronnie had a wonderful knack of showing his presence even though he had been locked up for many years. The password given by him to enter Browns was: 'The Colonel sent me.'

We had a drink or two in what was classed the Silver Card section, after which we were ushered upstairs to the exclusive Gold Card section. We met and had a drink with Joey Pyle, who then introduced us to Albert Reading. We got on instantly with both of them and, being boxers ourselves, we were soon chatting about the greats of the old days.

Albert had been told that on no account must he let Tony Lambrianou in, because Ronnie was still annoyed about the newspaper report. I felt it was a bit unfair on Tony but, even though Reg and Ron were not there, it was still a big night for them and we respected Ronnie's wishes.

Kate, along with others, came in from the premiere and that night we mingled with many famous people.

We found Charlie Kray and told him Ron wanted to see him. Charlie nodded. He appeared to know what Ronnie wanted. My idea was that Ron wanted to talk to Charlie about the film contract and Charles Rosenblatt's advice.

Tony turned up with Adrian Bullen but they were both turned away, which saddened me, but I felt it was between the old fold so I didn't get involved. Bullen later sent one of the doormen to ask me to allow him in on his own as Tony had left, so he was brought in with two of our people.

After our successful meeting with Charles Rosenblatt and Colin Fry, arrangements were made for a meeting to be held at The King's Oak with Colin, which was to include Martin Mitchell.

Martin Mitchell wanted Lindsay and me to present a cartoon deal to Charles Rosenblatt for his consideration, and told us that there would be £100,000 involved if we were successful. The animated movie was to be called *Floo Man Choo* and after looking over the package I was very impressed by its presentation. The cartoon was based on germs turned into characters, educating children about the dangers of disease.

The cast list of voiceovers was very impressive:

Floo Man Choo........Vincent Price
Ah Tee Choo............Dudley Moore
Rubella.....................Eartha Kitt
Penny Cillin.............Jerry Hall
Auntie Septic............Elaine Stritch
Auntie Biotic............Penelope Keith
Oral Higeen..............Lenny Henry

We could see how valuable the movie would have been to be presented in front of Charles Rosenblatt, in view of the success he'd had with the animated film *Watership Down*.

Lindsay was discussing the cartoon deal with Martin Mitchell while I was discussing possible musicians for a soundtrack on the new movie *The Krays*. Colin said that Roger Waters, formally of Pink Floyd, had shown an interest, but how true it was I didn't know. We also discussed possible contenders for parts in the film.

David Ley suggested his friend, Robert Powell, to play Charlie Kray. We were all in agreement for Barbara Windsor to play Reggie and Ronnie's mother, Violet. I had met Ray Winston on a number of occasions and he, along with Glen Murphy, was also being suggested. Ronnie was in contact with the American actor, Robert Duvall, who he suggested would be suitable to play part of the Kray's Mafia connections.

Suddenly, Colin went into some sort of breakdown, insisting that I was going to be shot. I was stunned. I didn't know what had brought this on. I didn't know what was happening to him. The atmosphere changed in an instant, and even though I wouldn't allow weapons to be present at meetings, we always had a team on standby armed to the teeth in case we encountered any problems, such as those being mentioned by Colin.

Lindsay was still chatting with Martin about the cartoon deal, so I called him over, but by then Colin was having a complete breakdown. Campbell tried to shake some sense into him but I told him to leave things alone, and we immediately arranged for Martin and the others to be taken from The King's Oak. With Colin blurting out about me being shot we couldn't take any chances. We decided to take him back to the flat in the hope that he would sleep it off and be able to give us an explanation the next day.

The armed team arrived and Lindsay went outside to check that all was in place, in case a shooting was about to happen. Everyone in The King's Oak began to get jittery; they were unnerved at seeing armed people running around and taking up their positions outside the pub.

We brought in cars to take Colin to the flat, but he became even more agitated at seeing weapons in the hands of people he didn't know. Eventually we managed to get him into a car and he seemed to calm down for a while. I told Lindsay to stay at the pub with the others and, sandwiched between two more of our cars, we headed towards the flat.

When we parked outside, Colin appeared to have calmed right down and I assured him I would stay with him to see he was okay. The car door opened and I got out first, helping Colin to his feet, but he bolted, screaming and shouting as he went. I instructed the drivers of the three other cars to get going, then went looking for Colin, but he was nowhere to be seen. Then, as I was making my way back to the flat, I saw police cars and an ambulance racing up the street.

I telephoned The King's Oak and explained the situation, and it wasn't long before the phone rang and I was told that it had been picked up on police radio that Colin had been injured. Campbell made enquiries about which hospital Colin would be taken to but no one seemed to know anything, so there was nothing we could do but wait for news.

The next day, after making more enquiries, Campbell found out that Colin was at Whipp's Cross hospital with a broken back and a broken foot. Of course, all eyes were on me. Even Lindsay asked what had gone on. I hadn't touched him. On the contrary, I felt rather worried about him, but what made matters worse was that Colin told Campbell a very bizarre story of how he'd received his injuries.

Back in Wales, Lindsay and I had secured a deal for a Welsh Office grant of £250,000, then it was a case of waiting for the completion of the factory. We decided to let Paul Edwards do the local driving. His father had kept on to me about giving him another chance.

I was still in touch with Colin Fry by telephone, but it was still a mystery to me how he had received his injuries. He invited Lindsay and me to a party at his twin brother's home; he also lived in the South Wales area.

When we met up with Colin at his brother's home, it was decided to get the film deal back on track, and after making many enquiries we had a number of people prepared to finance it. One major player was David Ley, who indicated that he wanted to have majority control. Martin Mitchell was another who wanted to have a financial involvement, but David and Martin were still on bad terms.

We had been told that, with David and Martin on the same side financially, they were a formidable force to be reckoned with, so we arranged a meeting with David and Martin at different times, to see if we could get them to reunite and put their differences behind them.

We had several other deals on the go besides the film, including T-shirts with Reggie and Ronnie on, and we were in negotiations with a company which made braces. The company had Michael Douglas wearing their Thurston braces and was associated with the film *Wall Street*. The company showed an interest in designing Kray-style braces, which would be part of the memorabilia if and when the second film came out. Also, Ronnie had come up with the idea of a board game based on Godfathers and Gangsters and, understanding the world of art and design, we set about having a prototype made.

Ronnie had a contact in Leeds, who in turn was in contact with Waddington bosses, so we arranged to go to Leeds and check it out. We met a couple there called Frank and Noelle, who we believed to be a nice couple. Frank told us that he was once the minder of Danny La Rue, but we soon realised that Frank only knew Ronnie through writing to him in jail, and had told him a load of bollocks about knowing the Waddington bosses.

Frank and his wife took us from club to club, but we soon cottoned on to the fact that it was only to make them look good as we were friends of the Krays. However, we liked Frank and he had other business interests which we liked the sound of, so it hadn't been a wasted journey.

We visited Kate at her home in Headcorn, Kent, to discuss various business ventures, and she introduced us to her ex-partner, Harry, a likeable chap who I came to respect. It came up in conversation that Reggie and Ronnie were unhappy with the treatment they were receiving during their visits to each other because the screws and nurses were present all the time, and we felt that it was an issue that could be brought up with the European Court of Human Rights.

We heard that Paul Edwards had been taken to prison for non-payment of fines, and one day, when Lindsay and I were preparing to go back to London, Edwards rang, asking if we would pay him out of Cardiff jail.

I explained that we were on our way up to London and would send one of our boys down to get him instead, but he asked if he could come to London with us. We made a diversion to Cardiff, and as we arrived at the jail a few screws we knew from our last sentence were on their way out so I asked them how Edwards was. Laughing, they said he was like a fish out of water and was shitting himself.

As we handed over the money to the screws at reception, Edwards was being brought out to the gatehouse, but what he didn't realise was that the reception office had a two-way mirror looking straight into the gatehouse, and as we looked through it we could see Edwards looking worn out, his face full of fear.

We went outside to wait as the big doors opened and Edwards came into view. We watched as he puffed out his chest and told us that it had been a piece of piss! Lindsay and I just looked at each other and smiled. Then we headed for London with Edwards sitting rather quietly in the back of the car.

When we arrived, we were met by Campbell who explained that the *Sunday People* wanted to run a story on us, but I told him we wanted nothing to do with it. Then he added that it would be good publicity for the new Kray film. I discussed it with Reggie and Ronnie who said that they would like the story to go ahead, so we reluctantly agreed and left it to Campbell to arrange.

At The King's Oak, Jim O'Neill introduced us to Ken Hilton, the owner of the pub. Ken had an interest in the Family Inn Consortium, which was good for us to know as we intended acquiring a few pubs in Wales.

We held a meeting with David Ley and asked him if there was any possibility that he and Martin could become partners again. After some thought, he said that he was prepared to let Martin deal with certain transactions within the film deal, but would not sit in the same room as him. As we felt that we had made a breakthrough, we didn't pry into the reason there was so much animosity between them.

When we were negotiating finance for the second film with David, he confirmed he wanted in and was prepared to give £50,000 as a token payment to show he was genuine. He also said that he wanted full control over the film if he was financing it. He agreed to pay Lindsay and me £15,000, as we knew our investment in the second film had reached £30,000 and David wanted to pay us his contribution, which was fine by us.

I told him that the first film contract didn't reach its full potential with royalties, and we had already been told by Charles Rosenblatt that we needed to sell the film throughout the world even before it was made, which we could do as representatives of Charles. David was offering a good deal, but when I talked about it with Ron, he decided that David should visit him so that he could hear it for himself.

When we met up with Martin Mitchell, we found he was more than happy to have a small part in setting up the film. He was putting together a glossy package of the animated film *Floo Man Choo* for presentation to Charles Rosenblatt but, of course Martin, along with us, had to wait until Colin had recovered from his injuries.

Pete Gillett was pissing off quite a few people, including Kate and Reggie, and there was talk of him being done. Ronnie knew it would have been a bad move on Reggie's part, so Kate came to see us at The King's Oak. We decided that we should go down and have a word with Gillett, telling him to keep his mouth shut because he was pissing a lot of people off: Reg more than anyone. But even Ronnie had had enough of him and sent the message, 'Shut it or I will rip your eye out and piss on your brain.'

Personally, I wouldn't have taken too much notice. We had told Kate not to worry too much as what was done was done, but we would point out to Gillett that Reg wasn't happy and it would be better for him if he let things go. That same night we sent down our boys to gather as much info as possible on Gillett.

The next night, we assembled the biggest team that we could put together, but it soon became clear that we were being set up and the place was crawling with armed response. Just for the cheek of it we showed how close we could get, leaving our marks in various places, then we withdrew. The task we were left with was to find out who had tried to set us up.

When we next visited Ron, we told him that we weren't happy about taking a message to Gillett as we didn't know the bloke and felt it was something and nothing compared with the deals we were hatching.

When we were taking David in to meet Ron, we could see he looked nervous. After the introductions, David explained about giving £50,000 as a token payment and said that the intention was for Reggie and Ronnie to receive £1 million pounds each. He also pointed out that he wanted exclusive rights – with no interference – to deal with the finance and construction of the film, and that he would only deal with Lindsay and me. Ronnie nodded his head in agreement and, as always, a firm handshake was given, sealing the deal as businessmen.

Campbell had arranged a meeting with two *Sunday People* reporters and, of all the venues for it to take place, the reporters picked the conservatory area of The Blind Beggar pub in the Whitechapel Road, where Ronnie had shot George Cornell. On walking through the door we noticed Tony Lambrianou, who was in discussion with a reporter from *Wales on Sunday*.

The *Sunday People* reporters seemed to be under the impression that Lindsay and I would be playing the lead parts in the next Kray film. It didn't help the situation when Tony came in and told the reporters that we were playing the parts. After many questions had been asked and photographs taken, the story was due to run that coming Sunday. But when I read it I wasn't happy with the way some parts had been worded as it gave a clear indication that we were dealing with Reggie and Ronnie's business affairs.

We had urgent business back in Wales concerning our land development, so we decided to leave Edwards in London with instructions to pick up the money from David Ley then take it to Campbell, who Lindsay and I agreed would take his cut.

They realised he had an outstanding fine which was why they sent him to jail. Then we had a phone call telling us that Edwards was throwing his weight around in London and causing a lot of bad feeling at The King's Oak and drinking himself stupid.

We knew then that we'd come to the end of the road with him. He was becoming an embarrassment to all concerned and he had to go. So we hammered up to London where we found him in the flat with all the lads.

He had failed to collect the money from David Ley: the thick bastard had threatened him for the money. David was a man of his word and didn't need to be threatened for the money, so he told Edwards to fuck right off.

We took Edwards into the bedroom – to save him the shame of having a bollocking in front of everyone – but he fell over the bed, bumped his head, cut his lip and made his nose bleed. I should have sent the thick fucker packing there and then, making him walk home to Wales, but I decided to take him back myself the next day and have a few words with him on the way.

The next day Campbell telephoned the flat asking if he could borrow Edwards; Campbell and Edwards had never got on very well, so I found it strange when he asked to take Edwards with him to try to get Gazza (Paul Gascoigne, the England footballer) to a phone in order to talk to the press regarding a report that Gazza had shot an air rifle from his hotel window. I told Campbell he could do what he liked as I had finished with Edwards and his bullshit, but I pointed out that whatever they did, they were on no account to bring their problems back to us.

After Campbell had picked up Edwards, Lindsay and I decided to have lunch at a local pub, but as we were leaving the flat, Campbell and Edwards returned and I found it strange that they seemed to be the best of friends, although what they had done I didn't have a clue. They decided to join us for lunch and I watched as Campbell told Edwards to do this and that, yet a day earlier – the same as every other day – they had hated each other.

Edwards was moaning about his ribs after his fall off the bed and decided to return to the flat for a rest. I tried to find out exactly what they had done for the reporter, but Campbell was being very evasive and getting pretty drunk.

It was then I noticed a letter sticking out of his pocket on *Sunday People* headed paper. I lifted it out his pocket without him noticing and put it in my inside jacket pocket, intending to read it later.

Then a phone call came asking for Bullen, who had also joined us. It was his girlfriend telling him that Edwards had grabbed his gear and left the flat. After arranging for drivers to take Campbell home, Lindsay and I headed up to the flat with Bullen where I asked his girlfriend about Edwards. But all she said was that he had made a phone call, then told her that he had to get back to Wales.

I checked the last number dialled and found it was the speaking clock. I knew that Bullen's girlfriend had rung us at the pub, so why was she covering up the last number? Then the telephone rang and it was one of our drivers saying that he was at Campbell's house but that he had lost his keys and couldn't get in, so I told him to bring Campbell back to the flat.

Remembering the letter I had taken from Campbell, I read that the Godfathers were to assist with the security services, tracking down and turning in Iraqi terrorists relating to the war with Iraq, and realised to my horror that Campbell was about to leak its contents to the press.

How Campbell had the information I didn't know, as it had only come to mine and Lindsay's attention when we had been sworn to secrecy when taking the message to Reggie from Ron. I decided not to mention it to Campbell when he came back to the flat, as he didn't know we had it and we felt that it wasn't really our problem.

When they arrived, I took Campbell into the bedroom to find out what he and Edwards had been up to, but he was so pissed he wasn't making any sense. Suddenly, Bullen came running in and tried to bully the information out of Campbell by ramming a gun into his forehead. I managed to calm the situation and made Campbell a coffee, then I left Lindsay and the others with Campbell while I went into London to see a few people.

After the meeting with Ronnie and David Ley, I received a telephone call from David telling me he was pulling the plug on the deal. A friend had telephoned him and told him to cut Lindsay and me out of the deal, but what he didn't realise was that David's word was his bond and he pointed out to him that if he didn't have Lindsay and me in on the deal, there was no deal. He obviously didn't realise that Ronnie had agreed the deal with David on the visit, and that Lindsay and myself, and also Reggie, were all in full agreement.

We went back to see Ronnie and told him what had happened. He was livid, and judging by his response it was obvious that he had no idea, but there was nothing we could do.

I think Ronnie felt pretty bad, knowing how hard we had worked to get the final finances on the table, and he sat with a look of thunder on his face. He couldn't go on to us – we had done our job. In fact, it had cost us quite a lot of money running around the country setting it all up and going through all the legalities.

Ronnie took off his watch – a gift from Kate – which was encrusted with many diamonds, and passed it over the table, telling Lindsay and me to keep it as a token of how sorry he was. I reminded him that it was a gift from Kate on their wedding day and said that I could not take it under any circumstances, but the more I refused the more he became enraged. It got to the point where I had to take it or he would have blown his top on the visit.

He knew as well as us that fifty grand would have been on the table within days, with a further million pounds to follow. It wasn't my place to tell Kate that she had blown the deal – that was between her and Ron – but I did tell her that Ronnie had given me the watch although I had no intention of keeping it, and that I would return it to her at the earliest opportunity.

She seemed to think that I was taking advantage of Ron; I think not. I don't think many people could put one over on him.

When I took a closer look at the watch, I noticed that one of the diamonds was missing. It may have been lost when Ron had it, but then again I may have lost it, so I took it to a jeweller's and had a new diamond fitted, at a cost of well over £100.

Kate telephoned me to say that Wilf Pine was coming to pick up the watch, so Lindsay and I arranged to meet him at the Severn Bridge car park. We introduced ourselves to Wilf and his friend and handed over Ronnie's watch for it to be delivered to Kate, where it belonged.

8

THE BOOK OF BAD LUCK

Everyone seemed more content once Edwards was off the scene. We were all sick to death of his bullshit. Nevertheless, even though he was gone, we decided to have him watched, and word soon came back that he had done a deal with the police. It appeared that he had teamed up with an old school friend who was a Detective Inspector, but we didn't worry too much as he was just as thick as Edwards.

An old friend named Andrew Chamberlain turned up at one of our meetings and said he'd just been released from prison. We had already been in talks with his brothers and I got on particularly well with his brother Paul, so as we felt that Andrew was a sound bloke we decided to give him a go. However, most of the lads didn't like him because they said that he and his younger brother had a stink about them, unlike Paul who got on well with everyone and put people at ease. But because of the uneasiness the lads felt, we knew we couldn't let them go off on any ventures with the brothers.

When we next saw Andrew, he told us that he was at a loose end, so Lindsay and I invited him and his brother up to London as a few of us were due to visit The King's Oak. Phil Regnard also brought his brother, Terry, along. Jim O'Neill, as usual, had prepared meals for when we arrived, but when we sat down to eat, both Chamberlain brothers began complaining about their food, which surprised me as I had every confidence in O'Neill's cooking. Then one of them brought out a device they claimed was a bug detector and I thought they were joking at first, thinking what a marvellous party trick it was, but they were serious.

We all sat watching as they drank themselves stupid and messed about with the device – which apparently was a genuine bug detector, but they had no idea how it worked. Then they started picking on Campbell, complaining that he had insulted them. I knew they were walking on thin ice. If they picked on the wrong man, I had no doubt they would have been taken outside for a long walk, so I called over one of the Regnard brothers and instructed him to take them back to Wales as soon a possible. They were not only embarrassing themselves by spewing all over the place, they were an embarrassment to me. So they were taken back, not realising how close they had come to some serious problems.

Ronnie seemed to have calmed down regarding both the film deal and the watch, and was thankful we hadn't sold it. We toyed with the idea of taking the film deal to Martin Mitchell, but decided against it because of the possibility of it being ruined again. I felt we needed to see David Ley, mainly to apologise for Edwards' conduct, but also to thank him for his loyalty in wanting to keep the film deal with us.

Ken Hilton, due to financial problems at The King's Oak, moved in with his family, and although I got on very well with Ken we decided to take our meetings elsewhere. Ken had a family and sometimes in the past things had got out of hand and we didn't want to risk anything going wrong when his children were around.

We decided to team up with David Ley on some business ventures he had in mind. He had heard that The King's Oak was in trouble, so asked Lindsay and me to negotiate on his behalf with a view to buying it from Ken. But when we approached Ken about David's offer, we found that he had already sealed a deal with his business partner, hoping it would get him back on track. Jim O'Neill had left; he had lent Ken £15,000.

When we next visited Ronnie, we told him of our decision not to use The King's Oak for meetings and that, although the place had served us well, we had a chance of buying a pub in south London called The Thomas-A-Becket. Ronnie immediately began shaking his head and told us that the place was bad luck. Then he asked if we could take Ken in to see him.

I sensed an uneasiness in Ron after we mentioned the pub, but he didn't mention it again during the visit. Instead, he leaned forward and began whispering that he wanted Lindsay and me to do him a very important favour. With our heads bowed into the centre of the table, he continued to talk in a whisper and told us that when he was a youngster he was a right tearaway and would often wander miles from home and hang around different bombsites.

One day in particular, before he was even a teenager, he was having a general mooch around an area where all the solicitors and barristers had their offices. He noticed an open window and on looking through, saw a great big book sitting there for the taking. Although he knew that nicking it would be of no financial gain, he jumped up to the window, grabbed the book and made a run for it. As he ran he heard a voice shout, 'Come back, you bastard,' but he ran and didn't look back.

I thought his story was leading to a joke and that we'd soon hear Ronnie laughing like hell at the punchline but, when the whispering went even quieter and I had a job to hear him, I knew it was something which was obviously troubling him. He said that when he got home he showed the leather-bound book to Reg. Then they opened it, but the pictures and writing seemed not to have any meaning, so it was thrown under the bed and given no further thought.

Moving briefly off the subject of the book, Ronnie told us that one day, when he was picking up bits and pieces from bombed-out houses, he was surrounded by a crowd of people and within the crowd he saw the Queen, now the Queen Mother, who was touring the East End, giving her support during the bombing. He broke into a laugh and said that a photograph had been taken of her and that he was also in the picture when it was published in the papers the next day. He said that he and Reg laughed when they told the story of how he was caught red-handed in the photograph, taking things away from bombed-out houses. He ended his story with, 'Not a lot of people know that!'

He returned to the subject of the book and, changing his tone back to a whisper, said, 'I still have the book after all these years.' He told us how the mention of The Thomas-A-Becket pub and its bad luck reminded him of the book. He said that he had looked at the book on a number of occasions and eventually realised that it contained writings and drawings on occult matters. He asked us to recover the book, which would be arranged through his brother Charlie, and then we were to destroy it as he felt it had brought him bad luck throughout his life.

Lindsay and I sat in silence for what seemed an age but was probably only a few seconds. I remember thinking, 'If it's been bad luck for you, it could well be bad luck for us.' But I had to shake myself out of those strange thoughts. After all, it was only a book.

We were soon taking Ken in to meet Ronnie, but we could see that Ken was nervous about the meeting, so we stopped at a pub in Bracknell for a drink, which seemed to do the trick. Ken had soon calmed right down.

Ron shook Ken's hand with a vice like grip and wasted no time in getting down to business. He proposed to fill Ken's pub with famous people and good friends, then split the profits fifty-fifty. Ken nodded in agreement.

We chatted and drank the usual alcohol-free lager and at the end of the visit, as Ron walked with us to the door, he pulled me to one side to tell me that he had arranged for Lindsay and me to pick up the book and then destroy it. He didn't need to repeat himself. He knew my word was my bond and it would be done with no ifs or buts.

As Jim O'Neill no longer worked at The King's Oak, we arranged to meet him at a new pub he was managing in Chelmsford, and as Ian and Phil knew the way, they came along. As soon as Jim saw us, he said that he wanted Lindsay and me to recover the £15,000 that Ken owed him, but we pointed out that we couldn't possibly do that as we classed both him and Ken as good friends. I also told him that he would be wise not to send anyone else after Ken.

Ian invited us all to a family party and Lindsay and I decided to go along before travelling back to Wales. We partied until the early hours, and were all feeling a bit the worse for wear when I asked Jim for the telephone number of the pub. As he wasn't familiar with the number, he passed me his diary and pointed it out so that I could write it down. The drinks were still flowing and Jim had moved on to chat to someone else, so I slipped his diary into my pocket until I bumped into him later.

When the party was coming to an end, we called on a driver to take us back to Bullen's flat so that we could get some sleep before showering and going back to Wales. I telephoned Charlie to arrange to pick up the book on the way and expected him to meet us at a pub, but he said he was busy and would meet us on the Roman Road. After a brief chat, Charlie handed over a box and we were on our way.

I looked inside the box and saw a smaller box, inside which were some old armbands for holding up shirt sleeves, a few brooches or badges, and a small pocketbook called *West End Rituals of Craft Freemasonry*. The badges had little tags saying 'The Grand Master' and 'Grand Director of Ceremonies', plus a little sword and a bent-up dove.

The whole box smelled of smelly socks and the book was wrapped in an even smellier cloth. I was becoming fascinated with the contents, and as I opened the book I saw a couple of loose pictures. The first one, called The First Tracing Board, showed angels walking downstairs; the second one was more sinister and showed a coffin with skull and crossbones. There was also some sort of parchment with what appeared to be Hebrew writing on it. I could see the pages of the book had been damp at some stage and it looked as if something had chewed some of the edges. I removed the pictures and turned over the next page, which had the title 'The Book of Law' and underneath was a picture of an eye with the words 'Aiwass LLL'.

I placed it all back in the box and decided to take a closer look at it when we were back home.

Our land development was hitting problems with the drainage and we found that it was the council which was causing the delays. We had gone through the proper channels when getting planning permission, so couldn't understand why the council was giving us aggravation over something which had been passed months previously.

The last thing we needed was conflict within the planning department; Lindsay and I knew we needed to have a good relationship with the planners in view of the bigger projects we had in mind. We needed to get the problem solved by way of legal argument, and if it meant taking our complaint higher we had friends in the business who could take on our case.

Several meetings were held throughout the week in the hope that the drainage problem would be resolved, and it was at one of the meetings that someone suggested we highlight our case on the television. We heard that HTV Wales had been running a number of programmes showing that councils in other areas were giving the same problems to other builders.

I made a telephone call to the HTV Wales studio and was soon chatting to the producer, Mr Bruce Kennedy, who showed an interest in our problem and agreed to take on our case.

Lindsay and I spent a few evenings reading through the old book that Ron wanted us to destroy. We had no doubt it was of occult origin and understood Ronnie being superstitious and believing it brought him bad luck. We placed it in an old box and, after packing it with rolled-up newspapers, we poured lighter fuel over it and it was soon burning away nicely. We threw the badges away.

We still held meetings with a select few and there seemed to be some concern about there being paid grasses amongst certain gangs. It was suggested that we set up a dummy police station so anyone suspected of being an informant would be put through their paces and think they were in a genuine police station. We knew it would have to be thought through very carefully and obviously would take a lot to finance, but when we took a vote on the idea everyone voted unanimously to go ahead.

I smiled to myself, thinking that it was like being in the chambers of the local council, yet we were the most ruthless criminals. I spoke briefly about what would happen if we found out who the grasses were after setting the process in motion. The room fell silent: not for want of anything to say, but because of the thoughts running through our minds of dealing with the ultimate betrayal.

9

ARMED ROBBERY

It was early morning and I heard the tinkling of milk bottles. Then suddenly police were through the door, arresting me for an armed robbery which had taken place some time during the summer. All I could say was, 'You must be fucking joking.'

I soon realised that Lindsay had also been pulled, and that Ian and Phil were on their way down from London. They too had been arrested.

One of the leading detectives on the case was Inspector Gareth Edwards, and as he was taking me to the cell he said, 'You are in it now, mate.' Without bothering to look at the little shit, I replied, 'Do you know something I don't?'

I was put in a freezing cold cell, while Lindsay was put in a cell with the heating turned up full. We could hear the desk sergeant complaining to the detectives that this wasn't what his job was about.

I was taken into the interview room with the heating full on and the two detectives asked why I was sweating. I went through the first interview knowing that I had an alibi, but the two detectives weren't having any of it.

After my interview, they opened all the windows to let out the heat before taking Lindsay in and asking him why he was shivering. The daft bastards must have thought we were in Cuba.

On the second interview they played the same game with the heating, and although we gave them an account of where we were on the day in question, we still had the same response. So we decided, after taking advice from our solicitor, that we would answer none of their questions in any subsequent interviews, which were becoming so frequent that I got to know the detectives as Sutton and Price.

What I found amusing was that they seemed more interested in the stripper we had arranged for Andrew Chamberlain at a party in The King's Oak, and the photographs we had taken of him and the stripper, which showed Chamberlain with a length of string tied around his private parts.

Sutton and Price, laughing like fuck at Chamberlain in the photo, asked me who he was. I didn't think they were being serious, neither did the solicitor, who looked at me knowing very well it was Chamberlain. He was laughing like hell and so was I because I knew that every copper in Gwent knew the Chamberlains, but Sutton was still rabbiting on.

'You went to London with Andy. This boy called Andy. There are a lot of enquiries to be made yet. We thought we had a lot before the enquiry, but things are coming out all the time. You see, Paul Edwards has thrown a lot of light onto things this morning and last night. I'm asking you again, would you identify Andy for us, please? If you are as innocent as you say you are, you've got nothing to concern yourself with in identifying this person named Andrew. Do you want to identify Andrew to us, please?'

'No comment,' I replied, smiling. I knew from that point that Chamberlain was the rat. Even the solicitor had cottoned on, but Sutton couldn't see it.

Sutton and Price were well happy with the photographs of the stripper and, still laughing, Sutton was off again:

'The photos I have here were recovered from your home today. Lovely ones too as you are smiling. There are some other lovely ones too, I can assure you. You've made me smile now. In the photograph that I'm showing you is a gang: Phil, Ian, Lindsay, you, the other boy – who we believe to be from Wales – we can't identify, and we don't know who the persons in the middle are. Would you accept from us that these photographs were taken on the night of the stag party up in London?'

'No comment,' I said.

'Would you accept that this is the body of the stripper you privately hired?' Sutton asked, with a daft look on his face.

I couldn't believe it. I was being interviewed for an armed robbery and I had these stupid fucking coppers, Sutton and Price, going on about a stripper.

But there was no stopping them and off Sutton went again: 'Well, we believe that the private showing did take place in London and, at this present moment in time, enquiries are under way to establish the identity of that stripper, so that she can be interviewed. Any comment about that?'

The solicitor jumped in. 'You're going to interview her, are you, the stripper?'

Sutton and Price, laughing like hell, nodded their heads. Sutton still went on: 'Can't you see what line you're going down, honestly? We're not pulling any strokes. Adrian Bullen is in a compromising position and he's talking. I will ask you again to identify Andy for me, please. You don't want to, do you?'

'No comment,' I said, thinking, 'Doesn't he go on?'

'Okay, I have no further questions for you. Leighton, is there anything you wish to ask us as your investigating officers?'

I didn't answer.

As I was leaving the interview, Sutton smugly told me that they had my father in a cell and that he was to be charged with armed robbery. I couldn't believe it. I thought I had Morcambe and Wise sitting there out to take the piss. But they weren't.

When they took me back to the cell I found that they had put my father in the cell next to me. I asked him if he was okay and, looking up at me from the bed, he gave a nod. He asked, 'Did you do the robbery, son?'

I replied, 'I did not.'

'Well then, son, you can't admit to something you haven't done.'

I knew my father wasn't too well, and Lindsay shouted down, asking what was going on. I shouted back, 'They've got Dad in the next cell to me.'

Lindsay went quiet.

One of the pip coppers came down, asking me some daft fucking question and that was it, I went off on one and the sergeant, along with some others, came running down. I was booting hell into the door. Then I heard a copper shouting, 'He's ripping the door off.' Lindsay had managed to get his fingers under the door, and with his feet either side, began to bend it open.

Their faces were full of terror. They were screaming at my father and yelling at us both to stop.

I knew that someone had framed us for some poxy armed robbery. Lindsay had a witness who had seen him go to my father's house at the time the robbery was taking place, yet Sutton and Price were more interested in interviewing a stripper than speaking to the bin man who would verify Lindsay's story.

They eventually let my father go, and Lindsay and I were taken back to court, as their three days, questioning time had run out. They needed to get an extension of two days for further interviews.

I was also being charged with dealing in drugs. It was on one of the interviews that the charge unfolded.

Sutton: I'm going to show you a diary now, a red diary. Do you agree I'm showing you a diary? Is this your diary?
Solicitor: I agree that you're showing him a red diary.
Sutton: Is this your diary, Leighton?
'No comment,' I replied.
Sutton: This was recovered from your home on Wednesday morning, and now I will take you to the date 8 August, bearing in mind that is the day we believe the stag night took place, and bearing in mind the questions I've just asked about you going into the toilets to make a deal. On the opposite page is writing. Is that your writing?
'No comment,' I said. I knew it was Jim O'Neill's diary from the party.
Sutton: No, or nothing to say?
'No comment,' I replied.
Sutton: You will see it says Billy's tab; it says q, which I believe is quarters of an ounce; 40 which I believe relates to £40; half an ounce £70; an ounce £120; quarter of a kilo £630; half a kilo £1,250; and a full kilo £2,500.
'No comment,' I answered.
Sutton: Obviously you know what I m getting at. I believe that those figures in your diary opposite 8 August relate to drug dealing. Have you anything to say on that?
'No comment.'
Sutton: That night, did you make an order for a controlled drug, called amphetamine?
'No comment.'
Sutton: The going rate for an ounce of amphetamine on the street is £120. I believe those figures on there was the deal that you were carrying out that night to purchase amphetamine drugs. Do you agree?
'No comment.'
Sutton: Were your buyers going to be Phil and Ian?
'No comment.'
Sutton: So you don't deny it?
'No comment.'

Sutton: If these figures here are easily explainable, Leighton, I am asking you to tell me what they mean.
'No comment.'

I knew very well whose diary Sutton was asking me about, but there was no way I could say anything. I knew I hadn't been set up with the diary, it was a genuine mistake, but it looked like I was going to get weighed off for dealing in drugs.

I wasn't a grass and never will be a grass, so it was down the pan I was going, for the simple mistake of forgetting to hand back O'Neill's diary.

My biggest shock was still to come as Sutton went on with the interview.

Sutton: Caroline, Adrian's girlfriend, she says that during one of your visits to London earlier this year, she walked into Bullen's flat after she had been out on a shopping expedition and she saw a shotgun.
'No comment.'
Sutton: Can you remember that? Her coming in?
'No comment.'
Sutton: She says that, at the time, you two were there, together with Paul Edwards and Adrian.
'No comment.'
Sutton: She also states that she was present in The King's Oak pub when a shotgun was on open display.
'No comment.'
Sutton: Jimmy O'Neill, James O'Neill, do you know him?
'No comment.'
Sutton: Well, we know him now. He is the former manager of The King's Oak. That's the pub that you frequented when you were in the London area. I think you mentioned that on your first interview, so will you accept that you know him?
'No comment.
Sutton: He tells us, and he states that, he has seen you and others, which has been mentioned in this interview already, in possession of a pump-action shotgun in his pub. We believe the pump-action shotgun he is talking about is that Mossberg there. Any comment to make?
'No comment.'
Then, concluding the interview:
Sutton: Now then, listen to this and listen to it hard. As you are aware, whilst you have been in custody, samples of blood, saliva

and hair have been obtained from you and your brother, Lindsay. A forensic scientist will provide evidence, bearing in mind that you and your brother denied any knowledge of the clothing, a forensic scientist will provide evidence to us that your brother Lindsay was one of the persons who entered the Halifax Building Society that day wearing one of those balaclavas.

'No comment.'

Sutton: Do you understand what I've just told you?

'No comment.'

Sutton: That we can now prove that your brother was responsible for the armed robbery.

'No comment.'

I thought, 'Hang on, mate. What the fuck are you going on about here? Forensic hasn't come back yet, so how can you say my brother was responsible?'

It became clear to them throughout the interviews that I wasn't the one who had done the job; I was being accused of planning it; dealing in firearms and also drug dealing because of O'Neill's dairy.

After five days, the interviews were over and it became clear who the rats were. They weren't just rats, they were part of the stitch-up to save their own little arses.

On my way back to the cell, Price seriously said, 'I hope we can have a drink when this is all over.'

I thought, 'What a fucking cheek. Five days of interviews over a poxy armed robbery and he wants a drink when its over. Yeah, bollocks!'

I heard them bringing in Ian and Phil, and realised we were all about to be charged. They had also arrested Ian's girlfriend Mandy, in the hope that Ian would give them what they wanted. However, during the course of the interviews they released her without charge.

Ian was shouting through the door, saying how Bullen was putting us all in it. I had a fair idea that there was another one who was stitching us, and Edwards was the main contender with his bullshit.

Lindsay and I, along with Ian and Phil, were taken out of our cells to be charged. Sutton and Price stood there with some others and said, 'Leighton Frayne, that you between 1 November and 24 July at London or elsewhere without the authority of the Secretary of State, had in your possession a pump-action gun, namely a Mossberg 12-bore, which was not chambered for 22 rimfire cartridges and had a barrel less than 24 inches in length. Contrary to Section 5(1)(ac) of the Firearms Act, 1968. That you, between 1 November and 24 July at Newbridge and elsewhere, conspired together with other persons to rob the Halifax Building Society, contrary to Section 1(1) of the Criminal Law Act, 1977.'

Lindsay was charged with armed robbery as well as the same two charges which had been made against me. It was clear that Sutton and Price thought Phil was the other robber with Lindsay. He was charged with the robbery along with supplying weapons. Ian was charged more or less the same as me, except that possession became supplier on his charge.

I could see the strain on Lindsay, Ian and Phil's faces, and knew that after five days of interrogation we needed to rest and recharge our batteries. It was at that point, when all hope of getting bail had gone right out of the window, that my mind began to welcome prison – if only to get away from the clutches of the police.

I knew we would be taken to court the next day to be remanded in custody. Lindsay and I both had the same thought, 'Let's get the fuck to Cardiff jail!' We also knew that once Sutton and Price had gone off duty there was the possibility of a visit.

It took a few hours to get back to the cell but, soon after we got there, when I tried to get some shut-eye, I heard a tapping on my cell door. I looked through the crack but couldn't see anyone. The tapping continued but this time someone was saying my name in a very low voice. I answered, thinking it may be Phil or Ian out of their cells (I knew Lindsay was at the other end).

'Leighton, Leighton,' the voice went on.

'Yes?' I replied.

'Andrew Chamberlain is a paid informer. Be on your guard!'

As I took the message in, I heard whoever it was go from the cell area back through the door to the police station. I knew then that I had been tipped off by a copper.

I lay on my bed thinking, 'Fucking Chamberlain. Someone's having me on.'

I knew Paul Chamberlain had just copped ten years for fire-bombing, but could have had less if he'd said who he was with – Paul was no grass. All I could think was, 'What's going on here?' I dared not shout up to Lindsay, so I left it until the morning when I would be able to talk to him in the court cells.

We were all taken to court the next morning in separate cars, with Phil and Ian segregated from Lindsay and me. When I got a chance to tell Lindsay about my visit the night before he was just as shocked as me.

Lindsay and I didn't bother going up for bail, we knew we had no chance. Phil and Ian did apply but were knocked back.

Sutton and Price were happy about bail being refused, and allowed us all in the same cell while we were waiting to be taken back to the police station.

Ian and Phil hadn't been to prison before and I could sense their anxiety. They were just as bewildered as Lindsay and me about all the bullshit we had been given throughout the five days.

Trying to relax Phil and Ian, I asked about the business card which Sutton and Price were so excited about: the card read 'Hutmar'. Sutton and Price seemed to be going down the avenue that Phil and Ian were our assassins.

We all began laughing like hell in the cell, and any coppers looking through at us must have thought we didn't give a shit about our situation.

I couldn't wait to get to Cardiff prison just to have a shower and put on some clean clothes, not caring whether they were my own or remand-issue.

The desk sergeant opened my door and told me I had a visitor, and when I went to the exercise yard for the visit I saw Andrew Chamberlain standing there. I knew in that instant that what I had been told was true. He had it written all over his face, and it crossed my mind to do the fucker there and then, but I thought, 'Fuck you. I will play your game.'

According to information given at our interviews, Gwent police had Chamberlain on their wanted list, yet there he was visiting me.

I thought, 'You fucking slag,' as he stood there asking if there was anything he could do for me. I didn't let on that I knew he was a rat but I cut the visit short and went back to my cell, and who should be there to greet me on my return but Sutton and Price.

They had already told Lindsay, Ian and Phil that we weren't going to Cardiff on remand as the prisons were on strike, and all remand prisoners were being sent to various police stations throughout South Wales and the west of England.

I had never heard of it before, prisons on strike, and I wondered whether it was another one of Sutton and Price's games, just to piss us off.

The desk sergeant informed Lindsay and me that one of us was being sent to Abergavenny police station, with three being taken to Bristol.

We finally got to talk to Ian and Phil and had to decide who was going to Abergavenny and who would stay with Lindsay and me. We decided that Ian should go to Abergavenny as he had the best chance of bail. Phil and Lindsay had been charged with armed robbery, but what Sutton and Price didn't realise was that Phil had a cast-iron alibi for his whereabouts when the robbery took place. Phil had also been charged with dealing in firearms, along with Ian. We felt Ian had the best chance of bail, even more so if he was separated from us.

Ian wasn't too happy about going to Abergavenny on his own and I could understand his feelings in wanting to stay with Phil, but in all fairness to him he listened to what I had to say and agreed to go to Abergavenny police station alone.

Lindsay, Phil and I were cuffed up and sent on our way to remand at a police station in Bristol. Lindsay and I knew the rules when on remand and assumed they would have to give us better conditions, which were our rights. Phil had never been to prison before, let alone remanded to a police station, so we knew we had to keep an eye on him.

When we arrived at the police station, we found that it had been converted into a sort of remand centre with the capacity to hold about a dozen prisoners, and we found the blokes remanded there were wandering around, giving it the big one.

The place was like a pigsty, so we set about cleaning it up as Phil looked at us, wondering what we were doing. I told him that we didn't know how long we were going to be there. Then, to the disbelief of the police, we asked for cleaning gear, such as bleach. I knew we needed to bleach the showers down, as the other remand prisoners didn't seem to care much about their surroundings.

We bleached our cells, the toilets and showers, which the police seemed to find amusing. Some of the other remand prisoners also seemed to find it extremely funny.

Phil was about to get his first lesson in prison politics as we went into the kitchen area where, on seeing sugar and used tea bags all over the place, we began cleaning and washing down the worktops.

Still bemused, a copper came in sniggering and told us that he had asked the other lads to keep the place tidy but they'd just laughed in his face.

'We are not living like fucking pigs in here,' I told him.

The copper looked rather stunned and when Lindsay started laughing I realised what I had said. The copper must have thought I was referring to him as the pig!

Once everything was shipshape, I pulled a copper, asking him about using the phone to let our families know we were okay. He told us that we could use the phone that was specially for prisoners' use, but said that the problem was getting on it. He was right – our so-called fellow prisoners were hogging the phone by ringing sex lines.

Some of them needed to be dealt with and it didn't take long to see who the leaders of the pack were. I enticed one of the big-headed bastards out of the way, while Lindsay and Phil kept watch, just in case any coppers wandered in.

I grabbed the bloke and smashed one hell of a head-butt into his face, busting open his nose. Then, grabbing hold of his busted nose, I warned him not to tell the coppers and suggested it would be best if he told them that he and his merry men wanted to fuck off to another police station.

It didn't take the coppers long to work out what had happened to the mouthy bastard and it was surprising how quickly the place changed, with everyone doing their bit to keep the place tidy.

After that, we had the police bringing us breakfast in bed with newspapers to read. Phil thought we were cheeky bastards, but Lindsay and I knew the police didn't have a clue how remand worked, so we took advantage of it.

Ian's solicitor went for judge and chambers, and as we expected he got bail.

We were due at Blackwood Magistrates Court and Blackwood coppers were soon there with a van to pick us up. When the cuffs were put on Lindsay, he complained that they were too tight, but the copper told him to piss off. Lindsay crunched the cuffs tighter and told the copper that he would have to explain at the other end how his hands had turned blue. Lindsay was telling the copper what a fucker he was, while I gave Phil the nod, ready to have a go in the van. I knew we could have given them some serious problems if we kicked off, but one of the other coppers loosened Lindsay cuffs and told everyone to calm down.

At the Magistrates Courts, we were taken from the cells to sit in the court. We decided that Phil should to go for bail. Lindsay and I held back applying for ourselves, as we knew we didn't have a prayer, and felt that if we did apply, it would have been a dead cert that Phil would have been knocked back.

A London solicitor representing Phil let it be known that he had a concrete alibi, and that even though he had replied 'No comment' in his interviews, it was not an admission of guilt. The magistrates took no chances and Phil was granted bail.

Lindsay and I were taken to Blackwood police station where we were told that the police in Bristol didn't want us back, so arrangements had been made for us to be sent to Cwmbran police station, another temporary remand centre.

When we arrived at the police station and were waiting to be taken through to the cell area, we saw a couple of lads watching television through the gates.

We were soon asked to go to be strip-searched, which was no problem – it was routine in the prison system.

We were told that we weren't allowed to have lighters or matches in our cells, but Lindsay and I, from a young age, were capable of sleight of hand, so placing my lighter – which was a brass Zippo – on the desk, I went through their strip-search. When it was finished, Lindsay stepped forward and I stood on the side as they prepared to search him. Before they started, he asked if it was okay to smoke, and they agreed. So, with his lighter hidden in his hand – also a brass Zippo – he leaned over, picked up the lighter on the desk and lit his fag and at the same time I picked up my cigarette. He then passed the lighter from the desk to me which I put in my pocket, Lindsay then placed his lighter on the desk, and with my lighter in my pocket I was taken to my cell.

As they didn't know how to deal with remand prisoners, our cell doors were left open but the corridor gate was locked. Lindsay had the cell next to me and, when we looked through the locked gate, we could see the desk sergeant sitting with a few other coppers, and at the other end there was a row of cells where the other lads were held.

The first couple of days were okay as it goes, with family visits in and around the cell area. The coppers, for once, seemed sympathetic about our surroundings, and one sergeant in particular was very good and was prepared to listen to any ideas we had regarding our conditions. We were offered tablets to help us sleep and the lads on the other side indicated that we should take them. I was never one for taking tablets just for the sake of it, but knew that the lads on the other side would be more than happy to have ours.

The police had decided to fit a shower at the end of our corridor as it was becoming awkward taking each prisoner downstairs to their personal showers. The shower had recently been fitted and I was the first to use it, and I was feeling refreshed, when the desk copper told me we had a visit.

It was Bruce Kennedy of HTV Wales, who had become very concerned with the way we were being accused of the armed robbery. The desk copper allowed the visit with Bruce to take place in the cell area, and he soon realised that the conditions we were being kept in were unsatisfactory.

After our visit with Bruce, we were due one from our family, but the shift was changing and one of the coppers coming on was a horrible bastard. He seemed to be hell-bent on getting our backs up, and told us that all visits were to be taken outside in the cage. I told him that we had previously been allowed visits in the cell area, but he wouldn't listen and told me to fuck off, as it was he who was in charge. Still arguing with me, he told me again to fuck off, just as my family walked through the door.

Pointing to the door, I told my family to go back out. They didn't ask why, they just turned around and walked out. The copper stood there sniggering at me so, as he locked the gate, I grabbed a mop stick, snapped it and rammed it into the lock of the gate. Lindsay, having rushed to put on his trainers, ripped out the shower and slid it against the gate, then we started smashing the place up. The copper suddenly didn't look so smug and, looking as if he was about to cry, pleaded with us to stop.

The water from the shower was pissing out and anything that came apart was thrown at the coppers. A lad on the opposite side had his head stuck in the serving hatch of a door. As bits of toilet went flying past, water was filling up the floor, Lindsay was smashing anything that would break and steam was filling the air. The coppers could only watch from behind the door as pieces of the cistern smashed into it.

Metal pipes were ripped out and Lindsay ripped the cover off the communication wires, making the electricity go off with a bang. Out of breath, we stopped to have a fag. By then a dog handler had arrived with a shield and protective clothing, but what good he thought he was going to do I don't know. He tried to push the stick out of the gate lock using his shield but I was beating him back with a metal pipe. Then Lindsay began spraying Lynx body spray. The dog handler just laughed at us, so I clicked open the Zippo lighter and rolled the wheel, and to his surprise he was looking at one hell of a flame, which set his shield on fire. He dived into the water, which was rising nicely, then scurried off through the door. It seems the steam carried the flame much further than we expected.

With pillows and bedding burning, Lindsay began to smash one of the cell doors off its hinges. It was making a hell of a racket and, as the police station was built on concrete legs, each smash shook the whole building. Then everything went quiet.

Lindsay had a nasty cut on his arm after smashing through a cistern, but even though his blood was dripping into the water, we stood there with two metal pipes ready for whatever they wanted to try.

A copper called my name from behind the door and asked if he could come out without anything being thrown at him. As his head emerged, I could see it was the sergeant who seemed to have some understanding of our conditions, so we knew we couldn't give him any grief, and as he stepped forward he said that he had a high-ranking copper with him.

As they slowly approached we saw the high-ranker, and the pips on his shoulder shone in what little light was left after the devastation we had caused.

Lindsay understood by the look on my face that if we had a chance, we would try to grab him and take him hostage.

As we approached the gate, we took a firmer hold on our metal pipes and the pip copper asked if we would stop what we were doing. After all his big talk of threatening to kill us we should have told him, 'Say "pretty please" and we will.'

'FUCK OFF,' I shouted, as I raised my metal bar, making the sergeant and pip copper dive straight back behind the door. The sergeant realised what his boss had said and asked to speak to us alone. We agreed. He told us that we had proved our point, and anyway, there was nothing left to smash up. He also said that what the bastard copper had said to us was very wrong. Lindsay and I knew we were in for a booting when it was over, but I'd already decided I would take one of them with me.

The sergeant guaranteed us that if we gave up we would be moved to another police station, without having a booting off his colleagues. Lindsay and I knew there was no more we could do. It was a matter of getting out of there with the least amount of damage off the ones hiding behind the door.

I knew that at least we had an option – if the sergeant was a man of his word – and, remembering his fairness on the previous days, I agreed. I told him to give us a minute and he nodded quite happily.

When I talked about it with Lindsay, I said that if they gave us any grief we would take one of them down and not let go.

We walked towards the gate and threw our metal pipes to the floor. The sergeant, not taking any chances, asked Lindsay and me in turn to put an arm through the gate so that he could fit on the cuffs. After digging the mop stick out of the gate lock, he opened the gate slowly and asked us to turn around with our hands behind our backs. I knew we were taking a hell of a gamble if the sergeant didn't keep his word. We could be battered with our hands behind our backs.

Once we were cuffed up, all the coppers came through wearing riot gear and the sergeant took us into separate rooms. The dogs were right by my legs, snarling like hell. The dog handler who'd tried to get the gate open started pushing me in the stomach, asking me for a go. I tried to lay the head on him but the others held me. The sergeant was soon back in, shouting at the dog handler copper to let it go. Then, to my surprise, he came up behind me and told the dog handler that if he wanted to fight me, he would take the cuffs off me to even it up. The dog handler wasn't so brave then and whimpered off into the corner with his mutt.

The sergeant had kept his word – unusual for a copper I thought – and arrangements were made to move me to another police station. I was surrounded by 20 or so coppers in riot gear, shields held high, not taking any chances.

They arranged police escorts to get me from there, and the sergeant told me that Lindsay needed to go to the hospital for treatment to the nasty gashes on his arms.

I was able to listen to what was going on and it appeared that quite a crowd of reporters and photographers had gathered outside, so they threw a blanket over my head and guided me out to a waiting car.

Sandwiched between two riot coppers in the back of the car, we raced off at high speed, escorted by a number of police cars, sirens going and lights blazing away.

10

THE COPPERS' LAIR

With riot coppers and shields either side of me, I was escorted briskly into another police station, which had been converted into a temporary remand centre.

I was met by the Inspector of Ebbw Vale police station, who began stamping and shouting that if I were to do the same to his police station I was in for it. I could only smile as I heard the shouts of some other lads who were banged up. 'Let us know when you want to do this one. We're all ready,' a voice shouted from one of the cells.

Still cuffed up and soaking wet, I was put into a cell with no lights and, getting as comfortable as I could, I drifted off to sleep.

The next morning I found the cuffs had cut into my wrists, leaving blood all over the mattress, then the door opened and it was the same inspector I had seen when I arrived. He asked whether I would give them any problems if he took the cuffs off me, but on seeing my bleeding wrists they were off before I could answer.

I was taken to a cell area, which must have been on the female side as there were only two cells and they had built-in shower facilities. Six lads were on the other side chatting through the gate.

The inspector came down and asked if there was anything I needed. The only thing I could think of was ashtrays. He went off looking rather perplexed, then came back with a couple of small baking pots.

I was waiting for a visit to see how Lindsay was after his hospital treatment and I found out they had taken him to Newport police station.

Some of the lads on the other side were shouting over that it had been on TV, and what a good job we had done smashing up the police station. As I listened to them I could tell they were either stoned or drugged up. I was offered a mug of tea, and without thinking I drank it with relish, but after just a few minutes I felt as if I had been drugged. The coppers were soon down in my cell giving me other tablets, I knew I was fucked and could hardly stand. My mind worked okay but my body wouldn't do what I wanted.

After a day or two, when I was still head-shot on the bed, a copper came in the cell to tell me that I was due in court.

'Fucking court,' I thought. I wasn't fit to have a piss, let alone be dragged to court. I was dribbling as a result of the drugs which had been pumped into me, but I refused to go to court and rolled over on my bed.

Then two policewomen came into the cell and began to take my clothes off me and put on my suit. The odd hand went astray but I wasn't complaining – they had even ironed my shirt. Dribbling, and with a big smile on my face, they could have taken me anywhere, just as long as the arms of the law were going to undress me when I got back.

Soon after, one of our local coppers came in telling me to be ready to go to court. He could see I was in a hell of a shape. He went storming off to the desk, asking what the fuck they were playing at, and said that taking me to court in this condition wasn't why he wore a uniform. Before long he was back with another one to help me into the van which was to take me to court for a hearing.

The high almighty had spoken to them, but as they felt sorry for me they took the long way to court in the hope I would come out of my stupor.

When I arrived I was put in a cell with Lindsay. My head was shot to bits and I asked Lindsay to pay my fine so I could get the fuck away from there! Lindsay saw the funny side of it. I was taken into court dribbling like hell and one of the magistrates stopped and asked if I needed any help, but after a few minutes it was bail refused and back in the cells. Lindsay was taken back to Newport and me back to Ebbw Vale.

I had a visit from the family and I informed the inspector that I was going on an official hunger and water strike. I knew my rights, as on previous sentences I'd seen others go on hunger strikes in Cardiff prison.

My solicitor visited me and said that detectives wanted to interview me over the Cwmbran incident. The detectives asked me what I had to say about smashing up the police station. I knew they couldn't do us for a riot because to be classed as a riot it had to involve at least three people.

I could only point out to them that I didn't really give a fuck about what they wanted to charge me with considering what I had hanging over my head. The cheeky bastard told me that if I got off with the charges already against me, they would charge me with smashing up their police station.

I was just about to leave when I was asked to make a statement against the copper who had caused the problem in the beginning. Now it was getting interesting. Sitting back down, I was all ears. He went on to tell me that the officer had more or less admitted he was in the wrong, and they were prepared to sack him. I thought that the copper must be a right horrible bastard and must have upset someone within their fold. However, I told the detectives that the copper probably had a family, and that I wasn't prepared to take away his career just because he couldn't do his job as a screw. My solicitor nodded to the detectives and said, 'I told you so.'

As I got up from my chair the detective said, 'Well, your brother will if you won't.' I smiled as I went through the door. I knew my brother a little better than he did!

The hunger and water strike was beginning to get to me and the daft bastards were still giving me all sorts of tablets, which I was saving up.

As I lay in bed in the early hours I heard the gate open and could hear two people walking towards my cell door, which was locked at night. I padded my bed up with pillows and hid by the door, then I heard one of the coppers say, 'Is he dead yet?' Laughing, the other asked, 'Are the body-bags ready?'

I had placed a folded piece of paper in the crack of the door and, taking a deep breath, I blew through the paper, which gave out an almighty screech. Then I rammed my arm through the serving hatch like something out of *Dawn of the Living Dead*. One copper fell on the floor screaming like a banshee and the other froze in terror.

The good old borstal screech had served me well, and I laughed so much that my stomach hurt from the lack of food and water.

I received a visit from Bruce Kennedy, this time visiting as a friend, not on behalf of HTV Wales. He was appalled by the conditions in which we had to live. I handed over quite a few of the different tablets that I had been given, and could see that he was extremely shocked by the cocktail of drugs prescribed by the police.

I spent about five days on the hunger and water strike, but realised that it wasn't going to get me back to prison, so I decided to come off it. The doctor was called and advised me to take soup for a day or two. The lads on the other side were having Chinese and Indian meals, and fish and chips from the shops surrounding the police station, and it wasn't long before I was tucking into the same, depending on which coppers were on the desk.

Occasionally, I was able to make a phone call to Lindsay at Newport police station. As we were going into our fourth week in the police stations, I, along with the others, became bored very easily.

I made a request for a bible but the only response I got was a number of coppers laughing in my face. I wasn't a religious person but I had been taught in the early stages of prison university to always have a Bible in the cell, as the pages were the same gauge as fag papers. Sometimes, when we found ourselves out of fag papers, the good old Bible came in handy, and those who smoked weed would often joke that they'd had one hell of a smoke as they smoked through Psalm 23, The Lord is my Shepherd.

I knew my rights as a remand prisoner. I was entitled to have a Bible provided by the prison. So, after being refused by the police, I thought it was time I called upon the good old Archbishop of Canterbury. When sending a letter to such an important person I had the right to seal the envelope, and if it was opened they would be breaking the law. I explained in my letter to the Archbishop, Dr George Carey, how I was being denied a Bible, and that I had spent five weeks in the most appalling conditions in a police station as the prison system was not taking remand prisoners.

With my letter sealed, I told the coppers on the desk that it could not be censored. They were very cautious, and rang through to their superiors, which I expected. I knew they had to check with the prison system. A phone call came back confirming that I was right, the letter could not be opened as it was being sent to a very important person. The desk copper, obviously feeling a little embarrassed, offered to post my letter in the mailbox just outside the police station. In the meantime, one of the lads on the other side gave me a white Bible, which his girlfriend had pinched from a shop: a very nice one at that.

To be honest, I didn't really think I would have any response from the letter. However, within a day or two, when I was taking some exercise in the corridor, the desk phone rang. Being nosey, I listened in and heard the desk copper say, 'Fuck off, and I am the fucking Pope.'

I knew instantly that my letter had been acknowledged and that this daft copper was giving someone stick right down the phone.

Then the copper started shouting down the phone, 'I'll stick that Bible up your fucking arse. Don't go ringing here taking the piss you cheeky fucker or I'll fucking nick you. Now fuck off!'

I couldn't stand up for laughing. The daft copper had just abused a man of the cloth. He looked over at me with tears rolling down my cheeks and asked what the fuck I was laughing at. I didn't dare tell him.

It wasn't long before he was being grilled by the High-Brass. The Archbishop had clearly been appalled by the outburst and could understand my plight regarding the conditions.

The door of the remand section opened and there were coppers in their droves ushering in an elderly looking vicar who held a great big Bible in his hands. The vicar, being gently guided to me, introduced himself as the vicar of Ebbw Vale and, to his amazement, he said he had just spoken to the Archbishop of Canterbury, Dr George Carey, who had instructed him to give me a Bible.

I told the Vicar that on no account could I take his family Bible, regardless of who had sent him. Besides, when I looked closely I saw that the pages were too thick to use as back-up rolling papers. The vicar seemed to be in a sort of a daze, going on about how he had spoken to the Archbishop. I thanked him for his generous offer and asked him to thank the Archbishop, but explained that I had received one from a friend.

The vicar, looking very disappointed, walked away with his big Bible in his hands.

I was receiving letters from friends throughout the country, and knew that if I had been in prison my letters would have to have been censored, but it came to my attention that my letters were going straight to the police at Gwent's HQ. Even my letters to solicitors were being opened, which under prison rule 37a was illegal. Even letters which were sent directly to Ebbw Vale police station were sent to their HQ.

I received a letter from Ronnie, which enclosed a cheque, and was given to me, already opened, by a very nervous looking copper. Ronnie, not pulling any punches, mentioned the possibility of dealing with the witnesses, and indicated that I only had to give the nod for his plan to be put in motion. I knew what Ron was capable of but also knew that the letter had been read by high-ranking officers.

I had to get a letter out to Ron without going through the normal police procedures, so I wrote explaining that my letters were being read by coppers. Then I arranged for a friend to visit me in order to smuggle the letter out.

One day, out of the blue, I had a visit from Andrew Chamberlain, and found it strange that he turned up with his niece, who was only about 13 years old. I knew that a copper had to be his handler and had primed him to visit me and, yet again, I was tempted to storm right into him. But, of course, the visit had been thought through very carefully: he was using his brother's teenage daughter as his shield. I was glad to see him go. The stench was overwhelming, and the idea of having witnesses dealt with was becoming very appealing.

It was decided that Lindsay and I would go through the courts in the hope that all the lies would surface, but we knew that a trial date could be months – if not a year – away.

I found that there were still a number of coppers prepared to give me inside information, and I was warned that a plant was being brought in to see what information I would reveal; not that there was any info regarding the robbery. It had been seen in the past that nine times out of ten the snitch would lie in court, thereby ensuring a conviction. Such tactics were commonplace in prison; the police would send one of their snitches, sometimes even into the cell of the man they were targeting.

When I had been in the cell on my own for almost six weeks, a lad was moved into the cell next to me. I found out that he was from the Newport area. He seemed okay and we got on pretty well. Besides, I was glad of the company.

A few days later, the gate opened and in walked the snitch. I thought, 'They cannot be serious.' They were being so blatant (or maybe they were just plain thick). They had sent their little snitch through in all his glory, and with all the usual amusing questions. I decided that hammering the fuck out of him would do no good. Besides, I was bored, and now that I had allied with the Newport lad I knew that he couldn't go off saying I had said things which weren't true. So I just smiled at the crap he was coming out with. Even the Newport lad smiled, and he didn't have a clue what was happening.

After the snitch left, I let the Newport lad in on my secret: that our visitor was in fact a police informer. As soon as he heard that he wanted to beat the crap out of him, but I told him to play it my way and we devised a plan, which I knew could work both ways for me.

I decided to write two letters, one of which I would ask the snitch to smuggle out through his friends. It would be a dummy letter in which I would write a load of crap. The second letter would be smuggled out by the Newport lad's girlfriend but, unknown to him, I would write a load of bollocks in that letter too. Neither of the addresses on the envelopes existed, but each one clearly gave my home address on the reverse side. Then, marking the envelopes with distinctive marks known only to me, we set about writing the letter for the snitch to smuggle out.

Laughing like hell, we headed the letter to: Freddie Mercury of Queen, and wrote that we'd had a visit from beings from outer space who had given us the cure for AIDS in exchange for a couple of concert tickets. As we sealed the envelope, the Newport lad was on the floor laughing, knowing that the letter was going straight into the hands of the police. We had given the snitch all the cloak-and-dagger bollocks and he readily agreed to smuggle the letter out through his mates, who were more than likely coppers.

As we expected, the next day the snitch was let through the gate back to the other side, unlocked by a copper who was trying to look like he was on the set of a James Bond film. The Newport lad passed my letter to his girlfriend, so both letters were on their way. It was a pointless exercise, but it relieved the boredom a little.

A few days passed and the letter posted by the lad's girlfriend turned up at my home, which I expected would happen, but the snitch was soon pulled out. I had taught them a lesson: not to take me for an idiot!

The prisons were still refusing to take in prisoners, and that included nonces. They brought in a fat bloke – he must have weighed about 30 stone – and one of the coppers on the desk tipped me off that he was in for interfering with young boys.

Normally, when nonces are sent to prison they are put in segregation (rule 43), with the rest of their kind, until they are filtered in with normal prisoners. Then they pretend to be in for crimes which are accepted by the others.

I had a number of PP9 batteries. So, taking aim, I threw a couple through the bars of the gate, which hit him on the body. But they just bounced off and had no effect. I gathered up a few more and ripped open the metal, leaving all the jagged pieces sticking out, then threw those through the bars and hit him, causing him to jump. We then stuck razor blades in bars of soap and lobbed them at him, hitting him a few times, but that didn't have any real effect either.

The only chance we had was to get in close and run a blade over his throat. So we all sat in wait like a spider waiting for its prey. We knew that the coppers didn't have a clue how to deal with the situation, but they had showed the same disgust as us. Nevertheless, they decided to move him to another room, which meant he had to pass my gate. As he walked towards me, I readied myself to slash him, but as I lunged at him he managed to move out of the way.

As the tension grew, the police decided to move him to another police station. I overheard the desk sergeant saying that they were moving him to Newport, the same place as my brother. I managed to make a phone call to Lindsay and told him that a nonce was being taken in and that he couldn't be missed as he weighed about 30 stone. He knew the score, so I didn't have to explain too much to him.

As the nonce was leaving he smiled arrogantly at us and I smiled back, knowing he had more to come.

In a day or two, Lindsay managed to get a phone call to me in which he said that the fat bastard nonce had arrived, but on seeing Lindsay a look of horror spread across his face and he refused to go into the cell area. He was moved over the border to an English police station.

I was told that one of the lads at Newport police station had died, and when I made a phone call to Lindsay he told me it was Robert Oats. He said he would tell me the details when we met up in prison.

Finally, the prison strike was over, and Lindsay was in the first bunch to be taken to Cardiff jail. I never thought I would look forward to being taken to prison, but as strange as it sounds I somehow felt envious of Lindsay going there. I had been at Ebbw Vale police station for just over six weeks, so I knew it was only a matter of days before I would be joining him. I was sick to the back teeth of the place. I asked the desk sergeant when I would be going to prison and he told me it would be soon. I thought how ridiculous it must have sounded, asking to go to prison.

I had been taking some of the medication to help me cope with being penned in such a small place; I really needed to get away from the police station. Meanwhile, I found out that a Chief Superintendent was making himself busy by keeping me there. I would have thought that after the Cwmbran incident they would be more than happy to see me go. I soon realised that it was becoming personal with those higher up the ladder within Gwent police.

Two weeks passed and I was still at Ebbw Vale. I felt I had been fobbed off too many times, so I asked one last time for them to move me. When the desk copper rang through to the Chief Superintendent, I could hear the copper on the desk telling him that I'd asked to be moved. It was obvious that he was being told no way was I to be moved to Cardiff prison, so I shouted back to the copper to tell the mug, the other end that, if I wasn't moved by the evening, they would have another police station smashed to bits. I heard the lads on the other side give a big roar. They, too, were pissed off with the place. To my delight, arrangements were made to move me to Cardiff prison that very evening. My threat had worked. If they hadn't moved me that night, I had decided to take a number of hostages to make my point.

I managed to make a phone call to Cardiff prison and asked one of the screws there to tell Lindsay I would be there by tea-time. Soon I was on my way with a big smile on my face. It only seemed five minutes since Lindsay and I had walked through the gates to freedom. Yet there I was, going back.

The old reception had shut down and the ground floor of the education complex had been converted to a new reception area. As the police were undoing the cuffs to hand me over to the screws, I heard one of them on the phone telling someone that Frayne had arrived, and I thought maybe they were letting Lindsay know. But within a few minutes, four or five screws turned up with big grins on their faces.

My mind went into overdrive, thinking that I was going down the block for smashing up Cwmbran police station, but when they held out their hands, I realised they wanted to shake mine. Confused, I asked them why and they explained that they considered the police doing the jobs of screws as scabs, and said that Lindsay and I had proved they didn't have a clue when doing the job with remand prisoners.

I was put into a holding cell with about a dozen other men who, like myself, were waiting to be allocated cells on the wings. The door was locked, leaving the serving hatch open, and as I looked around I saw that the tables and chairs were similar to those of a modern day cafe: the plastic chairs and table all in one.

Then I looked around the room. Everyone seemed to be on a downer, looking very sad indeed; but I was over the moon after spending eight weeks penned up in Ebbw Vale police station. I saw one of the reception boys when I looked through the serving hatch and asked him for a cup of tea.

'Hang on,' he said, with a bad tone in his voice. I knew from the past that if you give an idiot a good job he would soon think he was a screw. I called to him again and told him that if he didn't get me a cup of tea, I would pull his fucking eye out when the door opened. He looked rather stunned, so I pointed out that I couldn't see a screw's uniform on him. He soon came back with mugs of tea all round.

I noticed a black lad giving me a strange look. 'Are you Lindsay's brother?' he asked, smiling. I nodded.

'I thought so. I have heard a lot about you from your brother,' he said, holding out his hand to shake mine and introduce himself as Danny.

We were called to be taken to the wings and allocated our cells, but I knew Lindsay had a two-man cell ready for me. I hadn't seen him since the Magistrates Court, so I was looking forward to it, knowing we had a lot of catching up to do.

With a screw leading the way, we were led up to A3 landing, which is normally for convicted prisoners, and the A2 landing, which I knew as the remand section, was completely empty. Lindsay was soon out of the cell and walking down the gangway to meet me and help me with my gear.

He had also sorted our meals out, so I didn't have to bother going to the hotplate. As I made up my bed, we were chatting 19 to the dozen and not really making any sense at all, but we calmed down after an hour or so and he told me what had happened to Robert Oats.

Most of the lads who were well into their medication would pack the tablets up their backsides. Lindsay had noticed that the conditions in the police station were getting to Robert and that his state of mind had begun to deteriorate. He asked for help and was informed that he would be taken to a hospital, which could deal with the mental illness he was suffering from.

It was obvious that he had never recovered from the death of his son, which happened while Robert was in prison the last time. He made it clear that he didn't want to go back to prison, and if he did he said he would drop all the tablets he had packed.

Lindsay knew he was faced with a big problem and checked with one of the coppers at Newport to see if they really were taking him to a hospital, and was promised that they were. Lindsay knew that if the copper told Robert he was going to Cardiff, then he had no option other than to tell the coppers he was packing his medication.

The copper categorically told him that Robert was going to an outside hospital. But, of course, they had lied and he was sent to the hospital wing at Cardiff Prison. While he was in segregation he died, choking on the tablets he had hidden inside himself.

Within a day or two, we were moved down to A2 and were next to the cell where we had spent remand on our last sentence. Even though the place looked more or less the same, there had been a change. There was a small cabin in the middle of A2 from which the screws locked and unlocked the doors.

There were no cans of beer in the evenings like before, but we were allowed to have our beat boxes to play music or listen to the radio.

The medical staff had the major task of reducing the medication most of the lads were on, but the lads didn't see it that way. They wanted all the tablets they could get, so tensions were running very high at the dispensary hatch, with many fights breaking out most evenings.

When I saw the doctor myself, he was concerned about the number of different tablets I had been prescribed while in the police station, and to my surprise he told me that I had overdosed.

When I had a chance to look around the wings I noticed that there were a number of female prison officers, and a few of the lads joked with them, 'Are you a good screw?'

I also saw our old friend from our last sentence, GL, who had been promoted to Senior Officer (SO). GL was one of the fair screws, and the respect worked both ways.

Quite a lot of the screws I'd got to know on our last sentence had either moved on or retired, and most of the new screws were around my age or younger.

Lindsay and I knew we had to start preparing our defence as soon as we had been to the magistrates for committal, where we would receive our committal papers and be able to see exactly the way the police were building their case against us – and who the rats were.

I knew we would be looking at a long sentence if our defence was weak.

Through my father, we were in contact with Michael Mansfield's clerk, and we were pleased we weren't going to end up with any of the South Wales muppet barristers we'd had representing us in the past. I was far from impressed with them.

Our solicitors from Blackwood thought we were talking a load of bollocks, but I had no faith in them with a case as complex as we were facing.

Like most people on remand, we tended to condition ourselves to sleep as much as possible and, more often than not, when the door was opened at 8.30 in the morning, I would jump out of bed, slam it shut and go back to sleep until dinner-time.

Every afternoon we would shower, and later, when the cell doors were left open, we could associate with other prisoners. That was the time when all the wheeling and dealing took place, but the difference with those lads, compared with my last sentence, was that I noticed deals were being made with heroin – or smack as it was called.

Although I was never one for smoking the weed, I didn't see it as a problem when the lads smoked it, as it seemed to put everyone in a mellow mood. However, the use of smack sometimes involved needles, and proved to be a nasty drug if it was allowed to sweep through prisons.

The first fatality I witnessed was a chap two cells up from me. He died after mixing the stuff with liquid Tamazipan, another sleeping drug the lads got hooked on while under their system.

For some unknown reason, I often used to get some lads coming to me with their case papers, asking for advice. As I didn't have my own case papers, I would gladly go through it with them. Some would be on charges of robbery, grievous bodily harm (GBH), actual bodily harm (ABH), and even murder.

One lad who came to me was up on a number of charges of robbing several building societies throughout the city of Cardiff, and I couldn't help feeling sorry for him. He was going through a tough time with his wife and kids, and would jump on a bus to the city, walk into a building society masked up, and hand a note to the cashier, which demanded money. But his spelling was so atrocious that the cashier would explain to him what he had spelt wrong, and after apologising for the errors in his spelling, he was dubbed the polite robber.

With his lack of education, I could see the police had taken advantage of him in his interview, and with self-admission, it was a case of seeing how long he would get. Yet he thought he had a chance of a warning.

Another lad was up on a murder charge, and even though it sounded bad, it became clear that it was self-defence, with the man who was holding the knife falling on it during the scuffle. Although he was well educated, he wasn't familiar with the law, so Lindsay and I pointed out a few irregularities in his paperwork.

We advised him to bring the matters up with his solicitor and barrister, which he did, and when he was up in court on another charge – burglary – to his amazement, the judge threw out the murder charge. He was delighted with the advice we had given him and word soon went around that we had worked on his case, getting him off with murder.

Another lad was fighting at the dispensary hatch while getting his medication. The screws put him in an armlock, ready to cart him off to the block, when a bully screw smashed one hell of a punch into his face, causing black eyes and a nasty cut across one eye. The screw then became a target with us all for what he had done; it's a known fact that when prisoners get their heads together to give a bully screw back his just desserts, the methods can be quite devastating.

They kept the lad down the block while his injuries healed, but didn't realise he was due up in court for a hearing. When he came back up from the block, I told him to get a complaint in regarding his injuries, and the screw in question began to panic. Lindsay and I knew through our sources that the screw was giving direct information to the police, so he was approached and told that if the lad dropped the complaint, he could have a word with his police friends not to oppose bail when the lad was up in court. Also, we said, when he was out of jail, no one would be any the wiser about his injuries.

The bully screw seemed to think I was helping him out, when, in fact, I knew it had got the lad out of prison. He was given bail.

As I lay on my bed one day, chatting to Lindsay and a few of the boys, the cell door went black as a shape emerged through it. It was a young bloke who had just been remanded, and, after looking at Lindsay and the others, he crouched over in my cell. He was a giant of a man, 7ft 2in, and some of the other prisoners had told him to come and see Lindsay and me for advice. He had been to see a number of screws, asking for extra food. Another complaint he brought up was that his bed was far too small.

When he introduced himself as Stretch, we all fell about laughing, but on a more serious note I could understand his plight. I arranged to go the library to look up on giants and what rights they had when sentenced, and after reading the prison rules I found that because Stretch was over 6ft 7in, he was indeed classed as a giant. This meant that by law he was entitled to two men's meals. I also found out that the prison authorities had to extend his bed to fit his height.

When it was pointed out to one of the Governors, he was in full agreement with the terms that were requested by Stretch. For the sake of a bit of research, for which Stretch was more than grateful, I found that a few of the other lads were entitled to the same, with their height being around 6ft 7–8in.

When the door was open, I would often go around different cells looking for newspapers to read – anything to pass the time when banged up.

One particular day I came across a chap breaking his heart. He had been charged with murder, but as he'd never been in prison before, he told me that he was terrified. He told Lindsay and me his name was Jon.

We reassured him and told him not to think about the outside world. When he told us his story, it was clear that things didn't add up. So Lindsay and I spent some time going through his paperwork in preparation for a visit with his barrister and solicitor. When the visit came, he gave them a lot of legal talk and within a few days a deal was struck for him to plead guilty to manslaughter and a sentence of five years was suggested.

Lindsay and I knew that if we had been able to spend more time with him he would probably have had a chance of a walkout. However, he was more than happy with his legal team. In my opinion, he should have sacked them, knowing that he could well have had the prosecution representing him.

11

RATS IN THE SINKING SHIP

Lindsay and I were due at Blackwood Magistrates Court. As the law stood, we should have been committed to Crown Court after the statutory 72 days. However, the police wanted an extension, claiming they had further enquiries to pursue.

I knew that without the case papers we couldn't build a case to defend ourselves but, of course, the police knew that too. Asking for the extension clearly told me that they had nothing on us, and our solicitor from Blackwood told us that he would cross-examine the police and ask why the extension was needed. Lindsay and I knew we could ask for bail now that Ian and Phil were out of the way; we knew there wasn't much chance, but if the coppers couldn't give a good enough reason for our arrest and wanting the extension, there was a slight possibility in our favour.

Bruce Kennedy had arranged to send a colleague to take notes and, when the screws handed us over to the police at the court, Bruce's colleague introduced herself as Catrin.

We were soon called into court, where the first witness called was Price, the detective who was in on most of our interviews. Our solicitor wasted no time in asking him why he wanted an extension.

Price replied, 'We are still looking for an automatic shotgun in the London area.'

Our solicitor questioned him further. 'So you are telling me you are asking for an extension, while you look for an automatic shotgun in the whole of London?'

'Yes,' Price replied.

Just then, the door of the court opened and in walked Andrew Chamberlain with a few of his mates.

Price's expression turned to horror, and Sutton, the other detective, poked his head through with the same look on his face. Chamberlain was soon marched out.

I wondered whether Sutton recognised Chamberlain from the photograph with the stripper. If only we'd had the dummy police station set up months earlier, we would have known what he was, along with the other rats in the sinking ship.

Our solicitor had nothing further to say to Price, which I found rather odd.

Bail was refused so we were taken to Blackwood police station before being taken back to prison. Our solicitor called in briefly to tell us that he would be down to visit us soon, and we also had a brief chat with Catrin, who appeared to be just as amazed as us by Sutton and Price's behaviour.

We were back in court a week later to be committed. Sutton and Price were still trying to dig up more shit on us and carried on with their extension, a situation which was becoming very strange indeed. We were given a set of committal papers between us and were able to see who the rats were. Just as we expected, there he was on pages 96–111: Andrew Chamberlain!

On the way back to prison I was doubled up laughing as I read the bollocks the slags were coming out with.

The two plums, Sutton and Price, did eventually interview the stripper. I still couldn't believe it. They had even taken her diary as an exhibit, yet the bin man's statement didn't come in until a month later, when it helped Lindsay with his alibi.

Once we were back in prison, it was confirmed that Michael Mansfield was interested in taking on our case and, as promised, our solicitors visited us. At last it was time to start building our defence case.

Lindsay was in with one solicitor and I with another when I decided to check with Lindsay on a matter which I was discussing with him. As I walked in, I heard the solicitor tell Lindsay that he could have dyed his moustache ash-blond, as the two women cashiers had noticed a thick ash-blond moustache, even though both the robbers wore balaclava masks.

I told the solicitors there and then that they were sacked and to fuck right off. The solicitor I was with could see my point, but the damage was done. Our own defence was beginning to sound like the prosecution.

We were faced with finding a new solicitor who was prepared to fight for us and were advised, through Michael Mansfield's office, to take on a solicitor from London. Lindsay and I agreed, so a meeting had to be arranged for our new solicitor to travel from London to Cardiff to see us.

We were still going over the paperwork and I still couldn't understand how some people we had considered to be our friends had lied, making up stories along with the police just to save their own arses.

What I found very strange – and downright stupid from a police point of view – was that a shotgun was found in a park behind where the robbery took place. The area had been cordoned off, yet an 11-year-old boy had found a shotgun and said, 'I picked it up and saw that it was a gun. I then told the policeman and put the gun back down on the floor.'

What in God's name were the police doing letting an 11-year-old boy help them to look for items after an armed robbery had taken place? Saying that, it was police stupidity that we needed to help us build our case against them. This wasn't about an armed robbery; I knew we needed to fight against police officers on every level within the Gwent police force.

Our new solicitors from London were having problems getting our case paperwork released from the previous solicitors.

Our solicitors eventually received the papers and a meeting was promptly arranged at Cardiff prison with London solicitor Nan Mousley, who had picked up on the same inconsistencies we had encountered. She was giving off all the right signals and we were pleased with her fighting talk, so we went back to our cell confident that we finally had real solicitors preparing our case for trial. We knew the trial could be quite some time away but we wouldn't let the case take over our lives, we both knew we had to get on with remand as best we could.

As we had on our last sentence, we applied for cleaning jobs, knowing it would take our minds off the case. Cleaning jobs would come up far more often on remand than in prison, due to cleaners either being sentenced or acquitted.

We became friends with Jon, and found he was going through a tough time with the bang-up, so Lindsay and I decided to put his name forward for a cleaning job alongside ours. Fairly soon, two of the cleaners had been to court and sentenced, leaving two vacancies. Lindsay, Jon and myself were at the top of the list, and Lindsay decided to let Jon and me take the jobs. We agreed that after a while we would swap places.

We were approaching Christmas, which is a very low time to be in jail, and a time when depression and anxiety can be sensed throughout the prison. Tempers are stretched to the limit and, as a lot of the lads were on reduced medication after being held in the police cells, fights often broke out with some devastating results.

Our solicitors informed us that they had a hearing date at Newport Crown Court, and that they intended to find out why Sutton and Price needed extra time to further their investigation. Questions were also going to be raised about whether they'd had enough evidence to arrest us in the beginning. The judge at the hearing wasn't happy with the way the case was taking shape; under the law we had to go up in front of a Crown Court judge to be formally committed for trial, and the prosecution and police should have had everything in place for a trial to take place.

The judge ordered that they have a few weeks extension and if by then all paperwork had not been handed over to the defence, he would consider bail for us. At last we had a breakthrough. Nan Mousley felt that the prosecution case was beginning to crumble.

With Christmas out of the way, Jon seemed more settled and was dealing much better with prison life. Lindsay and I decided to knock the cleaning jobs on the head, as being on remand meant we could have money sent in to buy tobacco and toiletries. We also had contacts who would get anything we needed off the wing.

In his spare time, Lindsay decided to draw portraits of a few of the lads' families, charging them a pack or two of tobacco, which they were happy to pay as they were going away with first-class drawings.

The drawings soon did the rounds and attracted the attention of a number of younger screws, who also enquired about having a portrait drawn of a loved one. Lindsay wasn't letting a screw pay with a couple of packs of tobacco – that was only a favour to the lads – so we made it clear we wanted vodka, tobacco, etc., and the drawing was completed within a night. The deal was that the vodka and tobacco had to be handed over before Lindsay gave them the drawings, otherwise they would simply be ripped up.

One night, Lindsay and I got so pissed we almost forgot we were in jail. We had our music blasting, lights dimmed down and drank until we both collapsed on our beds. The next day, although I was hung over, I managed to get myself over to where I had hidden the hacksaw blades on my last sentence, and as sure as damn it they were still there. After a discussion with Lindsay, we agreed that if our court case failed we had to consider the option of going over the wall.

Each day, Lindsay and I would go through our case papers, taking notes and cross-referencing with the Archbold Law books. At first, we found the task quite difficult, but we soon got the knack of how the book worked in relation to the law.

We knew we had a bit of a dilemma regarding the two ladies who were the victims of the robbery. They must have suffered a frightening experience. I had been charged with the offence and knew they wouldn't be looking at me in a favourable light.

In the first statement she said that the gun pointed at her was quite long. However, four statements later she identified the shotgun found in the park by the 11-year-old boy, which was sawn off and rather short. What I found even more bizarre was that Sutton was wandering around with the sawn-off shotgun and visiting the lady at her home.

The second woman went down the same avenue, saying, 'The gun appeared to be a shotgun, and as far as I am concerned it was full length. It had not been shortened, i.e. sawn off.' She then went on to say, 'This man appeared to have a moustache, which was thick and ash-blond in colour.' Even more astonishing was that she described one robber as being 'big-built with broad shoulders', while the other was 'much smaller in build and his height was about 5ft 6in'.

Things simply didn't ring true. Lindsay and Phil had been charged with armed robbery, as their descriptions fitted those in the women's statements, but what Sutton and Price didn't know was that Phil was at work in London on the day the robbery took place, and Lindsay had been visiting my father, which the bin man verified. I was charged with conspiracy. In other words, I planned the robbery. The police had accepted my alibi; that I wasn't there.

I wasn't surprised to see Paul Edwards' name in the statements. His mission in life was to bullshit! However, I was shocked to see Chamberlain there as he, along with his brothers, were spoken highly of within criminal circles. As for Bullen, Campbell, O'Neil and Hilton, I was very surprised that they had to bullshit.

Our development business began to take a turn for the worse: the interest was overtaking the costs, so the receivers were sent in. However, that was the last thing on my mind as we were sitting in jail. We knew we had to pull in our trusted friends, unlike the shower of shit whose names were on statements against us. We needed to know who had carried out the robbery, so the word was sent out and the hunt was on.

The first few weeks revealed nothing, but left a trail of broken bones along the way. Another problem we had to contend with was that Edwards, along with Phil Regnard and his brother, had opened their mouths about a matter which had nothing to do with Lindsay and me: they each had a hit on them, to be carried out before the trial.

That was the last thing we wanted, bodies going down before our trial, so we made it clear to those concerned that we would deal with the people in question in our own time, which was agreed on a temporary basis. As far as I was concerned they deserved everything they got, as they were quite happy giving it the bollocks when they were in London.

Things were getting rather heated, with our lads leaving no stone unturned. Unfortunately, those who knew nothing could only be sympathised with after they had been visited, but those who made a big deal of it had to be pressured that little bit more, which didn't go down too well.

Lindsay and I knew that the robbery had to have been carried out by someone within the Gwent area, as it was such a small sum of money.

Just has we were beginning to draw a blank, we received a message that one of the robbers had, by chance, been found. Lindsay and I knew such a breakthrough would exonerate us, and leave the police with egg on their faces.

We soon received a visit from a friend who gave us the full details and I was shocked. One of the named robbers was Stephen Cook, who was going out with my sister. I didn't really know much about him, but I knew Lindsay hated him. Cook claimed that he was asked to do the robbery with Paul Edwards and, being frightened of Edwards because of his size, he decided to go along with him, hoping to get some cash out of the job.

As a result of our lot slapping a few people along the way as they tried to find out who had done the robbery, Cook had panicked and decided to hand himself into the police, fearing what we would do to him. To my amazement, the police had told Cook to fuck off. Sutton and Price were soon on the scene and they, too, began telling Cook to piss off. Cook, still in fear, insisted that he carried out the robbery with Edwards, and went on to tell them that he had left a pair of trainers behind and that he'd been bleeding in one of them.

At first Sutton was arguing with Cook over the colour of his trainers, but then decided to charge him as the other armed robber with Lindsay, and also with perverting the course of justice. He was remanded in custody, not to prison but to a police station somewhere in Gwent.

All charges against Phil were subsequently dropped.

I knew Edwards didn't have the intelligence to carry out an armed robbery.

Cook was kept safely out of the way in a police station; the police must have been scared stiff of us getting near him.

We informed our solicitors of Cook's arrest, and requested that they go for bail at the High Court in London. They then had the task of finding him, but the police were being very evasive. We couldn't apply for bail until our solicitors had a statement from Cook, but no one seemed to know where he was being held.

My father was in constant touch with Michael Mansfield's clerk, Mr Adam Bowles, but paperwork that had been sent wasn't arriving. We had been tipped off that the police were intercepting the mail my father was sending. So, in order for our mail to reach its destination, letters were posted from cities, such as Newport and Cardiff, and in some cases they were posted as far away as Bristol.

After quite a bit of legal wrangle, our solicitor tracked down Cook to a police station in Abergavenny. With his statement given, we could apply for bail at the High Court. Lindsay and I knew it could take a week or two before we would get a hearing. We also knew that bail was going to be set at £100,000, with the condition of signing on at a police station.

However, over the dinner period, two screws opened the door and told us to get our kit together, as we had bail. We were rather puzzled, but we grabbed our kit and were soon going through reception, being processed and out through the prison gates.

As we stood outside we knew a mistake had obviously been made, but we weren't complaining and very soon a few of the lads were picking us up. I rang Nan Mousley in London asking about our release, but she was just as puzzled and advised us to go back to prison. I couldn't believe what she was telling me. I most certainly wasn't going to walk back into prison after spending seven months on charges I fiercely denied. All our assets in the development project had been frozen, yet we needed to have £100,000 at the ready for our bail.

Nan rang back and told us to get back to jail as the police were classing us as escapees, and that we would more than likely be hunted down by the armed response units. But there were a few people we needed to see, so we decided to make the most of it and told Nan that we would hand ourselves in at Cardiff prison the next day. We knew we were walking on thin ice if we were to hand ourselves in at a police station though. Their case against us was falling apart.

We didn't sleep all night: it was a case of cramming a few weeks into 24 hours before heading back to prison. We had one last meeting with a few of our lads in Cardiff, then Lindsay and I were dropped off outside the prison.

We walked into the main reception and, speaking through the hatch to one of the screws on the desk, I explained that the prison had let us out by mistake. A couple of the screws began laughing, and thinking we were taking the piss told us to fuck off. I too began laughing, thinking, 'What the fuck am I doing here waiting to be let back into the shithole that we were mistakenly let out of yesterday?' But we couldn't take the gamble and leave again in view of how desperate the coppers had become.

The laughter gradually gave way when the screws could see that Lindsay and I were serious and not attempting to leave. Behind the hatch, the screw picked up the phone and asked to speak to the Governor, and a number of other screws appeared who also looked puzzled. It must have seemed very strange, but I knew we would be getting bail within a few days and that walking back to prison could only weigh in our favour eventually.

The face of the screw on the phone took on an expression of horror as he realised that we really had been let out by mistake, and as he replaced the receiver more screws gathered, waiting to hear what was going to be said.

'Yes, you are right, chaps. Both of you should be in prison.'

Then, with a look of 'I told you so' on my face, we were escorted back to the cells. As we walked down the landing flanked by God knows how many screws, all the lads on remand – and the convicted prisoners on the landings above – looked on in amazement, wondering what the hell we had done.

Our cell had been taken so we were put in a basic cell, which was a right shithole. As the door slammed shut we knew we would have to wait until our solicitors secured bail at the High Court. After an hour or so all the doors were opened after the dinner-time bang-up, but we had a job to get to the recess as we were surrounded by dozens of men on remand asking what we were doing back inside.

When we told them what had happened, many of the lads shouted that we shouldn't have come back. I was feeling worn out, so I just filled my water jug. All I wanted to do was get my head down.

The two lads who had moved into our cell kindly offered it back. As strange as it may sound, prisoners tend to get very attached to their cell, especially if they've been in it for a long time. It isn't an attachment for the love of the shitpit, it's more about scrubbing out other peoples stench and making the small cube a sort of home, so we thanked the two lads for their offer and said that we would move back in the morning, after we'd had a good night's sleep.

We woke feeling refreshed and our short day of freedom had become a distant memory overnight. We were back to the reality of the prison, with its stench, clanking of keys and slamming of doors.

We moved back into our cell and I paid the two lads a couple of ounces of tobacco, which seemed to please them. Also, Jon was good enough to return the drop we had given him a few days earlier.

I was expecting to be called to the Governor to get an explanation for their mistake but, even though it was such a huge error, they didn't seem too keen to give one. I wasn't complaining about having 24 hours out, though. We had managed to get quite a few things in order. Our solicitor, who had calmed down once we were safely back behind bars, told us that our case was up for hearing at the High Court in London, towards the end of the week. Steven Cook's statement, along with Lindsay and me walking back into prison, would, I was sure, be in our favour when bail was applied for.

Friday soon came and we were both ready to be released over the dinner period. I lay on my bed watching a programme on a pocket TV. Then the doors were unlocked with the dinner-time bang-up over. I was still optimistic that the High Court would give us a tea-time release, and told myself that it was just a matter of waiting a few more hours. Tea-time came and went, but still there was nothing. I was getting really pissed off and, knowing that the solicitor's office would have closed by then, I made a phone call to my father to see if he had any news.

He told me that we had been granted bail with a surety of £100,000 and a few conditions. My father also explained that some very good business friends of ours (and his) in the pub trade were prepared to put up bail.

Ronnie was more than happy to arrange bail, but Lindsay and I didn't think it would be wise to take him up on his offer given the connection brought up during the interviews. We didn't think it would look too good.

We had the weekend to think things through and were confident that it was only a matter of time before we would be let out. The bail money wasn't a problem, it was where it was coming from which was proving to be the headache. The weekend passed, the £100,000 had been arranged by a very good friend from south London, and friends were in place, ready for Gwent police and their intimidation tactics.

Word came back to us that Phil Regnard had been sniffing about, and I had no doubt he had turned tail and was working with the idiots at Gwent police. But, unknown to Regnard, it seemed that he had slipped through the net when he was about to be grabbed on other matters. He was lucky he got out of London when he did.

We were notified that all was in order in relation to our bail and that preparations were being made for our release. But, of course, the prison wasn't taking any chances by letting us go until they could see that everything was in place.

The police pushed for an early trial date – 1 June. Lindsay and I knew this could be a setback, and that a little more time would have given us the opportunity to find out why so many had turned prosecution, based on the police and their bullshit.

We went through the big prison gates again, but this time everything was above board. A few of the lads had come down to pick us up and, with two weeks to go before the trial, Nan Mousley wasted no time in travelling down from London for a conference to prepare us for it, and to discuss which barristers were to represent us.

We also had a meeting with Bruce Kennedy, who wanted to produce a programme based on the way some police officers and detectives in Gwent police were showing too many inconsistencies, and how their investigation hadn't followed police rules on procedures.

There was no time to enjoy our freedom as we had to hold meetings constantly in an attempt to catch up on lost time. We also filmed the programme with HTV, which was done over a period of days at our homes and in our local pub.

I visited our development site and found it had been gated off, stopping me from gaining access. I made an appointment to see our bank manager as the interest had eaten away at a considerable amount of profit. At the meeting, I asked how the receivers had been sent in, and said that, although I understood the bank's priorities, as the law goes in the UK, we were innocent until proven guilty.

I was then given access to the site – not that there was anything I could do at that particular time.

Our solicitors had arranged a meeting with our prospective barristers and, as was agreed with our solicitor, prospective meant that if we were not happy they could simply fuck off!

Just as we were about to leave to meet them, I received a telephone call from Nan Mousley, warning me that the barrister lined up to represent me was a former police officer. To Nan's amazement, I said that I had nothing against the police in general, it was the corrupt and bent bastards I didn't like; the ones who think they are above the law.

We met the two barristers who introduced themselves as Jimmy Beck, who was to represent me, and Michael Topolski, who would represent Lindsay. We had separate rooms in which to hold our meetings, and Jimmy Beck said that he had been a copper for 25 years and I can remember thinking, 'What the fuck am I doing, having a copper represent me against his own kind?'

However, the more I listened to him, the more sincere he became, and I knew I was finally listening to a barrister who was prepared to fight for me after being disappointed so many times in the past by barristers from South Wales. Jimmy seemed to be very concerned about the diary and, if Jim O'Neill hadn't turned prosecution witness, there would have been no way I could have mentioned that the diary belonged to him. In my defence I could explain that the diary wasn't mine, but I was to be charged with drug offences based on its content. Jimmy told me that we would deal with that particular problem at the trial.

I could see that he had done his homework on our case, and he picked up on several things which I had missed. He also wanted to visit sites which were mentioned in statements by some of the prosecution witnesses – something I had never experienced before. Barristers I had met in the past would meet me minutes before a trial and then prove themselves to be useless.

Lindsay and Mr Topolski joined Jimmy and me, and both barristers went over their strategies and tactics for the trial. Lindsay and I were very happy with their approach and began to feel more confident.

We still needed to find out for certain who Andrew Chamberlain's handler was within Gwent police, although we were fairly sure that Inspector Phillips was Paul Edwards' handler. We decided to have Chamberlain watched and soon came up trumps, discovering that his handler was next-in-command to Phillips, a bloke called Chief Inspector Johnson. Just as we thought.

12

THE TRIAL – THE STEPS OF DOOM

The cars were waiting to take Lindsay and me to Newport Crown Court. Bruce was also there with a number of camera crews, ready to film us leaving. Our defence had asked us to arrive early to enable us to go over paperwork and discuss any queries we might have.

When we arrived, we could see that new courts had recently been built and were very different from the dreary old Crown Courts. In all its splendid whiteness, the grand building with its long steps awaited us as we walked into the jaws of our fate.

We met up with Jimmy Beck and Michael Topolski, who told us that the prosecution barrister was our old friend Mr Patrick Harrington, who had defended me on my previous case.

Lindsay and I had always thought that Harrington was a bastard, and in a way I was glad he was for the prosecution. Arrangements had been made for him to represent one or other of us when we were with the Blackwood solicitors, but at least now we knew where we stood, knowing he was prosecuting.

Nan Mousley hadn't turned up, but I wasn't too worried; the barristers were the ones fighting on our behalf. I asked Mr Beck if he could make a request to the judge for me to have access to the toilets whenever necessary. I explained that a number of years ago I had been stabbed several times, and that one of the wounds had given me the long-term problem of needing the toilet regularly. It had been estimated that the trial would take approximately four long weeks, which was quite a disheartening thought. Sitting through one day of a trial is bad enough.

We were introduced to a lady who was a stand-in solicitor, brought in from a Newport firm but appointed by our London firm of solicitors. She said that if there were any messages we needed to pass to our barristers when we were in court, we were to write them down before attracting her attention, and she would pass them on.

Lindsay and I were soon called in and were pleased to see that the new courtroom was nothing like the old intimidating court; the decor was very much lighter, giving it the appearance of an American court.

We were guided to the accused area, which wasn't in the middle of the court as before, but was a comfortable seating area at the back which had a length of thick glass 18 inches high directly in front of it. Sitting with us were two screws, which was standard court practice. We knew the two screws from Cardiff prison and they gave a look which said, 'I hate sitting through these court cases, they are so boring.'

While we were waiting I remembered that it was Lindsay's birthday, so I whispered, 'Happy birthday.'

He smiled and whispered back, 'What a birthday this is turning out to be.'

As we faced the court and the judge's bench, I saw to my left the door which must have led to the cell area downstairs and, to my delight, just through that door were the toilets.

We had been told by our barristers that the judge sitting at our trial was Judge Gibbon. We knew that he was a fair judge but very sharp indeed. Everything was in place, then one of the ushers shouted, 'All rise and stand.'

The judge walked in wearing his robes, and on his head was the traditional judge's wig, or as Lindsay calls it a Rick Parfitt, from the band Status Quo. The judge took his seat and Jimmy Beck was soon on his feet, asking that I be allowed to use the toilet at will, before explaining my past injuries to him.

Judge Gibbon looked at me, paused and then said, 'Leighton, you may use the toilets at will.'

I nodded my thanks to him.

Addressing our barristers and the prosecution, the judge explained that, even though we were on bail, each day, during the lunch period and for 30 minutes after, we were to be kept in the prisoners' cell area. We were also told to report to the cell area each morning, which meant that Lindsay and I were not allowed to enter the courtroom through the usual entrance. I didn't mind – it was better than being remanded and it indicated that the judge was still prepared to give us bail throughout the trial.

The weather was so hot that even the modern air-conditioning didn't seem to cool the courtroom down, so Judge Gibbon addressed all barristers and told them that if they wished they may remove their wigs. They all agreed. Now the courtroom definitely had an American feel about it.

The morning soon passed with the barristers and judge going through all the legal talk, and the swearing-in of the jury was arranged for the afternoon.

'All stand,' a voice shouted as the judge retired.

We knew the procedure, so we walked through the door and down the steps to the cell area where we were to have lunch. A few of the lads I met when I was on remand greeted us as we were put in a cell. Also in the cell was a chap called Roger whose case we had heard about: he had kidnapped a bloke and had an armed stand-off with the police, which ended when he blew off his victim's hand.

The time in the cell soon passed and we were led back up the stairs for another boring session – listening to the jury being sworn in. The two screws with us were just as bored, so we would read newspapers off our laps, out of the judge's view.

As the selection of the jury began, we were asked by our barristers whether we knew any of the jury members and, if so, to inform them immediately. I took a quick glance just in case there were a few coppers amongst them, but not seeing anyone of any relevance I carried on reading my paper.

The day was drawing to a close and I whispered to Lindsay, 'Thank fuck for that.' He nodded and smiled.

The jury was sent out. So, as agreed by the judge, we had to spend 30 minutes in the cells where Roger and the others were being cuffed up ready to be taken back to prison. Roger told us that he wasn't happy with the way his barrister had performed in court, and that he intended sacking the useless bastard the next day.

I spoke to one of the lads who was on Crown Court cleaning duty and asked him to have a word with Dai in the kitchen to send up some decent food the following day.

When we arrived home, Bruce was in touch to tell us that an HTV Wales news team would be at the courts to film us in the morning. I told him that one of the cameramen had left a battery behind after filming, and he asked me to hand it to the news team the next day.

Before leaving for court the next morning, I emptied all my paperwork from my briefcase and filled it with cans of lager, ready for lunch break in the cells. I wasn't really breaking the law by having them. I was still on bail and was in a position to drink them after the day in court was over.

As we expected, there were camera crews and reporters lined up waiting for us, and as we walked up the steps of doom, as we called them, we were met by a number of photographers asking if they could take photographs of us. To refuse would have been pointless, so after many clicks and flashes, I looked around for a cameraman with an HTV sign on the side of the camera so that I could return his battery. I spotted one who was filming a report and walked towards him. The lady giving the report looked at me, horrified. She must have thought I wasn't happy with the filming, but when I explained about the battery she looked relieved and the camera followed me to the door of the court where Lindsay was waiting.

When we were let in, I kept the screws occupied by asking some daft questions about whether they had seen all the camera crews on their CCTV screens, while Lindsay went through to the cell area with the briefcase. After leaving it in one of the cells, we were taken up to the court and saw that the public gallery was packed with reporters, all ready for the prosecution's opening speech.

Mr Harrington began his speech and, as we expected, within the first few minutes he had mentioned the Kray twins. He knew exactly what reaction it would provoke and he was right. The jury sat up like meerkats and the reporters were scrabbling over each other, eager to hear every word.

Harrington went on to say that Stephen Cook had carried out the robbery with Lindsay and that I had helped with plotting it. He began going on about sawn-off shotguns, Browning automatics and a Mossberg shotgun. He also claimed that I had hit Paul Edwards in the face with the Mossburg and, supposedly, put a replica pistol in James Campbell's mouth, as well as slashing him with a knife on his upper arm and forehead.

The whole court was silent as Harrington lapped up the attention and reeled off his speech, and we could only sit and listen as all eyes bore into us. I looked at my reflection in the glass and checked to see if I had grown horns. This was the best I had seen Harrington perform, and I realised that he seemed more comfortable prosecuting than defending. As he brought his opening speech to a close, we were wondering who the hell he was talking about. He had said appalling things about us but not a word of it was true.

Silence filled the courtroom as Lindsay's barrister, Michael Topolski, slowly got to his feet. There wasn't a lot he or Jimmy Beck could say until they had cross-examined the prosecution witnesses.

Adrian Bullen was the first witness to be called, but the morning was coming to an end so the judge adjourned proceedings until the afternoon.

Dai from the kitchens in Cardiff prison had done us proud with salad rolls. We met Roger in the cell again, where he shared our lunch, but this time with cans of lager. He told us that he had sacked his barrister and was going to represent himself. Knowing he was still on remand, we decided to let him drink all the cans as we could have a drink at the end of the day. As we sat eating our rolls, which tasted so good they could have come from a top restaurant, Roger drank can after can of lager. As he finished the last one, the door opened and we went back into the courtroom and took our seats, eager to hear what Bullen had to say.

Harrington was to cross-examine him first, then hopefully our barristers would be able to ask him a few questions and show him up as a lying slag. He was soon called in and, as he took the stand, we saw that the slimy little rat didn't have the bottle to look at us. He wanted to make a big show of the trial and started his cross-examination by asking Bullen about our hairstyles. What the fuck that had to do with the trial I didn't know.

'Tell me, Mr Bullen, what was their physical appearance at this time? How did they dress? What did they look like?'

'Similar to myself,' Bullen replied.

'Dark?' Harrington asked, getting himself comfortable.

'White shirts, dark suits. Smart,' Bullen said, with his usual smug look.

'Smart?' Harrington enquired.

'Mm,' Bullen answered.

'Hairstyle?' Harrington asked, wanting every detail.

'Not similar to mine – brushed back,' Bullen said with a little pride in his voice. What he was getting at was: those who comb their hair back must be villains or gangsters!

Harrington went on, asking why we held meetings and what our habits were in London.

Time for Bullen's big performance: 'I believe it was mentioned, on occasion, that they were down to visit Ronald Kray in Broadmoor, but, you know, it could have been on subsequent meetings.'

We sat listening to Bullen responding like a puppet to Harrington, making Lindsay and me look like the villains of the decade.

It was only a year past that we were filling his cupboards with food, giving him money to get by and involving him in some of our business ventures. Lindsay and I had considered him to be a very good friend, yet there he was selling his soul. People like him never change; they will always be rats. I knew my comfort was that I held far more qualities than Bullen could ever dream about. He knew what he was doing was shameful. That was why he couldn't look me in the eye.

Harrington pressed Bullen on the purchase of firearms, asking, 'So, what was said at this Sunday meeting?'

Bullen's face went from smugness to a more serious look. 'The various different firearms that were, that could be made available to us, and how much they would cost,' he answered.

'And what sort of figures were discussed?' Harrington asked.

'Ranges from £600 to £2,000 per weapon,' Bullen replied, looking rather worried.

Harrington was on a roll. 'What sort of gun?'

Bullen, lowering his head, replied, '£600 was a Star 22 pistol.'

Judge Gibbon jumped in. 'What?'

'There is a make called Star,' Bullen explained, thinking the judge was looking on him as the expert.

Harrington, not letting the judge take his limelight, asked, 'Star?'

'Yeah,' Bullen replied.

Mr Harrington: 22 pistol?

Bullen: Yeah, it's a semi-automatic pistol. That came with a silencer. And up to basically some of the better 9mm side arms.

Mr Harrington: Such as what?

Bullen: Glocks, Brownings.

Judge Gibbon: And they were, what? About the £2,000 mark?

Bullen: Yeah.

Mr Harrington: How did Paul Edwards handle those two meetings?

Bullen: Same way he handled most. Not very well.

Mr Harrington: Not very well?

Bullen: No.

Mr Harrington: Is he very bright?

Lindsay and I looked at each other shaking our heads, knowing that Edwards is very dim indeed.

Bullen: I would say not, but I don't know what you're comparing him to.

I had to laugh under my breath. I could compare Edwards with many things of no intelligence and a thick plank of wood seemed to flash through my mind. Bullen and Harrington seemed to be dribbling on about a supplier of weapons, who for some reason Bullen didn't want to name in court, but wrote it down for the judge and barristers to view.

What I was finding very strange at that point was, why wasn't the person whose name he wouldn't mention sitting in the dock with me? The police would know his name because Bullen the grass would have told them.

I knew that if I was on the jury I would have been very confused at that point.

It became clear that the primary objective of Harrington and Bullen was to discredit Lindsay and me, not to explore the truth, putting the blame onto Lindsay or me. He even went so far as to discredit David Ley, claiming he was financing us to obtain weapons. Everything we were supposed to have done, such as cutting down a sawn-off in his flat or carrying weapons willy-nilly, was ridiculous. He was always there with us!

Harrington had more or less come to the end of his cross-examination and the day was at an end, so the judge adjourned, telling everyone to be back at 10am the next day.

Just before we were taken down to the cells for our 30-minute wait, Jimmy Beck told us that he wanted to visit a number of sites where we were supposed to have test-fired guns. So Lindsay and I arranged to pick him up at his Newport hotel.

Back down in the cells we saw Roger with a big smile on his face. His day had gone well, and he laughed as he told us that he had been rather tipsy earlier and had directed a few little digs at the judge.

We had little time to freshen up at home before going back to Newport to pick up Jimmy Beck. We took him up the valleys to the mountaintop where Andrew Chamberlain had claimed we test-fired guns. It was a short walk from where we parked the car to the spot in question, although Chamberlain, along with the police, had claimed the spot was secluded from the public.

We watched as a man jogged past us, before going on to another spot where an old derelict pub called The Double'd stood, and it was at that spot that some cartridges were found. The area was used by many people as a shooting range, and although some of the cartridges found there were compatible with the Mossburg found in the park after the robbery, none of them had our fingerprints on. When Jimmy felt he'd seen enough, we returned to introduce him to our parents. My mother had prepared a lovely tea for us. We ate as we discussed the day's events, before returning Jimmy to his hotel.

Day three of the trial saw us splashed all over the front pages of the national newspapers. The *Sun*'s headline, in particular, caught my eye: 'KRAYS II', based, of course, on Harrington's opening speech. I smiled when I saw the photograph they had taken, remembering the lagers in the briefcase Lindsay was pictured holding. The press and camera crews took more photographs of us walking up the steps of doom, but we were soon in the cells with further supplies of lager for Roger to have as his afternoon tipple before he went into court. All the screws had newspapers under their arms, obviously following our story, and many of them were asking to sit in the courtroom. It seemed that they no longer found it so boring.

When we arrived in court, the police told Harrington that either myself or Lindsay had made a threatening telephone call to Chamberlain the previous evening, warning him not to go to court. Harrington went straight to the judge and relayed the information, and I could hear Judge Gibbon say that he was going to revoke our bail. But Jimmy Beck asked what time the call had been made. When the time had been established, Mr Beck told the judge that it couldn't have been either of us because we had been on the mountain with him at that time. The judge then told Harrington that he believed Mr Beck, and said that we could remain on bail.

I was reading a newspaper on my lap again, but this time there was a difference: the story on the front page was about my own case. Michael Topolski informed us that he was going to raise with the judge the issue of the press reports and the effect they could have on the trial. Both of our barristers requested that the matter should be raised with the jury absent.

With the court standing, the judge took his seat. Then, looking at Lindsay and me, he gave a little smile. Mr Topolski pointed out that the front-page headlines could have an adverse effect on the trial. The judge, still smiling, said that it appeared from the photograph taken of us that we had posed for the camera, but I knew that wasn't true and I passed a note to the solicitor explaining that the photos were taken before we had a chance to refuse. But my note made no difference, and Judge Gibbon continued to allow the press to report at our trial. He allowed our barristers five minutes to chat with us and Michael Topolski indicated that he would pull front page on the next day's newspapers.

The jury was ordered in by the judge, and Harrington told him that he was almost finished with his cross-examination of Bullen.

Bullen was called to the stand and reminded that he was still under oath. Answering questions posed by Harrington, Bullen told the court how, apparently, I had informed him that Lindsay had carried out the robbery with a pump-action shotgun, and had got away with ten grand, and that Chamberlain had been with us on the mountainside, test-firing guns. Harrington concluded his cross-examination, leaving Bullen to be questioned by Mr Topolski.

Mr Topolski: I represent Lindsay, Mr Bullen. I have a number of questions for you. As his Honour said yesterday, if you want a break or you want to sit down, just ask the judge. It was 6.35 in the morning on Wednesday, 25 September, at your house, when you were arrested by police. That's right, isn't it?
Bullen: I think it was a bit later than that when I was actually arrested, but it was that morning, yes.
Mr Topolski: For conspiracy to commit robbery?
Bullen: That's correct.

Mr Topolski pointed out that Bullen had been searched for firearms and ammunition when he was arrested, and that he was also asked about imitation weapons. He then asked about a number of telephone numbers that the police found in a drawer, in particular Charlie Richardson's.

Mr Topolski: Who is Charlie Richardson? Tell the jury.
Bullen: He's a former … from what I read in the papers … a former gang member from south London.
Mr Topolski: A rival gang to the Krays?
Bullen: In the sixties he was, yes.
Mr Topolski: Why did you have his phone number in your house?
Bullen: No reason.
Mr Topolski: No reason? Who gave you that phone number?
Bullen: Either Lindsay or Leighton Frayne.
Mr Topolski: Did you tell the police that?
Bullen: Can't remember.
Mr Topolski: You didn't did you, Mr Bullen?
Bullen: Like I say, I can't remember.
Mr Topolski: Were you able, during the course of that search, to have a private word with your girlfriend, out of earshot of the police?
Bullen: There were police present all the time.
Mr Topolski: Answer my question. Were you able to have a private word with your girlfriend during the course of that search, out of earshot?

Bullen: Don't think so, no.
Mr Topolski: Did you ask her to remove some cartridges that were on top of a fridge – get rid of them?
Bullen: Yes.
Mr Topolski: Whose cartridges were those?
Bullen: Don't know who they belonged to.
Mr Topolski: Why did you want them got rid of?
Bullen: Cos I didn't want the police to find them.
Mr Topolski: Why not?
Bullen: Because I just didn't want them to find them.
Mr Topolski: Why not?
Bullen: Because they were live cartridges.
Mr Topolski: Whose were they?
Bullen: As I say, I don't know.
Mr Topolski: Don't you?
Bullen: No.
Mr Topolski: Yours? ... Sure?
Bullen: Yeah.
Mr Topolski: What gun were they used for?
Bullen: Shotgun.
Mr Topolski: Shotgun cartridges. Colour?
Bullen: Red.

I looked across at Lindsay, who was looking at me as if to say, 'What's going on here?' I wondered where Lindsay's barrister was going with his line of questioning. Bullen had just given a confession regarding the cartridges and a shotgun, but wouldn't say who they belonged to. I must admit I was somewhat puzzled – he could have said they were either mine or Lindsay's. After all, he was bullshitting about everything else, the same as the others.

Mr Topolski questioned Bullen about making his statement after the arrest – which had been done on a questions-and-answers basis – only to be released a few days later without charge. It came out during the questioning that, after he was released, he was telephoned regularly each week by Sutton!

It was becoming clear that if Bullen did not co-operate with the police, he, too, would have been charged. Yet he was released after three days of questioning, without charge. Mr Toploski began to question him further about telling the truth, which he must have been in the beginning, until the pressure was put on and Bullen decided to co-operate with the police.

Mr Topolski: Was it always your intention to tell the police the truth from the word go, Mr Bullen?
Bullen: Yes.
Mr Toplski: Did you do that?
Bullen: In what respect?
Mr Topolski: In every respect. Did you answer every question you were asked by the police truthfully?
Bullen: I have.
Mr Topolski: You tried to. Does it follow from that, that you have been telling this jury the truth?
Bullen: I have.
Mr Topolski: The first interview was on the 25 September and it began at 8.44 in the evening. The police officer showed you a Mossberg single-barrel pump-action shotgun, that had been sawn-off on the stock as well as the barrel. Question: 'Have you ever seen that weapon before?' Answer: 'I can't say that I have.' Was that true?
Bullen: I answered negative, yes.

This was Bullen's typical smarminess. The bottom line was, when shown the shotgun and asked whether he'd seen it before, he replied, 'No.' Mr Topolski knew he had the rat on the run, and asked whether the answer he had given was true. Muttering away to himself, like the dithering idiot he really was, the mask of Mr Intelligent was beginning to slip.

Bullen: Was it true ... that that's what I said?
Judge Gibbon: No, no, no. Was the answer true? There is no doubt about that's what you said.
Bullen: Oh, right, no, that answer wasn't true.

When Mr Toploski pointed out that what he had said to the police had been transcribed from a tape, Bullen realised he'd dropped a clanger.

Mr Topolski highlighted a further paragraph from the interview in which Bullen dug himself in even deeper, when he said that he had only seen Mossburgs on TV, but had never seen one cut down so badly.

Mr Topolski: You haven't seen that Mossburg before?
Bullen: I m saying that I have never seen a gun cut down like that before.
Mr Topolski: What, so badly?
Bullen: Yes.

Mr Topolski: You have seen them cut down very well. Haven't you, Mr Bullen? By professionals? Haven't you?
Bullen: Who do you mean by professionals?
Mr Topolski: I'll come to who I mean later. You have seen many guns cut down, haven't you?
Bullen: I have seen two.
Mr Topolski: Two?
Bullen: I have only actually physically been present when one has been cut down, but I have seen two cut-down guns.

Mr Topolski continued to point out inconsistencies between Bullen's statement and what he was telling the court. The judge even questioned him. He too must have been able to see what a lying rat he was. The thought of the whole court had to be: 'Can he wriggle his arse out of this?'

The air was thick with suspense, and eyes darted back and forth as everyone listened to Mr Topolski's questions and scrutinised Bullen's answers.

Mr Topolski: Is that true, Mr Bullen? You understand perfectly well what my questions are. Please try and help the jury.
Bullen: I am trying to help the jury.
Mr Topolski: Was that a truthful answer?
Judge Gibbon: Just read the question?
Bullen: Yes … I am just trying to read it all with the context of everything else.
Mr Topolski: If what you told the jury is true, that can't be a truthful answer, can it?
Bullen: I am with you … No … That explains it for me … No.
Mr Topolski: That's a lie. That is a lie.
Bullen: Yes.
Mr Topolski: Yes?

Bullen had cracked, and could only prattle on about not seeing guns cut down. Mr Topolski began moving up a gear, knowing that Bullen was wounded by the way he had been caught out. Bullen went on with a number of answers, admitting he had lied on a number of occasions when questioned by the police but, of course, in further interviews after he was released, everything he was asked by the police he agreed to. It was also pointed out that Bullen – along with the police – claimed I had spoken to Bullen and Edwards or, as was written in Bullen's statement, Paul.

Paul Edwards had gone off the scene in April, so he couldn't have been there for me to tell both him and Bullen anything.

Judge Gibbon: Well, you put Paul there.

Mr Topolski: I am just going to deal with that ... I will leave it to your Honour.

Judge Gibbon: No ... Well ... I won't take over your ... I am puzzled, that's all.

Mr Topolski: Who was there at that meeting, at that conversation about an armed robbery? What do you say now, Mr Bullen?

Bullen: The one in my flat?

Mr Topolski: Yes.

Bullen: Myself and Leighton.

Mr Topolski: Anybody else?

Bullen: No.

Mr Topolski: Not Paul?

Bullen: No.

Judge Gibbon: You made a reply there: 'No, not that much, because I was with Paul all night ...'

Bullen: Yeah, I've just looked at that and I can't figure out where that's come from.

Mr Topolski: I think the witness is trying to say – I don't want to put words in his mouth – but there may have been a conversation at The King's Oak, but the one when the robbery conversation takes place is back at the flat.

Mr Topolski (*To the witness*): Is that it?

Bullen: I am just trying to figure out who this Paul is at The King's Oak.

Mr Topolski: Mr Bullen, it's Paul Edwards.

Bullen: No.

Mr Topolski: Oh ... It's not?

Bullen: It can't have been.

I knew Bullen wasn't so stupid as to get that wrong, but I knew who would be, and looking at the expression on Bullen's face (the only time he looked at me), I knew and he knew that he'd been rumbled.

We were watching as Bullen's web was slowly being torn away. I was becoming intrigued, wondering what path he would take to get out of the hole he'd dug for himself.

Mr Topolski pressed Bullen further about Paul being part of a conversation which I knew had not taken place.

Mr Topolski: It's another Paul?

Bullen: That's what I am trying to figure out. Where did Paul come from? Cos Paul Edwards can't have been at The King's Oak.
Mr Topolski: Why not?
Bullen: Because he wasn't around.

But I knew that Paul Edwards had been around London, and The King's Oak, after we had sent him off, and that he had been wandering around with Inspector Phillips. It seemed there was the possibility that they had met with Bullen, and poor Bullen was becoming a little confused with the sequence of events. Whatever had happened, Bullen knew for sure that I would be working it out.

As the judge appeared to be taking over my defence, he too began to work matters out for himself.

Judge Gibbon: This is after he'd packed his bags and gone back to Wales?
Mr Topolski: Well ... Yes ... Supposedly.
Mr Topolski (*To the witness*): 'I was with Paul all night, just chatting.' Which Paul?
Bullen: That's what I am trying to figure out. It wasn't, certainly wasn't Paul Edwards.
Mr Topolski: Please take your time. Which Paul?
Bullen: I don't know ... Certainly wasn't Paul Edwards ... Probably more than one Paul in the country that I know.

I laughed under my breath. Here was Mr Intelligent, or so he made himself out to be with all his fancy talk of private-school education, yet that was the best he could come up with. It was clear he was stuffed. I checked the time, knowing it must be getting close to the lunch break. Mr Topolski knew he had to use what little time he had left with him on the stand.

Mr Topoloski: There's not more than one Paul mentioned in any of these seven interviews, Mr Bullen. You mention him there by his first name. You don't say Another Paul or Paul Bloggs or Paul McCartney, you just say Paul.
Bullen: Mm-mm.

Mr Topolski had pushed Bullen far enough on the Paul issue, and Bullen was then trying to say it may have been Phil, in which case the tapes had to be checked after lunch. Due to bundles of paperwork getting mixed up and not being in court, the Judge told Harrington to make sure he had the correct paperwork for himself and the jury. Bullen was asked about the cutting down of guns which were stored at his flat, and at other premises throughout London. As we adjourned for lunch, Mr Topolski told Bullen that he would continue his questioning after the break.

We met up with Roger and he joined us again for salad rolls and lager.

We were soon back in court, with Mr Topolski ready to cross-examine Bullen again and, as he had said earlier in the day, to pull a front page in the national newspapers.

13

GUN EXPERTS

Mr Topolski delved into why Bullen decided to assist the police after spending three days in the police cells, and why he hadn't mentioned a Browning gun up to that point. It was on the fourth interview, without a solicitor present, that he told the police about the Browning shotgun.

Mr Topolski asked him why he didn't offer the information in his first three interviews. Bullen replied, 'I wasn't asked.'

The only mention of a shotgun in his earlier interviews was when he said he'd seen Edwards cutting down a barrel.

The questioning went further, to armoured piercing shells and how we were supposed to have acquired them for use in shotguns, yet under questioning by Mr Topolski, the shells, or slugs, were never used as exhibits.

What Mr Topolski was pushing Bullen on was, when he was held in the Welsh police station, he was prepared to think up any old bollocks to get his arse out of there. He then made a more detailed statement in the November, a month after he was released from the cells, and claimed he didn't know if he was going to be charged or not.

Sutton was ringing him every week, as we already knew.

Mr Topolski made it quite clear that for 18 months, all those deals were going on around Bullen, cutting down guns and being surrounded by armoured piercing shells, side arms, etc, etc., yet none of it had anything to do with good old Mr Bullen, who was telling everything to the court, all in the name of justice.

Mr Topolski then took his line of questioning to Bullen's involvement with villains.

Mr Topolski: Does the name Lambrianou, mean anything to you?
Bullen: Yes.
Mr Topolski: Who is he?
Bullen: He is an out-of-work, whatever he does.
Mr Topolski: Keep your voice up, please?
Bullen: I am terribly sorry. I don't think he works. I don't know what he does.
Mr Topolski: Wasn't Lambrianou a co-defendant of the Krays?
Bullen: Yes, he was.
Mr Topolski: Aren't you a personal friend of Tony Lambrianou?
Bullen: No, I'm not.
Mr Topolski: Do you know him?
Bullen: Yes.
Mr Topolski: Have you met him more than once?
Bullen: Yes, on several occasions.
Mr Topolski: Several occasions. Has he been to your flat?
Bullen: Yes.
Mr Topolski: Have you been to his home?
Bullen: Yes.
Mr Topolski: Have you eaten with him?
Bullen: Yes.
Mr Topolski: Drunk with him?
Bullen: Yes.
Mr Topolski: Socialised with him?
Bullen: Yes.
Mr Topoloski: But he's not a friend?
Bullen: No.

Those sorts of questions had no bearing on our trial, but they gave a clear indication of the sort of person Bullen really is.

Mr Topolski asked Bullen if he had seen a jacket before and said, 'It is in fact Paul Edward's jacket,' to which Bullen replied, 'Yes, it is.'

Even the judge asked, 'Have you seen a gun inside that?'

Bullen replied, 'Yes.'

Mr Topolski questioned Bullen about meetings relating to the dealing of firearms and how, although he was always present, it had nothing to do with him. He then referred Bullen to his questioning the previous day by Harrington.

Mr Toploski: At about 4.20 yesterday afternoon, just before you finished your evidence, you were asked by my learned friend, Mr Harrington, what was going on that Saturday morning. Now, this involves Paul Edwards and James Campbell?
Bullen: Yes.
Mr Topolski: You smiled and you said Paul had been chauffeuring a certain football player.
Bullen: Well, that's what he said he had been doing.
Mr Topolski: Why did you smile yesterday at 4.20?
Bullen: Why did I smile?
Mr Topolski: Yes?
Bullen: Because it was an amusing kind of thing to say.
Mr Topolski: Is kidnapping an amusing thing?
Bullen: No.
Mr Topolski: Weren't Paul Edwards and James Campbell planning to kidnap Paul Gascoigne, the Tottenham footballer?
Bullen (*Laughing*): Not to my knowledge, no.
Mr Topolski: Sure?
Bullen: Yeah, positive.
Mr Toploski: Who was staying in a hotel down the road?
Bullen: Yes, he was.
Mr Topolski: Yes, he was, wasn't he?
Bullen: Mm-mm.
Mr Topolski: Yes. Didn't they plan to kidnap him?
Bullen: I have no idea.
Mr Topolski: Our Gazza?
Bullen: I have no idea.
Mr Topolski: Haven't you?
Bullen: No.
Mr Topolski: That's why you were smiling yesterday and misleading us by saying it was just about chauffeuring a football player around. That's a terrible little lie, Mr Bullen, isn't it?
Bullen: No.
Judge Gibbon: Well, that's bound to have got you another mention in the *Sun* tomorrow, Mr Topolski!

Lindsay and I watched as the reporters clambered over each other to get themselves outside the courtroom in order to file their stories for the next day's papers.

Mr Topolski suggested to Bullen that he was the sort of person who was prepared to say anything about anyone to get himself out of trouble, or off the hook. Bullen had even said how, the day before, he was handed a statement by Mark Sutton!

Mr Topolski made it clear that Bullen was being let down by the police, and even Bullen was beginning to realise how thick and dangerous the police were!

Questions went on regarding O'Neill and supplying drugs. After all, O'Neill had become a prosecution witness. Another one prepared to bullshit in order to get his himself out of the shit.

Moving onto Edwards, Mr Topolski asked Bullen whether Paul Edwards had told him that he had served in the SAS, to which Bullen replied, 'Yes.'

'Did you believe him?' Mr Topolski asked.

'No,' Bullen replied.

'Was that something Edwards was telling a lot of people?' Mr Topolski enquired.

'Yes,' Bullen answered.

Mr Topolski asked about Edwards carrying a knife, which was nicknamed Big Bertha, but Bullen said that he didn't really know. However, the point of the question was that Edwards claimed we called one of the shotguns Big Bertha.

I began to understand that Bullen and Edwards had gone to meetings enquiring about the purchase of firearms at times when Lindsay and I weren't present. It became apparent that the firearms they were asking about were Bernadelli PO18s, 9mm handguns, also Berettas and Browning fastbacks.

Those meeting were nothing to do with them at all, so I must admit I was confused by what was being said. Bullen became agitated when questioned about kidnap and murder. He wouldn't name the contact, so it was agreed within the court that the contact should be referred to as Mr X.

Mr Topolski was on a roll and he knew he had pulled the next day's front pages with the national press, but pushing Bullen on the name of the contact only made him shift the blame onto someone else and, as only Edwards had been with him, Edwards it was.

Mr Topolski: Let's forget the name.
Bullen: Okay ... Mr Edwards asked Mr X if he had a safe house in London that he could use for a few days to store somebody. Mr X said, 'Living or dead?' And Paul replied, 'Living'. Mr X replied, 'Yes, that's no problem. You can use a container if you want.'
Mr Topolski: 'Use a container if you want.' Any more?
Bullen: No, that was basically all that was said.
Mr Topolski: There was a second leg to this contract, wasn't there?

Bullen: What contract?

The whole court had their eyes on Bullen as Mr Topolski told how he had shifted the blame onto Edwards. He couldn't shift it onto Lindsay and me because we weren't there.

Bullen stood there denying everything thrown at him by Mr Topolski. He was asked about a double-contract killing, and how their heads, feet and hands were to be cut off and thrown in the River Trent. And how Bullen instructed Mr X that the torsos were to be thrown into an acid bath at a container supplied by Mr X.

When Mr Topolski asked why he was at the meeting, Bullen replied that he had been ordered by Lindsay and me to watch over Paul just in case he botched it up.

Mr Topolski was onto Bullen, asking him whether there was a right way or a wrong way regarding murder and kidnap. The question stumped Bullen and he could only reply, 'It came as a shock to me when he said it.'

Mr Toploski: Well, leaving your emotions to one side, what does it mean?
Bullen: What does what mean?
Mr Topoloski: Keeping someone in a container?
Bullen: Exactly what it sounds like, keeping ...
Mr Topolski: Kidnapping?
Bullen: Well yeah, I guess so.
Mr Topolski: Yes, you guess so. Did you breathe a word of any of this to the police when you were interviewed?
Bullen: Er ... I don't know. Is it in my statement?
Mr Topolski: No it's not in your statement, not in any of your interviews. You wanted to forget all about this aspect of it in September, for those four days when you were in the cells, did you?
Bullen: I had a lot on my mind.
Mr Topolski: Indeed you did.

Bullen was then questioned about a letter found at our development site, which contained many examples of car registration number plates. When the letter arrived I hadn't taken much notice and left it on the windowsill of a new house – along with the rest of the junk mail that had been delivered to the property.

After a bit of legal talk, Mr Topolski said that they had a fingerprint expert in waiting and, on hearing that, Bullen freely admitted that he wrote and sent the letter with the registration numbers on. The letter was postmarked 18 July; the robbery took place 24 July. Nevertheless, Bullen was quite happy to admit that he'd sent it to me.

When Bullen was asked what they meant, he said that he had no idea. Even the judge asked what he was doing running around getting car number plates on my say so.

The questioning went on until late in the afternoon when the judge adjourned until the next day.

As expected, next day we were again splashed all over the front pages, this time with the headlines: 'GAZZA KIDNAP PLOT'.

As Adrian Bullen was a prosecution witness, he was also mentioned in the paper, but more as a grass than anything else.

In court, in the absence of the jury, the judge and barristers again discussed aspects of press reporting of the case.

Bullen was soon called in for further questioning by Mr Topolski, who spent some time reminding Bullen of his previous questioning and asked whether he agreed or disagreed.

He also questioned Bullen about a reverse-charge telephone call he'd received from a Newbridge telephone box on the day of the robbery, something I'd noticed when I was at his flat. I had glanced at an itemised telephone bill and saw the call listed and had made it my business to find out which telephone box it had been made from. It was near the park in Newbridge where the gun had been found.

Then, coming to the end of his questioning, Mr Topolski suggested that Bullen was lying in order to get himself out of trouble, making up any story just to please the police but, of course Bullen disagreed.

Then it was the turn of my barrister to cross-examine Bullen.

Mr Beck told him that his questions wouldn't be as long, but would still rely on his answers, then more or less went over the same ground as Mr Topolski. He ended his questioning by saying that Bullen had lied to police and the court simply to suit his own purpose.

Bullen was then re-examined by Harrington in an attempt to put right the bollocks that he had come out with when questioned by Mr Topolski. When Harrington had finished, Mr Topolski spoke to the judge about the outstanding matter of Bullen's itemised telephone bill for the month of July, which would show up the reverse-charge call on the day of the robbery.

Judge Gibbon ordered Bullen to look for the bill, then forward it to the officer in charge of the case. Bullen agreed to the request but ended his sentence with, 'If I can find it.' Judge Gibbon told him that, in the event of him not being able to find it, he was to contact BT for a copy.

Paul Edwards was next to be called to the stand, so Lindsay and I settled ourselves down for some gripping entertainment. Edwards could truly bullshit his way through to Bullshitter of the Year.

As he stood in the witness box, we saw that he was another one who didn't have the bollocks to look our way. Getting the show under way, he was sworn in and asked his name and address, but he refused to give his address in open court, so the judge allowed him to write it down. However, he just stood there, like the lemon he was, until Harrington asked him what the problem was, and he replied that he couldn't remember his new address. Trying to give him assistance, Harrington approached the witness box, and the whole court heard Edwards tell him that he had moved to a new county, but Harrington pointed out that he hadn't moved very far away from his previous address!

Harrington began his questioning by asking about his moustache, his weight and height. He knew Edwards fitted the description of the heavily built robber and the ash-blond moustache was certainly going to cause a headache for him in view of the fact that Lindsay and I both have dark hair and if either of us grew a moustache it would be dark.

Edwards was being questioned about how he had met us, how often our trips to London took place and what our dress style was, e.g. whether we wore smart suits to conduct our business meetings.

When Harrington asked Edwards about visiting Ronnie in Broadmoor, he claimed that he had met Ronnie, but I knew that wasn't true. But then again, if Edwards was asked whether he'd met the Queen he would have said that he had.

Harrington then asked if he'd met Reggie, and this time I knew he had as I had introduced him to Reg briefly at Gartree Prison when we had arranged for Ted Hynds to meet Reggie.

Harrington wanted Edwards to name Reg and Ron, Tony Lambrianou and others, because the more shit he could throw at us while questioning Edwards, the blacker the picture would be painted for the jury.

What the meetings in London had to do with an armed robbery in Newbridge, I didn't know, but what I did know was that it was becoming apparent that we were going to be found guilty by our association with Reg and Ron.

When he was asked about Bullen, Edwards dropped him right in it by saying that Bullen was in the thick of it all and, just as Bullen had done, Edwards wanted to give the impression that whatever had been done was nothing to do with him.

Edwards was quite happy to name the Mr X that Bullen had so adamantly refused to.

As soon as Harrington started asking about makes of guns, Edwards was in his element. He named every gun, even spelling the make of one weapon to the judge.

I looked at Lindsay and began laughing. I knew it wasn't a laughing matter, but he really was very entertaining.

Mr Harrington: What sort of gun's that, Mr Edwards?
Edwards: That's a semi-automatic handgun. There was also mentioned a Beretta and a Browning fastback, SAS issue.
Mr Harrington: What sort of gun is the Beretta?
Edwards: A Beretta's a 9mm semi-automatic.
Mr Harrington: And the Browning fastback?
Edwards: That is, that is another semi-automatic weapon.

Still laughing, I leaned over to Lindsay, saying, 'He still thinks he is in the SAS.'

Lindsay smiled back, obviously thinking the same thing. That particular line of questioning went on for a few minutes before moving on to solid-shot cartridges.

Mr Harrington: Could you describe that a little more, please, Mr Edwards?
Edwards: Looking at the solid-shot itself, it is what you would use for shooting out engine blocks on cars or its armour piercing. It would pierce straight through and smash an engine block of a stock car, or anything like that.
Mr Harrington: I see. Was it full of shotgun pellets?
Edwards: No, it was just the head of the, the solid-shot piece itself.
Mr Harrington: Right.
Edwards: It wasn't in the cartridge. It had been cut away from a cartridge, taken out, and that's all it was.
Mr Harrington: Is it the sort of thing you can buy over the counter?
Edwards: No.

I was still laughing and biting my lip when Harrington looked around at Lindsay and me with an expression on his face which seemed to say, 'Fuck me, if they've got those sorts of weapons they could blow my fucking car to bits, and they are still free on bail.'

I had to head for the toilets, otherwise I would have laughed aloud in the court, and it wasn't long before Lindsay was behind me laughing as much as me. We had a drink of water and tried to ease our giggles, and when we returned to the dock we found that they had gone on to the Browning shotgun and spare barrels.

Mr Harrington: What happened there?
Edwards: The box was opened.
Mr Harrington: By whom?
Edwards: That was by Ian Hutley, the box was opened. Inside the box was a dismantled Browning automatic.
Mr Harrington: That's a shotgun?
Edwards: A shotgun.
Mr Harrington: You mentioned a little while ago a spare barrel.
Edwards: Yes, there was two barrels in the case. I believe the one was what they call full-choke and the other one, I think, was half-choke or ...
Judge Gibbon: One was what?
Mr Harrington: Full-choke and the other was half-choke.
Edwards: Yes.
Judge Gibbon: Choke?
Mr Harrington: Choke ... Does that mean the way that the shot splays?
Edwards: It's for the spread of the shot and one thing and another.
Mr Harrington: The splay of the shot, yes. Depending on what its use is intended to be for?
Edwards: Exactly.

Edwards was loving every minute of it. He thought he was the court gun expert and realised he had everyone's full attention. They were hanging on his every word.

What I found strange was that Edwards went on about cutting off a barrel in Bullen's flat, but there was no shotgun as evidence. Also, by their own admission, he and Bullen were party to what they say Lindsay and I were doing!

Harrington then asked Edwards about how we – allegedly – made him carry guns at all times.

Mr Harrington: How often did you carry the gun in that coat, Mr Edwards?
Edwards: I only ever carried the gun in the coat on a matter of four or five times. The gun was put inside the coat, the coat was left in the back of the car, and when we was back in The King's

Oak, go and fetch it, so you would go out and pick the coat up with the gun inside it already.

Mr Harrington: Right, and you have explained that it wasn't just you that carried the coat in with the gun.

Edwards: No, it was also Ian Hutley and Phil Martin.

Mr Harrington: Were Ian Hutley and Phil Martin friends?

Edwards: Yes, longstanding friends by all account.

Mr Harrington: What about ammunition? Was there ever any live ammunition with the gun when it was in a public place?

Edwards: The gun was always loaded on a weekend.

Mr Harrington: By whom?

Edwards: It would either be loaded by Leighton or Lindsay.

Mr Harrington: How often would you say the gun was actually taken into the public house?

Edwards: On most occasions.

Mr Harrington: Do you remember, for example, whether on the very day that it was cut down it was taken out?

Edwards: I believe it was taken out that night.

Judge Gibbon: I beg your pardon?

Edwards: I believe it was taken out that night, on a Saturday night.

Mr Harrington: Taken out, you mean taken from the flat?

Edwards: Taken from the flat to The King's Oak.

Mr Harrington: Apart from the people you have mentioned already, Mr Edwards, are there other names of people who used to come to The King's Oak?

Edwards: Quite a few, but ...

Mr Harrington: You don't know which I m referring to? Any others connected with the Krays?

Edwards: Connected with the Krays, the only ... I would say James Campbell. He was a regular. The only other people I can say that was anything to do with the Krays was Reggie's wife, Kate, and her ex-husband ... oh, Christ, what's his name? ... Harry.

Mr Harrington: Is that Reggie's wife?

Edwards: That is Reggie's wife, yes ... Ronnie's that is, sorry.

Judge Gibbon: Why were you party to carrying this loaded weapon round this public house?

Edwards: The only time that myself or anybody else had hold of the gun was under the instructions of Leighton and Lindsay.

Judge Gibbon: Yes, but didn't you think why this was necessary? Why was it being carried? Do you know?

Edwards: Well, from what I can understand, Leighton and

> Lindsay didn't take any chances, and if they were confronted by someone with a gun they wouldn't hesitate to use the weapon for their own protection, something like that, because of them running around London.

I got up to use the toilet and, on my return, Edwards claimed I had intimidated him and frightened him from the dock. I could only smile.

The day had almost come to an end, Judge Gibbon adjourned for the night and Lindsay and I were told that, due to legal implications, we need not attend court the next day and were bailed until the Monday. As a result of Edwards' outburst, we were told to stay in the cell area for an hour, allowing him time to leave the courts.

The weekend soon passed and we were back in court waiting for Harrington to continue cross-examining Edwards. As Lindsay and I watched Edwards walk to the witness box, we were amazed to see that he had cut his moustache right down to hardly anything, which was, of course, in our favour, but from the prosecution's perspective wasn't very clever. We wondered how he could be so dim. Our barristers turned around, letting us know that they, too, had spotted Edwards' moustache.

> **Mr Harrington:** I see you have altered the shape of your moustache since you last gave evidence.
>
> **Edwards:** Yes, I had a slight accident with it.
>
> **Mr Harrington:** A slight accident? As a matter of interest how does the moustache you are wearing compare to the way it was in the summer of last year?
>
> **Edwards:** Just a little bit thinner, thinned out a little bit more but basically the shape it is now.

Harrington had cleared that point up nicely, but I bet when he saw Edwards come to the court with his moustache thinned out he wasn't too pleased.

Edwards was then asked questions about O'Neill getting slapped, and again, not surprisingly, it had nothing to do with him. Questions then went on about how the Mossburg shotgun had supposedly come on the scene.

We could see what was going on: the Mossburg was the gun found by the young boy at the scene of the robbery, and Edwards was one of a number of people who said they had seen a Mossburg in our possession!

Edwards then went on to explain about the money he was asked to collect from David Ley; money which David agreed to pay, which bought him 50 per cent of the second film deal. But Edwards claimed the money was for weapons. Judge Gibbon picked up on what he was saying and pointed out to both Harrington and Edwards that the meeting with David was solely to deal with the second Kray film.

Mr Harrington: Then you were given instructions on the weekend in April?
Edwards: That was to get £14,000 out of David Ley, or tell him he had to pay up £14,000 and that was for finance of armament and weaponry and whatever like, you know.
Mr Harrington: Was that following any instructions?
Edwards: That was on the instructions of Leighton and Lindsay.
Mr Harrington: And is this the meeting that you told us about at the Traveller's Rest?
Edwards: Yes.
Mr Harrington: You have told us who was present: yourself, Adrian Bullen, Phil Martin?
Edwards: Yes.
Mr Harrington: And Ian Hutley?
Edwards: Correct.
Mr Harrington: In as much detail as you can, could you tell the jury what was then discussed?
Edwards: What was discussed with David Ley was about the £14,000. David Ley agreed to come up with eight instead of the fourteen. The conversation was just basically that and we said, 'All right, fair enough, we'll let Leighton and Lindsay know what you've said, like, and leave it at that.
Mr Harrington: Was anything said in conversation about guns or armaments?
Edwards: David Ley did ask when there are weapons acquired that he would like a small one himself, but that was it basically.
Mr Harrington: What was the first thing said about guns?
Edwards: To my recollection, the first thing that was said to David Ley about guns was, it was discussed about the extra money for finance for weaponry and one thing or another, and he seemed quite content with it and happy. But like he said, like I just said to you, that's what he wanted, that once weapons had been required he wanted one for himself for his own use, whatever he was going to do with it.
Judge Gibbon: Yes, but what was he going to get out of this except one little hand weapon? It seems a lot of money to pay for a hand pistol.

Edwards: Well, just to have the thing, that Leighton and Lindsay would be about if anything was going on, and he wanted anything done, that he could call on Leighton and Lindsay to sort people out or do anything, you know. It was just for being around them and all that. That's all I can say.

Edwards by then was well on his way to blowing a fuse. The judge had asked a valid question but Edwards was renowned for going off the subject and babbling about anything other than the question asked.

Harrington soon jumped in, bailing him out.

Mr Harrington: Is there any doubt in your mind, Mr Edwards, that guns were mentioned at that meeting?
Edwards: None whatsoever.
Mr Harrington: That same week, Mr Edwards, did you have any meeting with anyone else?
Edwards: Yes, we had a meeting with the gentleman I mentioned earlier on.
Mr Harrington: Where did you meet him on this occasion?
Edwards: That was a pub in north London.
Judge Gibbon: North London?
Edwards: Yes.
Mr Harrington: Was this your own meeting or were you acting on instructions?
Edwards: On instructions from Leighton and Lindsay.
Mr Harrington: And who was present with you?
Edwards: Myself and Adrian Bullen.
Mr Harrington: What was discussed at this meeting?
Edwards: The price of armaments again, which from the original price had dropped drastically. 9mm Browning fastbacks at that time, we were told they could have them somewhere between £600 and £800.
Mr Harrington: Were any other guns discussed?
Edwards: Only weapons that I mentioned before.
Mr Harrington: You say only Mr Edwards, but it's of interest to us to have the details.
Edwards: Yes, PO18s, Bernadellis – that is a Bernadelli, the PO18 – a Berretta 90 model and shotguns, you know. We was told whatever the boys wanted they could have.
Judge Gibbon: Had the price of those weapons also dropped?
Edwards: Yes, your Honour.
Mr Harrington: Were you under instructions to order any weapons?

Edwards: No, not at that time.

Mr Harrington: What was the purpose of this meeting?

Edwards: The purpose of the meeting was after we had seen David Ley, we had to find out exactly how much they was going to pay for weapons, or he wanted for weapons, and then it would be sorted out when Leighton and Lindsay returned back to London.

Mr Harrington: Did you have the authority to order weapons, for example?

Edwards: No.

Mr Harrington: Were other things discussed at that meeting?

Edwards: Yes, Adrian Bullen brought up about a person that lives up North, and was he still interested in doing the job up there.

Mr Harrington: What was said about the job? What sort of job was it?

Edwards: It was a job that was discussed from the past, in the company of Leighton and Lindsay as well.

Mr Harrington: Yes?

Edwards: From what I could gather, he owed out debts of somewhere in the region of £200,000. Leighton and Lindsay had been approached a long time back to try and recover some of the money or all of the money, which I had gone with them to sort out, if we could catch him.

Judge Gibbon: When had you been on this job, then?

Edwards: Oh, this was 12 months before I ever went to London, your Honour.

Judge Gibbon: And you had gone there with the defendants?

Edwards: Yes.

Judge Gibbon: Both of them?

Edwards: As a driver, yes.

Judge Gibbon: Did you see the man?

Edwards: No, we didn't.

Mr Harrington: Was there a discussion about what needed to be sorted out, what was going to be done?

Edwards: What was going to be sorted out, from what I understood and believe, that they was to go up North, pick up one target, returning back to London. At the same time pick up two other targets from Leeds, bring them back to London to be put in separate containers.

Judge Gibbon: When you use the words "picked up" is that a euphemistic term for kidnap?

Edwards: Yes, your Honour.

ve: Boxing for Newbridge ABC as a young man. If any bullies on the streets
untered my fists, they'd invariably end up in hospital.

w: The Frayne brothers with their dad.

Above: Lindsay and I with Tony Lambrianou and Wendy.

Below: The Kings Oak pub in Epping Forest, where I met James Campbell.

ove: Brothers enjoying a night out.

ow: Lindsay and I at the grave of Reg and Ron's mother and father.

REG KRAY

Reg writing to me at Ashworth hospital:
'Leighton, Hope you and family are well.
I'm Ok this end. You would be Ok here its
relaxed. Say hello to Lindsay for me.
Is he at Long Lartin !?
Ron gave me your address.
Take it easy.
God Bless,
Friend
Reg Kray

Letter from Ron:
20th Oct Ron Kray
Dear Lindsay Leighton
I wish you all the luck
in the world when you
go to court
God Bless
friend
Ron

Letters from Reg and Ron to Lindsay and I.

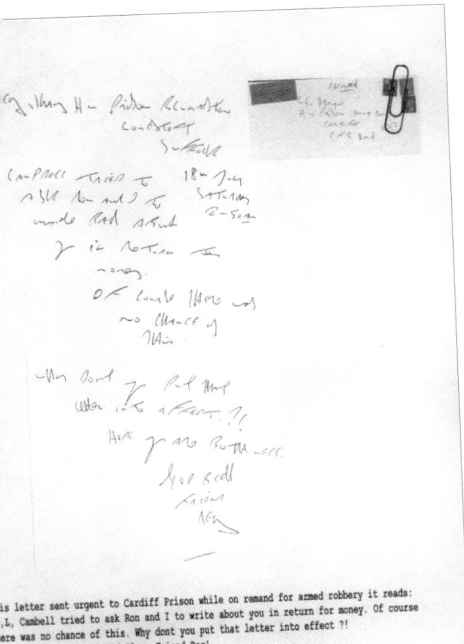

is letter sent urgent to Cardiff Prison while on remand for armed robbery it reads:
,L, Cambell tried to ask Ron and I to write about you in return for money. Of course
ere was no chance of this. Why dont you put that letter into effect ?!
ope you are both well God Bless Friend Reg'.

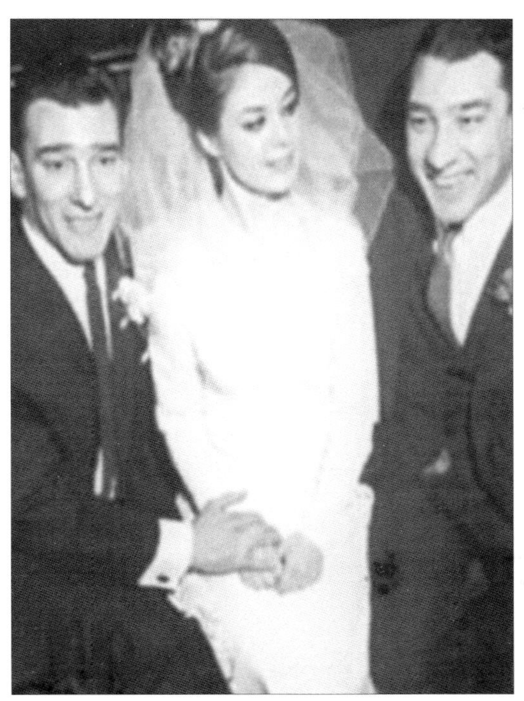

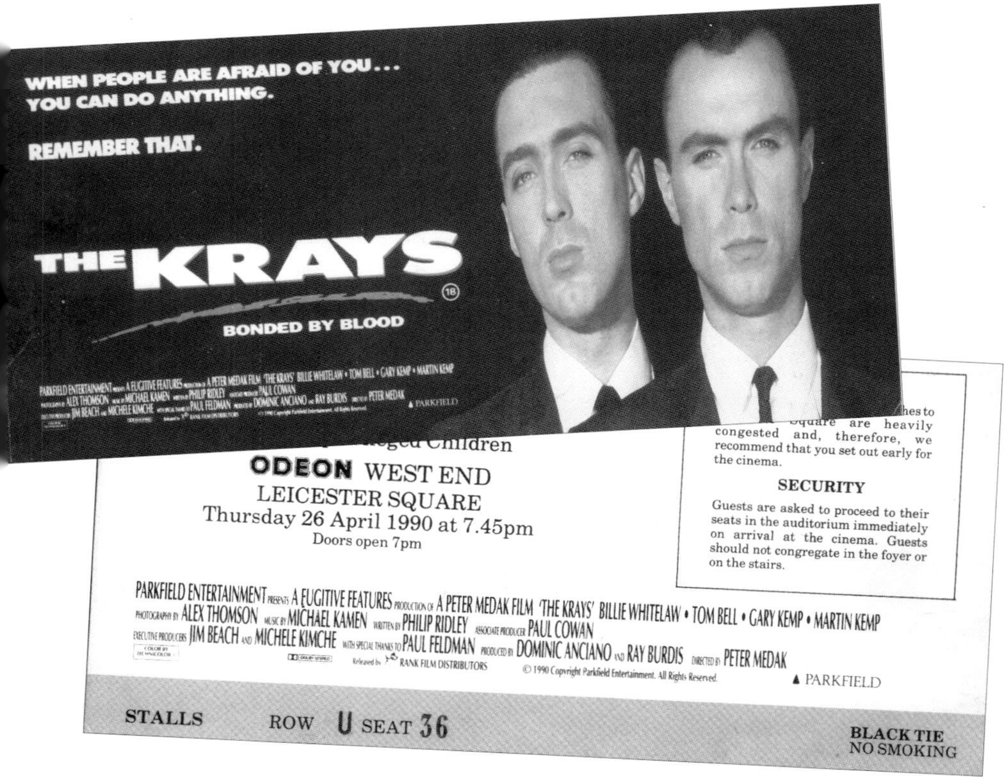

WHEN PEOPLE ARE AFRAID OF YOU...
YOU CAN DO ANYTHING.
REMEMBER THAT.
THE KRAYS
18
BONDED BY BLOOD
ODEON WEST END
LEICESTER SQUARE
Thursday 26 April 1990 at 7.45pm
Doors open 7pm
congested and, therefore, we recommend that you set out early for the cinema.
SECURITY
Guests are asked to proceed to their seats in the auditorium immediately on arrival at the cinema. Guests should not congregate in the foyer or on the stairs.
PARKFIELD ENTERTAINMENT PRESENTS A FUGITIVE FEATURES PRODUCTION OF A PETER MEDAK FILM 'THE KRAYS' BILLIE WHITELAW • TOM BELL • GARY KEMP • MARTIN KEMP
PHOTOGRAPHY BY ALEX THOMSON MUSIC BY MICHAEL KAMEN WRITTEN BY PHILIP RIDLEY ASSOCIATE PRODUCER PAUL COWAN
EXECUTIVE PRODUCERS JIM BEACH AND MICHELE KIMCHE WITH SPECIAL THANKS TO PAUL FELDMAN PRODUCED BY DOMINIC ANCIANO AND RAY BURDIS DIRECTED BY PETER MEDAK
Released by RANK FILM DISTRIBUTORS
© 1990 Copyright Parkfield Entertainment. All Rights Reserved.
PARKFIELD
STALLS
ROW U SEAT 36
BLACK TIE
NO SMOKING

bove left: Another letter from Reg, sent when I was on remand for armed robbery.

bove right: A rare one from the wedding album: Ron and Reg with Reg's wife Frances.

elow: Stars for the night! My ticket to the première of the Kray Brothers film.

Above: Lindsay with the signed platinum Dire Straits disc.

Below left: The labels designed by Lindsay for the Hooch bottles we sold inside Long Lartin.

Below right: Ian, a trusted and loyal friend.

selection of Lindsay's and my drawings. In prison, both inmates and screws would ask
n to draw portraits of their loved ones.

Time on the outside – relaxing on the beach.

Mr Harrington: Was anything said as to what was to happen to the two targets?'
Edwards: 'There was a lot said about them. How far it would have gone I can't say.
Judge Gibbon: Who was saying this?
Edwards: This was the defendants, your Honour.
Mr Harrington: You must be careful because this is a meeting that they weren't at.
Edwards: They weren't at ... It's going back to the first meeting. What was said about the two targets, they had crossed Leighton and Lindsay on some deal or other. They wanted to bring them back down to London, lock them in a container ... Like they said, they couldn't afford to release them again, so it was a case of topping them as far as they was concerned.

There was a clear pattern emerging with Edwards. When he was pulled up, as he had just been by Harrington, he would blow a fuse, and knew that an elaborate story would capture the whole court. He had started talking about murder for the first time.

The atmosphere was electric, and Edwards' bullshit was getting everyone's full attention. I could only look at Lindsay and smile as I wondered how Edwards was going to bear up under cross-examination by Mr Topolski and Mr Beck.

In all fairness to Judge Gibbon, he, too, could see what Edwards was playing at and knew it was getting out of hand.

Judge Gibbon: Let's get this straight. It was a case of what? When was this discussed? They couldn't afford what?
Edwards: After they had kidnapped them, your Honour, as far as they was concerned they couldn't afford to release them again.
Judge Gibbon: The two targets?
Edwards: The two targets.
Judge Gibbon: What about the man with the £200,000 debt?
Edwards: He was just going to be up for ransom, your Honour.
Mr Harrington: You say, "just going to be held for ransom", Mr Edwards. Did these things really get discussed?
Edwards: Yes, and also at Adrian Bullen's flat later on in the day after the meeting.

Edwards seemed to forget that Lindsay and I hadn't been present at that meeting because, as he'd explained earlier, we weren't in London. So Harrington had to steer the daft bastard out of deep water.

Edwards was then questioned about when Lindsay and I returned to

London. He claimed that I had hit him with the Mossburg across the side of the face and then, supposedly, held a knife to his throat while telling him to go and kill David Ley, and that if he didn't I was going to kill him.

I sat biting the inside of my cheek, trying not to laugh as the jury looked daggers at me, and Edwards reeled off one outrageous story after another.

Judge Gibbon: You were smacked in the mouth, across the side of the mouth by Leighton with the Mossburg?
Edwards: Yes.
Judge Gibbon: The knife was held by whom?
Edwards: That was by Leighton. He just, how can I put it, like, freaked out.
Judge Gibbon: And he said?
Edwards: You know, basically, 'You'll do as you're told or I m going to kill you', like. And that's it.
Judge Gibbon: And then you were instructed to go back to David Ley, next day was it?
Edwards: Sometime the following day and shoot him.
Judge Gibbon: And shoot him?
Edwards: Yes.

At that point I think Judge Gibbon had had enough of Edwards. He had been told by Bullen that Edwards was a fantasist.

However, instead of Harrington steering Edwards away from such bollocks, he jumped on it as well.

Mr Harrington: You used the expression, 'blow him away' …
Edwards: The same: blow him away, shoot him, kill him, whatever. It's slang then.
Mr Harrington: But what did you understand you were being ordered to do?
Edwards: To actually go and kill the man.
Mr Harrington: Was anything said as to what would happen if you did or didn't do that?
Edwards: Yes.
Mr Harrington: What was that?
Edwards: I was told, 'You might get away with it you bastard, but you've got a missus and kids at home and they'll suffer for it.'
Mr Harrington: What effect did that have on you, Mr Edwards?
Edwards: Can we have two minutes break because ... (*Edwards*

began crying) ... You've got to appreciate it's coming back in the end with what happened just before the weekend.
Mr Harrington: Mr Edwards, can you compose yourself, because you are going to have to go through this evidence at some stage. It may be better if we get it over with.
Edwards: Okay.

Edwards was right on cue. I couldn't believe he had the front to stand there crying, when he was the one giving all the bollocks. Therefore, we, along with Harrington, had come to the grand finale.

Mr Harrington: I don't know that I need to ask you this question, but I am going to anyway. What effect did it have on you when that was said to you?
Edwards: Well, can you imagine the effect it would have on you if your wife and kids were threatened?
Mr Harrington: Mr Edwards, did you have any intention of complying with that order?
Edwards: None whatsoever. I even lost my wife and children because of that. I couldn't even go home, I was too frightened to. I went and stayed in Swansea for I don't know how many weeks, some friends down there. Just so nobody could get hold of me, no contact with anybody.

I looked to the ceiling and swear I heard violins playing as Edwards gave his speech. I leaned over to Lindsay and said, 'The court witness? More like the fucking court jester.' Lindsay smiled. One of the screws overheard me and he, too, was biting his lip trying not to laugh.

Harrington furthered his questions by asking Edwards if he had been involved in the robbery. Edwards replied, 'No.'

Then they went through photographs of clothing left at the scene of the robbery, but there was nothing of any bearing. Harrington indicated that he had finished his cross-examination, so the fun was about to start, when Mr Topolski could start firing questions at Edwards.

Was Edwards going to crumble?

14

GRASS

Mr Topolski began asking Edwards questions. Edwards began to answer either 'Yes' or 'No'. However, it was only a matter of time. He enjoyed giving his bullshit, yet the more he babbled on the more he hanged himself.

The one-word answers went on until lunchtime and Mr Topolski hadn't been able to budge him at all.

After the lunch break, Mr Topolski wasted no time in steaming into Edwards with a barrage of questions, and it worked. Edwards was off again, to the dismay of Harrington but the delight of our defence.

Mr Topolski: From your evidence, and please listen carefully and correct me if I am wrong, what you told his Honour and the jury is that you have or had not spoken to, seen or in anyway communicated with any police officer about any of these matters before your interviews on 25 October.

Edwards: I had not discussed anything to do with this statement or the written statement with police officers until these statements were written.

Mr Topolski: Or anything whatever to do with the Fraynes or Frayne business before 25 October?

Edwards: The only other time that I spoke to anybody was when a police officer that I know from a long, long time ago asked me what I was doing, in passing interest, and I mentioned I was going back and forward to London trying to sort out a film and all that with Leighton and Lindsay Frayne, and that was the end of the subject.

Mr Topolski: Well, now you have raised that, I must deal with that. We will get back to the interviews, Mr Edwards, I promise you. Just leave them to one side for a moment. First of all, who was that officer?

Edwards: Er, that was Mr Phillips.

Mr Topolski: Mr … ?

Edwards: Phillips.

Judge Gibbon: What's his full name?

Edwards: Andrew Phillips.

Mr Topolski: What rank is he?

Edwards: I believe he is ... He's an inspector anyway.

Mr Topolski: An inspector?

Edwards: Yes.

What Edwards had done was give the name of his handler, Inspector Phillips, who had been running around London with him just after he left in April and, now that Edwards had mentioned his name, Mr Topolski had to work on getting information out of him a bit at a time.

It had also interested the judge, because he knew that Cook was claiming to have done the robbery with Edwards.

Mr Topolski knew it would have been a mistake to press him hard on revealing too much about Phillips, so he withdrew until he felt the time was right.

Edwards, during his questioning from Mr Topolski, tried to make out he was still our friend – something I found extremely amusing.

Mr Topolski: You just couldn't walk away?

Edwards: I didn't want to see Leighton or Lindsay in trouble that they are allegedly in now.

Mr Topolski: You have had a change of mind about that, of course?

Edwards: No, I have not.

Mr Topolski: Haven't you?

Edwards: I dislike what they have said with the threat towards my family, which any man would.

Mr Topolski: Is that why you are telling lies about them?

Edwards: I'm afraid I didn't come to court to tell lies. I came here to speak the truth, as I see it and as I believe it. All I can do is give you, or give the prosecution, an account of things that I can

recall. I couldn't turn round and say exact dates here, there and willy-nilly, which I made quite clear, but if I turn round and you are going to start calling me a liar again, I shall stand here and just totally ignore any questions you throw at me, because I did not come to this court to put my family in the jeopardy I have put them in, which you know yourself. Last Friday there was another threat made. I'm not having it, and I'm very sorry but that's it. As far as I'm concerned, *finito.* You've got everything there that you want and I am not prepared to take it any further.
Judge Gibbon: Now, you will end your speech there and answer the next question.

That subdued Edwards, at least for the time being. Mr Topolski then asked Edwards why, if he objected so strongly to guns, he didn't just leave.

Mr Topolski: Who took the guns from the car?
Edwards: It could have been anybody that Leighton and Lindsay caught hold of or was nearest to them at the time when they wanted it.
Mr Topolski: Who took the guns from the car?
Edwards: Myself, Ian, Phil and Adrian Bullen on occasions have even done it, and also the defendants have gone out and taken ...
Mr Topolski: You had no choice but to do that? Is that what you are telling us?
Edwards: You was told to go and fetch it and you fetched it.
Mr Topolski: Your family hadn't been threatened at that stage, had they?
Edwards: Not at that stage, no.
Mr Topolski: No? What was to stop you saying, 'That's it, I'm off. I'm having nothing to do with this any more. Get someone else to do your dirty work for you.' What was to stop you at that stage?
Edwards: What was to stop me at that stage?
Mr Topolski: Yes.
Edwards: As you have read in my statement, I thought I was in too deep, and the way that they was acting at the time. I was still a bit suspicious about what would go on afterwards, because they always said once you are in there's only one way out.
Mr Topolski: What was to stop you leaving and saying, 'I've had enough of this. I'm off home to Wales'?
Edwards: I have just explained it to you.

Mr Topolski: Just some vague feeling you had that they were in it too deep and you wanted to be around?

Edwards: No, everybody was in too deep at that time, and like I have said to you, they turned round and said straight: 'Once you're in you're in and there's only one way out.'

Mr Topolski: Or was it you wanted to stay around because you thought you could benefit from some of the criminal activity that was going on, Mr Edwards?

Edwards: No.

Mr Topolski: Mr Edwards, you have been shown the dark-coloured parka type jacket. Do you see that? And your answer is that it's Lindsay Frayne's. That's the one we looked at earlier on. Over the page you say, 'Yeah, he used to wear it regular. Where did he get it from? I don't know, but to be honest with you Newport or somewhere like that it was.' You actually remembered where Lindsay Frayne got this jacket from, did you?

Edwards: Because he had actually mentioned it.

Mr Topolski: He mentioned it?

Edwards: From the Army and Navy Stores.

Mr Topolski: You remember Army and Navy Stores now? Why didn't you say that then to the police, 'Army and Navy Stores'?

Edwards: I just didn't think of it. It's just as you were questioning there's things coming back which you must appreciate where the prosecution, with the questions I have been asked and one thing and another, there is certain things that will come back in my memory, the simple reason is that I do suffer with a form of dyslexia, so I do rely on my memory quite some bit.

Edwards was off, blowing a gasket again! What he was talking about I had no idea, but as I took a quick glance around the court I saw that everyone had the same expressions on their faces; expressions which said, 'What on earth is he talking about?'

It looked as though the judge had washed his hands of him, as he didn't seem to take any notice of anything he had just said.

And so it went on.

Mr Topolski made many valid points, but Edwards still seemed to lose the plot on some occasions, and his evidence was differing dramatically from his statements. It was as though we were sitting in a different court, listening to someone else's trial.

Mr Topolski was nearing the end of his questioning.

Mr Topolski: Listen to this, please. 'Welsh. Valley type accent. 5ft

10. Very heavily built. Sandy-coloured hair with a moustache. 33 years old.' Does that sound like you?

Edwards: That could fit no end of people, I should imagine.

Mr Topolski: That's a description of the robber who robbed this building society on 24 July, Mr Edwards. That was you, wasn't it?

Edwards: No, it was not. I am afraid if you keep on with that, let's be honest, the way this robbery went off, what I have seen of the evidence, if it was me that planned the robbery it would have been with much more military precision than it was. It would have gone off with expert timing, not like having stuff left round and all that. As you said yourself, I'm a true professional, so I would have known what I was doing before I even went in there and there would have been no evidence left behind.

Mr Topolski: And because you wanted to implicate my client, that's why you planted the gun in the wood so it would be found, didn't you?

Edwards: How would I get the gun? Because the gun was already in their possession, not mine.

Mr Topolski: You did that with your military precision and your thinking, didn't you, Mr Edwards? That was your tortured way of getting back at Lindsay Frayne, wasn't it?

Edwards: That is your duty and you are doing it, but I did not have anything to do with the armed robbery. I did not plant anything anywhere. I had nothing to do with it whatsoever.

The day had come to an end, but I had no doubt there would be more entertainment from Edwards when he faced my barrister, Mr Jimmy Beck, the next morning.

When we arrived back in court, Mr Beck told me that he had picked up on quite a lot of inconsistencies while Edwards had been questioned by both Harrington and Mr Topolski.

He was soon questioning Edwards, asking when he had first heard about the robbery. Edwards replied that he had heard about it on the television and read about it in the papers.

Mr Beck: Help me again. I think immediately after lunch yesterday, you were asked in cross-examination specifically about this. You never spoke to any police officer about the Fraynes, the robbery, anything like that, shotguns, other than the one casual conversation you told us about, until 25 October?

Edwards: That is correct.

Mr Beck: When you were arrested?
Edwards: That is correct.
Mr Beck: You may not be able to help with what I ask you, and if you can't, just say so.
Mr Beck (*To the judge*): Your Honour, I'm looking at the interview of my client, which is page 333 of the exhibit bundle. It's actually exhibit 115.
Mr Beck (*To the witness*): So on 27 September, in other words almost a full month before you were arrested, a police officer said to Leighton Frayne: 'This Paul Edwards has told police officers this morning ...' Do you understand that?
Edwards: Yes.
Mr Beck: What do you say about that?
Edwards: I have no idea whatsoever. It's something I couldn't help you on.
Mr Beck: It goes on to say: 'So Paul Edwards says because he's a bigger lump that he puts his weight on it.' Talking about the Browning shotgun: 'And held it firmly while Ian Hutley sawed the barrel off.' That is what your evidence is, isn't it?
Edwards: My evidence, as I have said in court, I did sit on the Browning gun while the barrel was cut, but that was by Lindsay Frayne. That was cut by Ian Hutley, Lindsay cut half way through the stock, I finished cutting the rest of the stock.
Mr Beck: All right. Let me just stop you, Mr Edwards. I don't want to be unfair, but it's right that you sat on it?
Edwards: That is correct.
Mr Beck: And here's a police officer putting it to my client a month before you say you had ever spoken to a police officer. Can you help me with that?
Edwards: I hadn't spoken to no police officer on any weaponry that was cut or anything else to do with the case at all prior to my arrest in a Gwent police station, so where you've got your information from I have no idea whatsoever.

I looked over to Lindsay and said, 'Edwards is going to blow a gasket now.' Jimmy Beck had him on the run, and Edwards had no way out!

Mr Beck: Well, let me make it clear to you, if it's not. I am looking at an interview …
Judge Gibbon: I don't think you are entitled to take it further than that, Mr Beck.

Lindsay and I looked at each other. What was going on? Jimmy Beck was onto Edwards and yet the judge was bailing him out.

Mr Beck: Your Honour, I would like to take the witness to other parts of the interview.
Judge Gibbon: You will be able to make your comment to the jury in due course. He has said affirmatively that he didn't see a police officer until October, and in due course you will be able to comment to the jury about the questions which were asked during the course of this interview, having possibly cross-examined the officer concerned.
Mr Beck: Your Honour, I am obliged. (*To the witness*): There's nothing at all that you can help me with, Mr Edwards?
Edwards: Nothing at all. Everything I have said yesterday and in my opening statement, to my best belief and my best knowledge, is things that did occur. I cannot elaborate on anything else and the only thing I can say is, are we going to go over the same ground as we went yesterday? Because, as I said, I have never turned round and accused either defendants of anything, for the armed robbery or any knowledge of the armed robbery.
Judge Gibbon: Stop making speeches, please. We understand.
Edwards: I'm sorry, your Honour.
Judge Gibbon: But you are quite certain in your mind, until you were arrested in October, and interviewed on the 25th day of that month, you had not spoken to a police officer about your activities in London with the defendants?
Edwards: That is correct your Honour.
Mr Beck: Your Honour, I am most grateful.
Mr Beck (*To the witness*): Mr Edwards, help me with this. After the argument in London in April, you left London and the company of the Fraynes suddenly. Is that right?
Edwards: I parted from their company, yes.
Mr Beck: What I don't understand, and what I want you to help me with, is this: was it because your wife and children had been threatened? Is that right?
Edwards: That is correct.
Mr Beck: How did your leaving London in any way prevent the Fraynes carrying out their threat to your wife?
Edwards: The way I understood the threat to be, that if I had left and gone home it was my wife and children that was at risk, not myself basically, and I turned round when I left them, as I have said, I went to Swansea and stayed with friends in Swansea.

Judge Gibbon: Yes, but the question is, how was that protecting your wife and children?

Edwards: The way I looked at it was, your Honour, by not being anywhere in the vicinity of my wife and children, they would turn round and find out I'm not anywhere in the area so hopefully they would leave them alone.

Mr Beck: Mr Edwards, the threat was, wasn't it, that you had to carry out their orders or your wife and children would be hurt? That was the threat?

Edwards: As I have said.

Mr Beck: Is it right, then, that there was nothing at all to prevent them harming your wife and children, because you hadn't carried out the orders, had you?

Edwards: I put that down to their own integrity to a point, that I was not anywhere in the vicinity. It was me that they had disagreements with and they would leave my wife and children alone.

Mr Beck: But you agree with me that they knew where your wife and children were living?

Edwards: Yes.

Mr Beck: And that there was nothing to stop them, if they so wanted, carrying out that threat, was there?

Edwards: Nothing at all.

Mr Beck: You didn't remove your wife and children to Swansea, did you?

Edwards: No.

Mr Beck: It's right, isn't it, that just before that April trip to London, you had arranged for your invalidity benefit to be paid at one of the property addresses owned by the Fraynes?

Edwards: Yes, I did.

Mr Beck: And the reason you did that was because your wife had thrown you out, hadn't she?

Edwards: No, she hadn't.

Mr Beck: We touched upon it yesterday. I would like to go into it in more detail. It's right, isn't it, that in February of that year you and your wife split up, had separated?

Edwards: Approximately about February, yes.

Mr Beck: You weren't living there with her?

Edwards: Correct.

Mr Beck: So how in any way were you protecting your wife and children from the Fraynes?

Edwards: Because I had been visiting my ex-wife on a regular basis. On a Wednesday I turn round and see my children on a regular basis.

I said to Lindsay, 'I wish he would turn round and fucking roll away. He's been caught out big time, the lying rat.'

Lindsay nodded and laughed, along with the screws who heard what I said.

Mr Beck: Yes, that may be so, Mr Edwards. What I am trying to grasp is why, by leaving London as you did, you were in any way protecting your wife and children.

Edwards: That's how it seemed to me at the time, as I have explained. I thought I was doing the best thing by not going back anywhere near her and the children at the time.

Mr Beck: This is an address that the Fraynes knew?

Edwards: Yes.

Mr Beck: You leave London in April, and go to live in Swansea?

Edwards: Correct.

Mr Beck: And that in some way, as you have explained, was because of the threat made to the wife and children?

Edwards: Made to me about my wife and children, yes.

Mr Beck: All right. Let me suggest to you that, in fact, that threat was never made. What the Fraynes were incensed about was your behaviour in London while they had been in Wales.

Judge Gibbon: Well, was the threat made? That's the first question.

Edwards: Yes, your Honour. It was made.

Judge Gibbon: And were the Frayne bothers incensed about your behaviour in London whilst they were back in Wales?

Edwards: The only thing that happened in London while they was back in Wales, your Honour, was on their instructions, which we have already gone through.

Mr Beck had made his point. It was clear that no threat had been made to Edwards' wife and children because he was no longer in a relationship with his wife, and she wasn't actually his wife.

Mr Beck continued his questioning about Edwards visiting London after we had sent him packing, the same time that we knew Edwards and Inspector Phillips had been asking questions.

We knew Edwards was an informer and that his handler was Inspector Phillips, but under disclosure rules, Edwards had immunity as a paid police informer, which was why Mr Beck couldn't push him on the point that he had made a statement, either on our arrest in September or before – not in October, as Edwards had claimed.

I knew there was to be some legal talk on the matter after Edwards had been cross-examined by all three barristers. However, the immunity appeared to let Edwards have carte blanche with his lies. It was also proving that our barristers hands were tied during questioning.

Mr Beck moved to question Edwards about weapons, which we knew would please him no end.

Mr Beck: You yourself, of course, from your army experience, know about military weapons, don't you?
Edwards: Yes.
Mr Beck: You know, presumably, what a Bernadelli PO18 is?
Edwards: Yes.
Mr Beck: I mean, do you know things like rate-of-fire, that sort of thing?
Edwards: Bernadelli, I never had any contact with. From what I have read about the Bernadelli, it's supposed to be one of the fastest self-loading handguns that you can get.
Mr Beck: What about the Browning Fastback SAS issue? I think that is what you described it as.
Edwards: That is what was ordered by the two brothers, yes, if that's what you are referring to.
Mr Beck: What do you know about that as a weapon?
Edwards: Browning Fastback has got a wide-pore ejection unit and less chance of stoppages.
Mr Beck: I'm terribly sorry, I interrupted you.
Edwards: I said it's basically a standard 9mm pistol with a wide ejection pore. So if you get a stoppage with it, it's very rare.
Mr Beck: Something that you've read about?
Edwards: It was just common knowledge.
Mr Beck: Common knowledge amongst whom, Mr Edwards?
Edwards: Amongst the armed forces.
Mr Beck: What about a Star make? Does that mean anything?
Edwards: A Star.
Mr Beck: No?
Edwards: No.
Mr Beck: So on any meeting, you certainly didn't get offered a Star pistol for £600 or a Glock for £2,000?
Edwards: No.
Mr Beck: Presumably if you had, you would have remembered?
Edwards: If I had I would have remembered.
Mr Beck: Is that something like a solid shot for a shotgun? You know what that is, don't you?

Edwards: Yes.

Mr Beck: Something which replaces the standard cartridge and in essence is a big bullet, if I can put it in simple terms.

Edwards: Yes.

Mr Beck: For shooting out engine blocks on cars?

Edwards: Exactly.

Mr Beck: And where does your knowledge about that come from?

Edwards: From the army.

Mr Beck: You see, what I suggest is that it's you and Mr Bullen who are the people with knowledge with guns, not the Fraynes. Do you understand?

Edwards: Yes.

Mr Beck: Is that broadly true, if I can put it in an academic sense?

Edwards: Military weapons, yes, because I have served in the military, but the Fraynes do have a knowledge of weaponry as well, and it's not a broad one.

Mr Beck drew his questioning to a close by taking Edwards through suggestions that he was involved in the robbery, which, of course, he denied. Mr Topolski then asked a number of questions relating to Edwards' first statement in October, which showed that he was mentioned in my interviews in September, also in Lindsay's interviews and, no doubt, Ian and Phil's.

Harrington furthered his cross-examination, covering the questions which Edwards had botched up with our defence. As Harrington finished off with Edwards, he found that he wasn't going to have the last word, as Mr Topolski jumped up and questioned Edwards further. He had discovered that while Edwards was in London in April, he had been on police bail, and although this fact was insignificant as far as the case went, it proved that Edwards had breached his bail conditions.

When all questions to Edwards were finished, the jury was dismissed so that time could be spent on legal talk in preparation for the afternoon session.

To my surprise, our barristers addressed Judge Gibbon on a new ruling which had come into being. It was known as the Judith Ward ruling. Judith Ward had been acquitted at the High Court after spending almost 20 years in prison for IRA crimes it was later proved she did not commit. This ruling opened up a completely new avenue for our defence, as it stated that the prosecution had to disclose all their material relating to our case, including who their informants were.

That meant that the likes of Edwards and Chamberlain could no longer hide behind the police and the courts were no longer obliged to protect them.

Our barristers had been up against a brick wall when questioning Edwards about the statement he'd made in October, knowing full well that he'd given the police information before we had even been arrested in September. There was also the danger that when paid informants were being protected, they could tell whatever lies they liked about a person in order to secure a conviction, which certainly seemed to be happening in our case.

Even though Edwards had slipped through the net of being exposed as a paid police informer, our barristers could now make the fact clear to the jury without any hindrance from the judge. It was going to be very interesting when Andrew Chamberlain took the stand, as he would also be exposed when under cross-examination.

That afternoon the next person to take the stand should have been Chamberlain, but Harrington had brought in Edwards' girlfriend to confirm his whereabouts on the day of the robbery.

Harrington began his cross-examination by getting her to confirm that Edwards was with her on the day of the robbery.

There wasn't a lot our barristers could do except to question her in a delicate way in the hope she may make a mistake and let the truth slip out. But, of course, Harrington was lying in wait just in case such a mistake should occur.

She was soon leaving and next to take the stand was Andrew Chamberlain.

Harrington opened by taking him through his statement, and didn't take too long to question him before leaving him to Mr Topolski.

Mr Topolski: You were arrested, weren't you, on 17 December, for conspiracy to rob? That's right, isn't it?
Chamberlain: Was I?
Mr Topolski: Weren't you?
Chamberlain: I don't know.
Mr Topolski: At 12.25pm on Tuesday, 17 December, were you spoken to by a police officer who said, 'I am making enquiries into an armed robbery which occurred on Wednesday, 24 July. I believe you know something about this and I am arresting you on suspicion of conspiracy to commit armed robbery.' To which you replied, 'I know what you are on about, but I had nothing to do with it.' You were then taken into an interview room and interviewed.

Chamberlain: Right.
Mr Topolski: I will ask you again, were you arrested on 17 December for conspiracy to rob?
Chamberlain: Right.
Mr Topolski: And you were interviewed, weren't you?
Chamberlain: Yes, I was.
Mr Topolski: On tape? That's right, isn't it?
Chamberlain: Yes.
Mr Topolski: Of course, 4 days before that, on 13 December, you had been in another police station, hadn't you, being questioned. Is that right?
Chamberlain: For what?
Mr Topolski: Burglary.
Chamberlain: That's correct.
Mr Topolski: Of a large amount of clothing.
Chamberlain: That's right.
Mr Topolski: Some of which was hidden up the mountainside?
Chamberlain: That's right, yes.

The point Mr Topolski was making was that Chamberlain had claimed he was first interviewed on 13 December, when it had now been revealed that he was on the mountainside with Chief Inspector Johnson and Inspector Phillips – where they picked up the cartridges – in August, which was the month before our arrest.

The Judith Ward ruling revealed statements which would not previously have been shown at our trial, and it was clear that the police hadn't told Chamberlain he was about to be exposed as a paid police informer.

Chamberlain was hitting some serious problems while on the stand as his statements weren't making any sense.

Mr Topolski: You had been at the mountainside in the August. Did it come as a surprise to you that you were being asked to go up the mountain again in December?
Chamberlain: No, I was just looking at it more in the way of to gather more evidence.
Mr Topolski: Yes. That, of course, is something that you help the police with from time to time, isn't it Mr Chamberlain, gathering evidence?
Chamberlain: How do you mean?
Mr Topolski: You are a police informer, aren't you?
Chamberlain: No.

Mr Topolski: You are paid by the police when you give information to them, aren't you?
Chamberlain: Who pays me?
Mr Topolski: The police?
Chamberlain: The police ... ? Have you got records of that?
Judge Gibbon: Well, no, just answer the question, please. Have you been paid by the police for giving them information?
Chamberlain: No, I haven't.
Mr Topolski: Have you given the police information on a regular basis about this and other crimes?
Chamberlain: No I haven't.
Mr Topolski: Are you what is known as a registered police informer?
Chamberlain: Why am I registered?
Mr Topolski: Are you a registered police informer?
Chamberlain: No, I'm not.
Judge Gibbon: He probably doesn't know that the police register their informants. I don't know.
Judge Gibbon (*To the witness*): Were you aware that the police keep a register of persons who give them information?
Chamberlain: Well ... Your Honour, I wasn't ...
Judge Gibbon: Were you aware?
Chamberlain: No, I'm not aware. What I'm aware of is, I'm not a police informer and I don't get paid by the police for to give evidence for them. This is the first I've ever been to court to give evidence.
Mr Topolski: Ah, well, that's where we may be misunderstanding each other.
Chamberlain: So am I a police informer?

Under my breath I muttered, 'Of course you are, you fucking prat. What do you think you are doing in the witness box, waiting for a fucking bus? You are a fucking grass mate.'

Mr Topolski asked him what the word pretext meant. The word was in his statement and, judging by how dim he was in the stand, I think Mr Topolski knew it was a fair bet that he wouldn't know. Mr Topolski pointed out that the word was contained in his December statement, and asked him whether he had just signed it without reading it through. Asked again what it meant, Chamberlain said, 'It means to publicise, no, to seek publicity in the wrong order. Something like that. I can't really explain it.' Then he said that a police officer had written down what he told him to write. One of the screws sitting beside me asked what school he went to. I could only shrug my shoulders.

Mr Topolski told the court that Chamberlain had been in and out of court 18 times and to prison on a number of occasions, the last sentence being five years for arson. The information was sure to discredit him. He was also asked about meetings he'd had with Inspector Phillips and Chief Inspector Johnson as an informant, and he was quite happy to mention their names.

He admitted to making a statement five days into the trial, in which he claimed I had told him that Lindsay had done the robbery with either Edwards or Cook, and yet none of that was mentioned in his December statement.

Mr Topolski: Have you ever passed on information, about crime or criminals? Not in return for money. Just simply passing it to a police officer or police officers? Have you ever done that in the past?
Chamberlain: No, I haven't.
Mr Topolski: Well, then, I'm afraid I must just press this slightly. These are your own words. Why do you feel it's necessary to say here you weren't acting as an informant? Why should the word informant come into your head in making this statement 5 days ago?
Chamberlain: Because I'm not an informant.
Mr Topolski: But why did you feel it necessary to say you weren't?
Chamberlain: Well, this is the first time I have ever given evidence against people. You see, where I come from, when they find out you have given evidence against someone, they call you an informant. So I made it quite clear I'm not an informant.
Mr Topolski: I think the word probably used is 'grass'. Certainly where I come from, Mr Chamberlain.
Chamberlain: Well, where I come from it's ...
Mr Topolski: Informant?
Chamberlain: Yes.
Mr Topolski: Proper use of the word, all right.
Chamberlain: I didn't have to come here today. I give my evidence and I'll come and go then, you know? That's what I m trying to put over.
Judge Gibbon: Yes, just wait for the next question.
Mr Topolski: Is this the first time you have been into court when the Fraynes have been in court, Mr Chamberlain?

Chamberlain: Yes.
Mr Topolski: Are you sure about that? Think very carefully. Weren't you a fairly regular visitor to Blackwood Magistrates Court?
Chamberlain: Yes.
Mr Topolski: You were. You visited that court regularly when the Fraynes were appearing there, didn't you?
Chamberlain: No, twice.
Mr Topolski: You listened when no doubt prosecuting solicitor or prosecuting counsel stood up and told the court some facts about the case against you?
Chamberlain: Yes.
Mr Topolski: Perhaps you even listened to the odd bail application, I don't know. Is that right?
Chamberlain: That's right.
Mr Topolski: What was the purpose of those visits by you to the Magistrates Court, Mr Chamberlain?
Chamberlain: Just to see them.
Mr Topolski: Just to ...?
Chamberlain: See them.
Mr Topolski: See them?
Chamberlain: Yes, see them.
Mr Topolski: Were you allowed a visit with them?
Chamberlain: No.
Mr Topolski: They were remanded in custody, weren't they?
Chamberlain: That's right.
Mr Topolski: Cardiff prison. No one is permitted a social visit with a prisoner at a Magistrates Court except in very rare circumstances. That's right, isn't it?
Chamberlain: No, what I meant is, see them, as in, I'll sit in the public dock by there.
Mr Topolski: Not to find out a bit more about what was being said about this case? Not to help you in doctoring some of your evidence that you don't start writing until 21 December, Mr Chamberlain? You smile.
Chamberlain: No.
Mr Topolski: No?
Chamberlain: No, I was there because my friends was there on in court. Leighton and Lindsay came in for the bail application. I sat in the court and listened to what went on. That's all what went on.

Another day had come to an end and, as usual, we were kept a further half-hour to allow Chamberlain to leave.

Mr Topolski and Mr Beck had spotted that Chamberlain mentioned during cross-examination Paul Edwards having been on the mountain, test-firing the guns with him. On hearing this admission, both our barristers agreed that they would have to listen to the tape to check that what they had heard was right. This shed new light on the robbery: Chamberlain was involved with Edwards and seemed to have contact with Inspector Phillips, who was Edwards' handler.

We were into day ten of the trial, and Mr Topolski wasted no time in pointing out to Chamberlain that he had mentioned Paul being on the mountain with him.

Mr Topolski: Yesterday, you were giving evidence and answering questions, first of all from Mr Harrington.
Chamberlain: Yes.
Mr Topolski: You were dealing with the visit on the mountainside.
Chamberlain: That's right.
Mr Topolski: And you spoke of going up the mountainside, you say, 'With shotguns and a pellet gun', and you say that you had with you Lindsay and Leighton Frayne.
Chamberlain: Yes.
Mr Topolski: You talked about going to the boot of the car.
Chamberlain: Yes.
Mr Topolski: You said Paul was there, didn't you, yesterday?
Chamberlain: Paul.
Mr Topolski: I would like you to listen to the tape of your evidence, please, at that point. Listen very carefully to what you say.
(*Appropriate part of tape played*)
Mr Topolski: Unless, of course, the truth is it was you and Paul Edwards up that mountain and it wasn't a slip of the tongue, you just made a mistake.
Chamberlain: It wasn't me up the mountain, nor Paul Edwards either.
Judge Gibbon: Well, you were up the mountain.
Chamberlain: Yes, I was up the mountain with Leighton and Lindsay. What I meant was, I wasn't up the mountain with Paul Edwards.
Mr Topolski: You do agree, don't you, you did say the word 'Paul'?

Chamberlain: Yes, I do.
Mr Topolski: You have never seen Lindsay Frayne with a moustache, have you?
Chamberlain: No.
Mr Topolski: Just to confirm the position at around the time we are talking about, would you be good enough to look at this photograph? It comes out of a bundle of photographs out of exhibit 64. This, I can help you, Mr Chamberlain, is a group photograph taken at the night of the stag night show, so-called, on 8 August. Do you see Lindsay there?
Chamberlain: Yes.
Mr Topolski: He very much looks as he looks now in the dock, doesn't he? Clean shaven.
Chamberlain: Yes.
Mr Topolski: Thank you, you can put that down. We also know from the evidence now, Mr Chamberlain, that on 13 December you were interviewed and confessed to your participation in a burglary.
Chamberlain: That's right.
Mr Topolski: I think it was a burglary of about £10,000 worth of property wasn't it?
Chamberlain: Yes.
Mr Topolski: Clothing?
Chamberlain: Yes.
Mr Topolski: And a judge gave you probation?
Chamberlain: Yes, me and my co-defendant.
Mr Topolski: Before coming to court for that case, did the police suggest they could give you any assistance as far as a sentence was concerned?
Judge Gibbon: Well, Mr Topolski, I will want this discussed in the absence of the jury if you are taking the point I think you are going to take. I'm not going to have the sentencing policy of the courts discussed in public.
Mr Topolski: Your Honour, I don't pursue it. The position I put to you, Mr Chamberlain, is this: I suggest that at all times, all the Fraynes' business was legitimate. Do you understand what I mean by the word legitimate?
Chamberlain: Yes.
Mr Topolski: You are, I suggest, a police informant and you have told lie upon lie to this jury to serve your own purpose.
Chamberlain: And what are my own purposes?
Mr Topolski: I can't explore that, Mr Chamberlain. You are the

only one who knows the truth and I suggest you have not been telling it.

Chamberlain: You make a lot of suggestions. None of them are true, as far as I'm concerned, and I certainly ain't a police informer.

Mr Topolski: You certainly aren't a police informer. I will leave it there.

Judge Gibbon: I am bound to ask you then, why did you go to London the second time? The police asked you to go there?

Chamberlain: That's right.

Mr Topolski: Perhaps you would be good enough to answer his Honour's question.

Chamberlain: What's the question?

Mr Topolski: Why did you go to the Fraynes on 6 August if it wasn't to gather intelligence?

Chamberlain: It wasn't to gather intelligence, as you say, for the police.

Mr Topolski: Why did you go?

Chamberlain: They are my friends.

Mr Topolski: I will leave it there.

It was then the turn of Mr Beck to cross-examine Chamberlain.

Mr Beck: I ask you questions on behalf of Leighton Frayne. So that you know the position from the outset, I adopt my learned friend's cross-examination and the case he has put to you. In other words, I call you a liar on exactly the same basis. You understand, don't you?

Chamberlain: Yes, I understand.

Mr Beck: Let me move to this question, Mr Chamberlain. You told my learned friend that you never visited either of the Frayne brothers after they were remanded in custody on this charge.

Chamberlain: That's right.

Mr Beck: I suggest that you visited Ebbw Vale police station and visited Leighton Frayne whilst he was remanded in custody on this charge. What do you say about that?

Chamberlain: I visited Leighton Frayne at Ebbw Vale police station.'

Judge Gibbon: 'When he was in custody?

Chamberlain: No, I visited Leighton Frayne whilst he was at Ebbw Vale police station. I didn't visit him at Cardiff prison or any other prison.

Judge Gibbon: Yes, but was he in custody? Was he in the cells or was he remanded?

Chamberlain: Yes, he was in the cells.

Mr Beck: Let me just clarify this with you, Mr Chamberlain. Leighton Frayne was being held in Ebbw Vale police station on remand, wasn't he, because there wasn't a space in prison?

Chamberlain: That's right.

Mr Beck: So he was in custody and you visited him.

Chamberlain: Yes that's right.

Mr Beck: What was the purpose of that, Mr Chamberlain?

Chamberlain: Just to see how he was.

I sat looking at Lindsay in utter disbelief. Chamberlain was in the witness box stitching us up with his bullshit, yet he had the cheek to say he was visiting in the name of friendship. What I was looking at as he stood in the witness box, was a greedy, slimy rat and, as had been pointed out to him time and time again by our defence barristers, he is and always will be A GRASS!

Mr Beck continued with questions about his two statements and the visit to the mountainside with Chief Inspector Johnson and Inspector Phillips. Chamberlain was getting mixed-up because by then Cook had come forward admitting he'd done the robbery with Edwards.

It was clear that Chamberlain had been asked to make another statement five days into the trial. Mr Beck was quick to ask why the police did nothing about having the name of the second robber, bearing in mind Phil Martin had been charged as the other robber with Lindsay.

Chamberlain was trying to make out that when Sutton and Price were interviewing him, he had been arrested on conspiracy to robbery, when, in fact, he had been on the mountainside with the two high-ranking detectives having an informal chat.

He wasn't making any sense and Mr Beck, through his perseverance, managed to show the inconsistencies between his past statement and about the meetings on the mountain.

Our barristers decided that their only chance was to cross-examine Chief Inspector Johnson, Inspector Phillips, Sutton, Price and a few others.

15

A TASTE OF THEIR OWN MEDICINE

Jimmy Beck told me that he was extremely concerned about the diary which I was claiming was O'Neill's. He knew that if O'Neill didn't admit it was his, I was in hot water and there was no doubt I would be charged with major drug dealing. The only thing in my favour was that I had never written in the diary, and Mr Beck could tell O'Neill that he had handwriting experts waiting to prove that the diary was his.

However, we were informed that O'Neill couldn't make the trial because, while travelling down the M4, his car had been rammed off the road and it was discovered that his brakes had been tampered with. Mr Beck shot me a stern look, and told me he hoped we weren't interfering with witnesses as the judge could revoke our bail.

Whether there was any truth in the story we didn't know; O'Neill would have known about the diary.

In the absence of O'Neill, James Campbell was called.

When Harrington started firing questions at him, Campbell was only too pleased to tell the court we were armed at all times with sawn-off shotguns, but even so, I couldn't help feeling sorry for him. Lindsay and I had always considered him to be a valued member of any business meetings he'd been on.

There wasn't much that could be said to Campbell.

Next to be called was David Ley.

Under cross-examination by Harrington, he said that he couldn't understand why we would want to rob a building society of £10,000, as we had access to far greater amounts of money from him if we'd needed it. That was the last thing Harrington wanted to hear, so he accused David of being our financier to buy weapons, but David was no mug and soon put Harrington in his place. Our barristers made it clear that our business dealings with David were confined to setting up the second film as he was prepared to finance part of the preparations.

After all the barristers had finished with David Ley, Colin Fry was called, but the police couldn't find him anywhere. It seems he had moved on and couldn't be found. The papers ran a story that Lindsay and I had arranged to get rid of him, which did us no good at all as far as a fair trial was concerned. Adrian Bullen's girlfriend was called to the stand and she went down the same avenue as Bullen, but she did point out that any weapons she had seen had been in the hands of Edwards.

We had to return to the cells for the time between witnesses being called, and we usually used that time to discuss the way the trial was going with our barristers.

Roger was in the next court representing himself and was no doubt tipsy from the lunchtime drinks. All the barristers, including Jimmy Beck and Michael Topolski, were eager to sit at the back of the court and watch Roger piss the judge off, and it seemed Roger was doing a far better job than the barrister he had sacked.

We knew our mail was being tampered with when it was sent through the normal channels, so we had arranged for any letters being sent from outside Gwent to be posted directly to Cardiff prison. The screws brought them to the court for us and because we were on bail they were not allowed to open them.

A letter had come in from Ronnie in which he said that he was following the trial, and wanted to bring in people from America to begin getting rid of witnesses but, even though the thought had crossed our minds, we knew that any interference could jeopardise our case, and strange as it may seem, at that point we still felt we had a chance. So a message was promptly sent back telling him that we still wanted him to hold off – for the time being.

Jim O'Neill was finally brought to court, with a police escort, but even then they claimed they'd had problems on the way down, although again I didn't know how true that was.

Under cross-examination by Harrington, we had to listen to O'Neill going on about guns and how he had been treated. In fairness to him, as with Bullen's girlfriend, he explained that Edwards was always the one seen with weapons, never Lindsay or myself. Yet strangely, Edwards wasn't in the dock with us.

I had always got on with O'Neill, apart from the time he threatened me and I'd thrown a wine glass at him. As for the slaps, they seemed to have come from Edwards at all times. It was only after reading through the statements that Lindsay and I realised what a pain in the arse Edwards was, considering he had only been employed to drive us around London. We could now understand the relief that had been felt by those we thought were our friends, when we had sent the halfwit packing in April.

When O'Neill was going on about the tabs which I had paid Hilton on a number of occasions, he seemed to forget that when there was trouble at The King's Oak – one example being when a number of people had been stabbed up – they were more than happy to have us around, giving us what we believed to be free drinks. I had brought up such matters with Hilton at the time, as there were a number of clubs and nightclubs where we were welcomed to have drinks and meetings, but we found The King's Oak ideal because it was so near to the M25.

We realised that there was treachery amongst them all and, as David Ley pointed out, through him we could have bought The King's Oak and got rid of all the rats.

When Harrington had finished with O'Neill, Mr Topolski had little to cross-examine him on, so Mr Beck took over the questioning, beginning with the monumental question: Was O'Neill going to admit the diary was his?

Mr Beck wasted no time in asking O'Neill, and told him that he had handwriting experts on standby to prove the diary was his. He was quick to admit it was, and explained how he had forgotten to take it back after I had jotted down his new number.

That was a massive blow to the prosecution, as part of their case was based on that diary alone, and I could have got 20 years as a drug supplier. Harrington knew he had been using a prosecution witness who admitted he was the owner of a book that was intended to incriminate me. Mr Beck had what he wanted. He hadn't thought O'Neill would admit he was the owner, especially in view of what was written in it.

Once O'Neill had been finished with in the witness box, my barrister, along with Harrington and the judge, had legal issues to discuss in view of O'Neill's admission. After a lot of legal talk and a bit of whispering, Jimmy Beck informed me that they were dropping the conspiracy case against me, but, to my amazement, Mr Beck told me that I was to be charged with the armed robbery itself. It just didn't make any sense. However, Mr Beck said that it would be very unlikely that I could be found guilty of armed robbery as only two people went through the door. He seemed very confident that he had my case in the bag.

If I had been on trial in London I would have shared his confidence, and although the nationals seemed to have eased off, the local papers were still taking us to the cleaners, claiming we must have idolised the Krays, as we dressed like them.

What we felt was unfair was that we had been asked by a number of national newspapers to give a story, but our defence told us that it had been stopped by the judge, yet reporting by the local press continued.

The time had come to call the police to the stand, and first up was Detective Chief Inspector Michael Johnson. It was going to be very interesting to see our barristers put them through their paces.

Harrington opened his cross-examination by asking about cartridges which had been found on the mountainside, where we had supposedly test-fired shotguns with Chamberlain.

The judge soon jumped in, asking Johnson who had picked up the cartridges and how they had been picked up. He then asked Johnson whether he had signed the exhibit form and, to the judge's surprise, Johnson replied that he had not. The judge then explained to Johnson that the exhibits could only be identical to those which had been recovered.

Harrington, rescuing him from such a blatant mistake, told the judge that Johnson wasn't responsible for signing it, and Johnson wasted no time in blaming Inspector Phillips.

For some unknown reason, a box was put in with the cartridges which had contaminated them, but even though Johnson was the senior officer overseeing the whole investigation, he had no knowledge of the box, or how it had got there.

I thought how unprofessional this made him look, as the cartridges were important exhibits.

After asking Johnson if he was the one in the local newspaper showing the shotgun the little boy had found, Harrington handed over his cross-examination to Mr Topolski. He also asked Johnson about the box contained with the empty cartridges, and pointed out that not knowing about it showed his incompetence as a Chief Inspector.

Mr Topolski: Mr Johnson, you'd agree, wouldn't you, as a matter of principle, that the finding and bagging of exhibits is something that must be done with the utmost care?

Johnson: Yes, sir.

Mr Topolski: And nothing should appear in the bag with an exhibit that wasn't found at the same time; and ideally items of a different nature, I compare a box and a cartridge, really ought to be separately bagged?

Johnson: Well, I would say that if it was sent up for forensic examination it would have been sterile. What has happened since it has come back from the forensic lab, and been on the desk here, I can't answer that.

Mr Topolski went on to ask about a press report in a local paper where Johnson had been photographed with a story about the armed robbery.

Mr Topolski: I don't ask questions about how photogenic you are, Mr Johnson! That article is written by a journalist.
Johnson: Yes sir.
Mr Topolski: And I make clear, I don't hold you in any way responsible, but I have highlighted something he's written there, Mr Johnson, and this is relating to what had allegedly occurred inside the building society. Is that right? Do you see what I've highlighted there?
Johnson: In pink sir, yes.
Mr Topolski: It says, doesn't it, in terms, that it was thought that the robber with the gun, had brandished the gun covered by a cloth?
Johnson: That was correct sir, yes.
Mr Topolski: That's right and that was your understanding, was it? Were you responsible for that information going to the press?
Johnson: Yes, sir, I think I probably was. That was the evidence that was available at the time.
Mr Topolski: Indeed. Well, thank you for that, because my next question is your source. Your source material for that would have been one or both of the two women who were in the building society at that time?
Johnson: Or from interviewing officers, because I never spoke to the two ladies that were robbed.
Mr Topolski: So the jury understands, the police go and visit and speak to your victims in these circumstances and, if they're up to it, take statements from them and it would be from those that you would have based that on. Is that right?
Johnson: Yes sir. I can't remember the exact press release, but ...
Mr Topolski: No. Is it available somewhere in the file, Mr Johnson, your press release?
Johnson: I don't know.
Mr Topolski: Thank you. That's all I ask you about that. I want to ask you again, taking the opportunity of you being here, about something else, and that someone else being Andrew Chamberlain?
Johnson: Yes sir.

Mr Topolski: Would you please tell the jury first of all, Mr Johnson, what a registered informer is?
Johnson: A registered informer is a person who wishes to give information to the police and remain anonymous. For administrative purposes he is registered.
Mr Topolski: Registered with who?
Johnson: He would be registered with the head CID man of the department who the informant is talking to.
Mr Topolski: So the jury understands, Mr Johnson, a person in such a position is not necessarily somebody who receives money for that information that he or she passes on?
Johnson: No sir.
Mr Topolski: It can happen though?
Johnson: It can happen, yes sir.
Mr Topolski: And on the subject of money, I digress slightly, did the Halifax Building Society offer any reward in this robbery, for information leading to the arrest of the perpetrators?
Johnson: I don't think they have, sir. I would have to recheck but I don't think they have.
Mr Topolski: If I may say so, you sound doubtful. You would like to check it would you?
Johnson: I don't believe that they have.
Mr Topolski: Would you be good enough to put in train a checking of that, and no doubt we can get that from other officers in the case?
Johnson: The officers in the case could answer that.

Mr Topolski asked Johnson about Chamberlain being a police informer, which he could now do, but Johnson claimed that Chamberlain had only come forward out of self-preservation because he thought his fingerprints were on the gun.

Mr Topolski: The man Chamberlain came to you, we understand, because he had seen that photograph of you with a gun?
Johnson: That is correct, sir, yes.
Mr Topolski: That he thought his fingerprints may be upon it, for example?
Johnson: That is correct.
Mr Topolski: Because he was saying, 'I've handled it'?
Johnson: That's right, sir. He didn't come to give information, he came because he was ... Self-preservation was his words, I believe, he used to me.

Mr Topolski: Those are certainly the words that appear in his most recent statement.
Johnson: His words, sir.
Mr Topolski: But he came to the police on 3 August, not as an unknown quantity. By which I mean, he had been registered as an informant beforehand, hadn't he?
Johnson: Yes sir, he had.
Mr Topolski: How long for?
Johnson: I can't answer that. I don't know.
Mr Topolski: I am sorry?
Johnson: I can't answer, because I don't genuinely know.
Mr Topolski: Was he assisted by the use of any mechanical devices in doing that, Mr Johnson? Bugs, tape recorders, anything of the kind?
Johnson: I don't think that's relevant, sir.
Judge Gibbon: Would you answer the question?
Johnson: No he wasn't sir, no.
Mr Topolski: Are you sure?
Johnson: Positive, sir. Not to my knowledge.
Mr Topolski: A tape recorder, for example?
Johnson: No sir.
Mr Topolski: You weren't interested in having the Fraynes on tape, speaking about this robbery?
Johnson: No, sir.

Mr Topolski obviously knew that the police had to disclose everything. He knew Chamberlain had bugging equipment, and needed to know that no conversation had been taped, but, of course, Lindsay and I knew there would have been no conversation concerning the robbery.

When he was convinced that no listening devices had been used, everything was hanging on Chamberlain's word, and he had already been proved a liar.

Mr Topolski and Mr Beck were going to have to dig deeper if they were to get to the root of who was involved in what, and it became clear that Johnson was meeting Chamberlain on a regular basis. On one occasion, Inspector Phillips was also present, meeting Chamberlain near his home. Johnson said that on those occasions Chamberlain was speaking to them about matters not connected with Lindsay or myself.

Mr Topolski: Mr Johnson, you are a very experienced officer of course. Been in the force how many years?
Johnson: Twenty-seven years, sir.

Mr Topolski: It's difficult, isn't it, to differentiate between a titbit of gossip and a bit of good information?
Johnson: Anything that Andrew Taylor ... Andrew Chamberlain spoke to me outside of the enquiry with regards to the armed robbery, and the two defendants and the other persons who had come into custody, I have never made an arrest on any information that he has given, because there was insufficient evidence there. What he had given me was titbits of information and gossip on what was happening.
Mr Topolski: Yes, but the report back he gave you, *vis à vis* the friends, was regarded by you in a higher category than titbits and gossip?
Johnson: Well, it was an armed robbery, sir.
Judge Gibbon: The quality of his information you are being asked about, rather than the seriousness of the offence.
Mr Topolski: I am grateful to your Honour.
Mr Topolski (*To the witness*): You regard it as better quality information he was giving to you about the Fraynes, than about other things he was talking about?'
Johnson: 'Well, it was information about an armed robbery that I and officers under my command were investigating. That was all that I wanted to glean from Chamberlain.
Mr Topolski: You'd drawn a distinction between the quality of this man's information, *vis à vis* other things which you've called titbits and gossip, and the quality of the information you say he was providing you, *vis à vis* the Fraynes. That is your evidence, isn't it?
Johnson: Yes, but what he was giving me on other matters was just titbits and gossip and tittle-tattle that was going on in and around the area.
Mr Topolski: Are you aware that much later in that year, in December, there were further visits to the mountain, after your visit on 3 August?
Johnson: Yes sir, I am aware of that.
Mr Topolski: Were you party to that? I don't think you were.
Johnson: 'No, sir.'
Mr Topolski: But you were [aware], your officers Sutton and Price, either together or separately, had made two further visits to the mountain in December. The jury will hear this evidence in due course?
Johnson: Yes, I believe they will.

Mr Topolski went further, asking about the mountainside visits and how many cartridges were supposed to have been fired off. Johnson replied that there were about 45 to 50, and that was supposed to have corroborated Chamberlain's story!

Mr Topolski then asked Johnson why he hadn't told Sutton and Price about his visit on the 3 August. Johnson answered that he was keeping Chamberlain, in his role as an informer, out of the picture.

Mr Topolski then quickly pointed out that Johnson had claimed Chamberlain had only gone to him out of self-preservation.

Mr Topolski: I put it again, Mr Johnson. Isn't it beyond doubt that you would have reported back, leaving Chamberlain's identity out for a moment, to your colleagues and your junior officers, the finding of these cartridges? You agree you would have done?

Johnson: Yes, I would have done and I did. But I can't remember when: what space of time between finding the cartridges and sending them to the laboratory. I can't remember, but I did, I did initially ... I didn't initially tell them the first day that we recovered the cartridges and then, eventually, then it was vital to the enquiry and it came into the enquiry.

Mr Topolski: Are there notes kept of briefings, Mr Johnson?

Johnson: Not in this case. I don't think there was, sir, no.

Mr Topolski: Minutes, or anything like that?

Johnson: I don't think so, no. You see, the cartridges were recovered and immediately, immediately, handed to a scenes of crime officer who dispatched them to the laboratory.

Mr Topolski: Of course they were.

Judge Gibbon: Well, Mr Johnson, what I want to know is why nobody in this case knew anything about this until a week or so ago? It was never part of the prosecution case up until a week ...

Judge Gibbon (*To counsel*): I am sorry. I have stolen your thunder.

Mr Topolski: I wouldn't describe it as thunder, more of a rolling cloud!

Judge Gibbon: What's behind it all?

Johnson: Andrew Chamberlain did not want to give evidence in this case. He came to me out of self-preservation, having been with the two defendants several days before the robbery.

Judge Gibbon: Yes, but he was a witness, you see, by the time this matter was committed to the courts. I mean, his witness statement was taken in December?

Johnson: Yes, sir, because once the enquiry then ... well, the

> information that Andrew Chamberlain gave us, the enquiry was commenced, and Andrew Chamberlain then became mentioned in the case by other persons and he was then, having been brought into the case by other persons who were being interviewed, he then had to be interviewed.

It looked like Johnson was blowing a gasket big time. I looked at Lindsay, who shrugged his shoulders, as if to say, 'What the fuck is he on about?' There was a Detective Chief Inspector dribbling in the stand. He even had the jury on the edge of their seats. I leaned over to Lindsay and said, 'Now it's warming up.' He nodded and smiled in agreement, and I got myself comfortable as I watched Johnson go down the pan.

> **Judge Gibbon:** Do I understand you to be saying that you did not want Chamberlain to know that you were responsible for him becoming a witness in this case?
> **Johnson:** Andrew Chamberlain didn't want to become a witness in this case, but the defence gradually overtook it, and what he didn't want to do was be labelled an informant. I mean he was refusing, he was refusing to make a witness statement and, for want of better words, come up front from the start.
> **Mr Topolski:** What I am going to suggest, Mr Johnson, is this: that there was a deliberate policy decision taken at the highest level to withhold the finding of these cartridges and the evidence of the finding from the defence, in order to protect the identity of Chamberlain as an informant. What do you say about that suggestion?
> **Johnson:** I totally disagree with it, sir. Andrew Chamberlain came forward, not as an informant, he came forward, again I repeat myself, in self-preservation, because he didn't want to become involved in this case, and he was afraid that he'd become involved because the defendant had allowed him to touch the gun and get his fingerprints on it and then leave it at the scene of a robbery.
> **Mr Topolski**: Now explain to the jury why it wasn't until 5 June of this year, 4 days into this trial, that you made your first ever reference in a statement to the finding of these cartridges on 3 August, if it wasn't because there had been a deliberate policy decision at the highest level not to try and conduct this case without revealing Chamberlain as an informer.
> **Johnson:** There is no way I could bring Andrew Chamberlain to this court to give evidence if he didn't want to and he did not want to make ... once he was interviewed in the middle of the

enquiry, he gave full and frank, not confessions, full and frank confirmation of what had gone on in the enquiry, but he did not want to be labelled as an informant from day one. To answer the question, when I asked him for about the fourth or fifth time, would he come up front and make a statement from start to finish, telling the whole truth on why he came to me and how it all unfolded, I don't feel I can answer that directly in front of the jury and to be fair to your clients.

Mr Topolski: It doesn't explain why you held back a piece of vital evidence from this jury until 5 June.

Johnson: To produce that would have given ...

Mr Topolski: Would have revealed Chamberlain as an informant?

Johnson: Would have given his identity, sir.

Mr Topolski: Yes, exactly. So there was a policy decision made by you to withhold this material if you could. You may have had good motives, Mr Johnson, you may have had very bad ones, I do not know, I'm not really interested. What I want you to agree to, because I think it is what you are saying, is that in order to prevent Chamberlain being exposed, you withheld this until you had no choice but to make a statement about it. That's what I'm suggesting.

Johnson: The choice wasn't mine, sir. The choice was Andrew Chamberlain's. I'd asked him from day one to make a full witness statement and he wouldn't.

Judge Gibbon: Yes, but what you are saying is, as long as he wouldn't talk about this in the form of a witness statement, you were not going to adduce this evidence.

Johnson: He might be a man of previous convictions, but I've still got to protect anybody that gives evidence, who was prepared to give information to the police on serious matters, such as armed robberies, and I wanted to keep his identity, keep his faith, and keep his identity secret.

Judge Gibbon: Keep his identity as an informant?

Mr Topolski: 'Secret', is that the word you use?

Johnson: I didn't. He didn't want his name to come forward and I didn't want his name to come forward, because he didn't want to.

Mr Topolski: But, Mr Johnson, as at midnight of 21 December, Andrew Chamberlain had made this witness statement that you were so anxious for him to make, he'd committed himself in writing, he'd signed it with the usual declaration. Shall we remind the jury what a declaration says at the top of anybody's witness statement: 'This statement, consisting of X pages, is true to the best of my knowledge and belief and I make it, knowing that if it is tendered in evidence, shall be liable to prosecution if I have wilfully stated in it anything which I know to be untrue, to be false or do not believe to be true.'

Of course, it says, 'If it is tendered' but he'd made a witness statement by Christmas, Mr Johnson. You'd got what you wanted out of him, but yet you wait until 4 days into this case to reveal a crucial bit of evidence, if it is true evidence, that these cartridges were ever found and I'm asking you why, and I am not sure there is very much between us. There was a policy decision taken, wasn't there?

Johnson: There was not a policy decision taken. He did not want ...

Judge Gibbon: Yes, but it was your decision. Informants don't decide what evidence the Crown Prosecution Service are going to bring forward in a case. It was your decision to protect your source of information.

Johnson: That is correct, yes, your Honour, and to have revealed the going to the mountain and recovering the cartridges, there is nothing better that I would have liked to have put that in initially on day one, but to be fair to him, I have had to go along with his wishes that he didn't wish to be mentioned.

Mr Topolski: So you'd rather be fair to a witness than to the defendants. Is that it, Mr Johnson?

Johnson: I don't see how I'm being unfair to the defendants.

Mr Topolski: Don't you?

Johnson: By virtue of what you've declared now, there's putting the guns with the two defendants several days before the robbery. Now, if ... I would have liked that on the initial interviews, but I couldn't because Chamberlain wouldn't make the statement. Now, I couldn't then declare the original 12 cartridges, because the obvious question is, where did they come from? They come from a source who wanted to remain anonymous, for whatever reason.

Mr Topolski: You would have been content, I don't use the word happy, would you, to have had this entire case conducted without revealing the finding of these cartridges?

Johnson: I m not saying that, sir, no.

Mr Topolski: Aren't you?

Johnson: No. What I would have liked was for this case to have

been conducted without the identity of ... as long as Mr Chamberlain was happy not to have his identity revealed, I would have been happy, or I would have had to let the case develop along those lines.
Mr Topolski: That's all I ask.

Mr Topolski had put Johnson through his paces, and giving credit to Judge Gibbon, even he had worked out that things weren't right.

Lindsay and I knew that what Chamberlain was saying about test-firing guns on the mountainside was nonsense, and Johnson had claimed throughout cross-examination that Chamberlain had told him about guns and arranging to do an armed robbery before it had happened.

They had pulled in quite a number of people before arresting us in September, but they just weren't making any sense. They didn't know their arse from their elbow.

Johnson was to be cross-examined by Mr Beck, but I doubted if he knew Mr Beck was an ex-copper and would know police procedure. It was going to be interesting to see if Jimmy Beck could get Johnson to blow a gasket or even crumble. What was certain was that he was lying through his teeth.

Mr Beck: Officer, I ask you questions on behalf of Leighton Frayne. If I just pick up the point you've been asked about, after he made his statement in December, Andrew Chamberlain was saying, 'I went out shooting with the Fraynes; I've identified where the cartridges were recovered from.' That's in his witness statement, isn't it?
Johnson: That is, yes, sir.
Mr Beck: So from that moment on, his identity is revealed and the fact that he's giving evidence of that nature?
Johnson: That is correct, sir, yes.
Mr Beck: And that's available to the defendants, because it is part of their committal bundle, part of the bundle of statements available to them as of 7 January?
Johnson: That is correct, sir, yes.
Mr Beck: What additional protection was there, then, in not revealing the 12 other cartridges?
Johnson: For whatever reason, he didn't want his identity brought forward as being the original person coming to the police and saying, 'This is what happened.'
Mr Beck: So it's his original co-operation with the police that was troubling you, is that right?

Johnson: For whatever reason, yes, sir.

Mr Beck: When the cartridges were taken to be examined they were accompanied by a form, weren't they?

Johnson: Yes, sir.

Mr Beck: Are you aware that it was DC Sutton who took that form and the cartridges for forensic examination?

Johnson: I am not aware, sir, no. He may well have.

Mr Beck: Would you take it as a matter of fact from me?

Johnson: Yes.

Mr Beck: That it was DC Sutton and he signed that form as the officer dealing with the transmission, does that make sense?

Johnson: Yes, sir, it makes sense, yes.

Mr Beck: There's a specific paragraph, 15 on the form. Method of delivery of articles to the laboratory. And that bears his signature?

Johnson: Yes, sir.

Mr Beck: So certainly on 8 August, DC Sutton would have been aware that cartridges had been found and presumably what that lab form says about their finding?

Johnson: That's correct, sir. I've never said that I never talked ....

Judge Gibbon: Well, you've answered the question.

Mr Beck: When Andrew Chamberlain went to the police station on 17 December, what instructions did you give the officers who were going to deal with him?

Johnson: To interview him as the other people were interviewed as a potential ... be involved in the robbery.

Judge Gibbon: As someone under suspicion?

Johnson: As someone under suspicion, interview him under PACE.

Judge Gibbon: And the distinction, you think, about someone who gives information to the police when he's been arrested and been questioned, and someone who goes to the police, not under suspicion which was worrying Chamberlain?

Johnson: I am sorry, your Honour ...

Judge Gibbon: Well, there are two ways a person can give information to the police: he can go and enter a police station and want to see Detective Chief Inspector Johnson and you see him and he gives you information, he's not suspected of any crime, he's there helping you?

Johnson: That's correct.

Judge Gibbon: There's another way: you arrest a man on suspicion of robbery, as you did in this case, and he is then interviewed and says things about other people. He's informing on them, but he's only informing on them once he is under suspicion himself and he may be thought to be doing it to protect himself?

Johnson: That is correct, your Honour, yes.

Mr Beck: Put shortly, officer, what I suggest is that on 17 December the interview was a smokescreen?

Johnson: No, sir, he was ... his name, by this time the enquiry was continuing and his name had come forward as being there when this was said, being there when that was said and he had to be arrested and dealt with as per the law. If he was shown, and there was evidence to show, that he was in any way involved in this robbery, he would have been sat in the dock now. It was not a smokescreen, no, sir.

Lindsay and I looked at each other. What the fuck was he on about? The whole court was hanging on his every word and I wondered if they could understand any better than us what was going on.

Mr Beck pointed out to Johnson that when Chamberlain was interviewed, he would have been told that they, the police, had evidence to prove he was involved in the robbery. What Mr Beck was asking Johnson was, what evidence did they have against Chamberlain if the interview wasn't a smokescreen? Harrington was soon to the rescue in the hope of bailing the babbling idiot out of his predicament. Harrington suggested that Mr Beck should ask the officer who had conducted the interview with Chamberlain, and said that no doubt that particular officer would have the answer when it was his turn on the stand.

Mr Beck said that Johnson must have briefed Sutton and Price beforehand, revealing the cartridges on the mountainside as a scenario in order to conceal the fact that he'd given information earlier.

I was beginning to have a different view. Chamberlain must have been brought in around December and backdated the cartridge find to October. But the cartridges on the mountain had nothing to do with us.

When Johnson was asked whether they had fingerprinted the cartridges, he replied that they hadn't.

Mr Beck also said that Chamberlain was worried about his fingerprints being on the shotgun, and yet the shotgun revealed no fingerprints at all.

When asked about sending Chamberlain in taped-up or carrying a bug, Johnson was quick to point out that we knew how to find bugs, which, of course, was true, but not the rubbish Chamberlain used – we had access to top-of-the-range gear.

However, as far as Lindsay and I were concerned, there was nothing to tape or bug and Johnson knew that. If we had done the robbery and been quite open in telling Chamberlain, as he claimed, I am sure the conversations would have been recorded, but it didn't happen, and we had to sit though listening to what Chamberlain had to say, along with the rest of his bullshit.

Mr Beck had finished with Johnson, and Harrington tried to repair the damage that Johnson had done, but what was said was said.

Next up was Inspector Phillips, and being a friend of Paul Edwards – they had even gone to the same school – there was no doubt he was as thick as Edwards! He had been cross-examined by Harrington and was soon handed over to Mr Topolski, and just a little way into his questioning Phillips was in trouble!

Mr Topolski: Chamberlain was an informer. That's right, isn't it?
Phillips: Was or had been, sir?
Mr Topolski: Had been.
Phillips: My understanding is that he may have been, yes.
Mr Topolski: When were you first asked, and by whom, to make a statement concerning the finding of the cartridges?
Phillips: When was I first asked? I made a statement on, I think it is dated on my statement, sir.
Mr Topolski: The 5th of June, four days after this trial started?
Phillips: Yes.
Mr Topolski: When were you asked to make that statement?
Phillips: Where?
Mr Topolski: When?
Phillips: That day, sir.
Mr Topolski: By whom?
Phillips: It came, as I thought, with instructions from the court.
Judge Gibbon: From the?
Phillips: It came, as I believed, on instructions from the court that I had to make a statement regarding my finding of the cartridges.
Judge Gibbon: It certainly wasn't instructions off the court. Do you mean the Crown Prosecution Service?
Phillips: From the Prosecution Service, yes. That's quite right, your Honour, yes.
Mr Topolski: It came out of this building?
Phillips: That's right, yes.

Further into Mr Topolski's cross-examination of Phillips:

Mr Topolski: This was an ongoing investigation, which, certainly by 25 September, had led to the arrest of and, very shortly thereafter, the charging of two men?

Phillips: Yes, sir.

Mr Topolski: The Fraynes?

Phillips: Yes, sir.

Mr Topolski: And others?

Phillips: Yes.

Mr Topolski: A man called Phillip Martin, for example?

Phillips: Yes.

Mr Topolski: Was also charged with robbery. Why no statement until four days into this trial?

Phillips: The officer in charge of the enquiry, Mr Johnson, hadn't required me to make a statement.

Mr Topolski: Or were you party to discussions that suggested to you a policy decision had been made not to make any mention of the finding of these cartridges ... Please listen carefully ... in order to protect the identity of Chamberlain as an informant?

Phillips: It was discussed as to whether or not the finding on behalf of the police by us involving Mr Chamberlain would be made public at that stage. I was asked, regarding my statement, I said if they want a statement they can have one, which is quite obvious. I've got to make a statement as to the finding of them. As far as any other discussions are concerned, sir, no it was Mr Johnson's decision as to when, when and if I made a statement.

One of the screws leaned over to me and said, 'He is thicker than the last one, and he was thick.' I smiled back.

Phillips seemed to blame everyone but himself, and if he couldn't answer a question he would just babble on about any old bollocks. If Lindsay and I hadn't been sitting in the dock, I would have thought it was a comedy show.

Mr Topolski: So you were a party to discussions that touched upon, at the very least, whether statements would be made disclosing the findings of these items, and then discussions centred upon Chamberlain as the informant. Is that right?

Phillips: It was quite some time later, sir. I wasn't directly involved in the case all the way through. I came in and did little bits, if you like, if that's the best way to explain it to the jury, and did certain enquiries as and when I was required under the direction of Mr Johnson.

Mr Topolski: In order that the men or women charged with a crime can see the case against them?
Phillips: That is quite right.
Mr Topolski: The principle is, Mr Phillips, the vital principle, for a just and fair trial isn't it, is that all evidence, admissible and relevant evidence in the hands of the police, should be disclosed to the defence?
Phillips: That's right, yes, sir.
Mr Topolski: So a man charged can see what he's facing?
Phillips: That's right, yes, sir.
Mr Topolski: There should be no trial by ambush, should there, Mr Phillips?
Phillips: Quite right, that's right.
Mr Topolski: Material lurking in the shadows to be thrown in at the last minute to try and hurt a man's fair trial. That is no part of proper policing is it?
Phillips: Are you inferring that this is something that's thrown in at the last minute?
Mr Topolski: I haven't come to any inferences yet. Just agree with the principle, if you feel able to. Do you agree with the principle?
Phillips: The principle is that all evidence will be, at some stage, be admitted to the courts, yes, sir.
Mr Topolski: You would be very uneasy, wouldn't you, if anyone said to you, 'Mr Phillips, hold back making a statement about that, we don't want to disclose something.' That would cause you unease, wouldn't it?
Phillips: I didn't think of it either way, sir. Any decision as to when I made my statement was Mr Johnson's.
Mr Topolski: So you were content to, of course, he's your superior officer, bow to any judgement he may have made about that?
Phillips: Well, whatever judgement he may have made, sir, I accepted finding of cartridges. As I said, I was not involved directly with it right from 3 August, right through to the present time. I did certain actions and I was involved in the enquiry and in conducting certain enquiries. The man in overall charge was Mr Johnson, and it wasn't until that stage that I was asked to make a statement on the day in court that I made my statement.
Mr Topolski: So if there was, is this the effect of what you're saying, if there was what I am describing as a policy decision made to suppress this information about the finding of the cartridges, you were no party to that policy decision?

Phillips: Not to suppress. At some stage I'd have to make a statement. How could it be suppressed?
Mr Topolski: Can you help, and it may be that you can't, did money change hands between Chamberlain and the police during the course of Chamberlain's dealing with the police?
Phillips: Money was given to Mr Chamberlain for expenses, yes, sir.
Mr Topolski: Do you know how much?
Phillips: I think there was £10 given on one occasion. On another occasion I gave him £100.
Mr Topolski: There's a fund available for that. It doesn't come out of your pocket?
Phillips: No, it didn't come out of my pocket, no, sir.
Mr Topolski: There's a fund available for that?
Phillips: That's right, yes.
Mr Topolski: And it's all, of course, recorded?
Phillips: Yes, sir.
Mr Topolski: And the purpose of it?
Phillips: Yes.
Mr Topolski: Described as expenses, I think. Is that right?
Phillips: That is right.
Mr Topolski: He requested other sums of money, but didn't get them?'
Phillips: 'Not that I'm aware, no, sir.
Mr Topolski: Can you help with this? Are you aware of whether any reward was offered by the Halifax Building Society, or the company which was robbed?
Phillips: I don't think there was one, sir, because I think their policy was that they didn't want to issue rewards because it can sometimes invoke crime just to get the reward, if you know what I mean.

Mr Topolski moved the questioning back to the cartridges on the mountainside and whether it was only him, Johnson and Chamberlain that knew. Phillips replied, 'Yes.'

When asked why he didn't take photographs, Phillips explained that he just happened to be in the office when Johnson received the phone call, so Phillips just sort of tagged along. Mr Topolski then asked why photographs hadn't been taken of the find, but Phillips could only shift the blame onto Johnson, at which point Mr Topolski asked him if he was a puppet, and reminded Phillips that he was a Detective Inspector and could have suggested that Johnson photograph the site. Phillips said that he would not dare suggest such a matter to Johnson, just as Johnson wouldn't suggest it to him.

Mr Topolski ended his questioning and took his seat, leaving Mr Beck to cross-examine Phillips.

Mr Beck picked up where Mr Topolski had left off, asking why photographs hadn't been taken and stating that usually a systematic search would have taken place, before informing SOCO (Scenes Of Crimes Officers).

Mr Beck went on to educate Phillips on how a real detective should have dealt with such a find. But it was becoming much clearer that their find was a complete load of bollocks.

Mr Beck: Are you aware that when a pump-action shotgun is used, after each cartridge has been fired off and the pump is activated, a cartridge is ejected?
Phillips: That's quite right. One is ejected and the other one is put back automatically, back into the breach.
Mr Beck: And that, therefore, given the type of gun, it's possible to determine from where cartridges are found where the weapon was fired?
Phillips: That's news to me, sir. I have never known that happen.
Mr Beck: You are not aware that a scientist actually can estimate how far the cartridge would be ejected?
Phillips: I should imagine, I'm not a scientist, but I should imagine, on the tension of the springs and the ejection mechanism, that he could say that the cartridge would be ejected a number of feet from a gun, but if a gun is being fired indiscriminately in a copse, with a person moving all around the area, it would be difficult to pinpoint any particular position when a gun was fired. That is my understanding and it is my own, sort of, thoughts on the matter.
Mr Beck: But, of course, even more difficult, I think you'll accept this, if we can't actually locate where the cartridges were found?
Phillips: I am sorry, sir?
Mr Beck: If we don't know exactly where the cartridges were found, then we can't begin to estimate where the gun was fired?
Phillips: The cartridges were found in amongst the undergrowth in that small copse. There was a large amount of damage done to trees and various other foliage, which indicated to me, although I'm not an expert, that there was a lot of indiscriminate firing had taken place of a shotgun; large numbers of shots had been fired.

Mr Beck: Oh. Did you ever think to photograph the damage to the trees?
Phillips: No, sir. As I say, Mr Johnson was the officer in charge, the senior officer in charge of the case, and I am not trying to abdicate my own field of responsibility in my own sub-division.
Mr Beck: I think we have heard that the cartridges went to the Scenes of Crime Officer?
Phillips: Yes, they did, sir.
Mr Beck: Was it your instructions to him that they should be dealt with speedily. Is that something you recall?
Phillips: No, sir, all I did to scenes of crime, as I said yesterday, is when I collected them. I had nothing to put them in. I had an old envelope in my pocket. I haven't got them in these pockets because it's my Crown Court Suit as we call it. My day-to-day suits that I wear in work, there is numerous bits of paper in various pockets. I took out an old envelope from there, and as the cartridges were collected, I placed them into the envelope, gave the envelope and the cartridges to SOCO, so that he could then ensure that they were protected for, ready for future examination.

Mr Topolski asked why the cartridges had not been submitted until five days after the find, but, of course, Phillips didn't know and could only answer in the babbling language that we were all getting used to.

Mr Topolski had Phillips boxed in a corner regarding his meeting with Edwards.

Mr Topolski: You may not be aware of this, Mr Phillips, but Mr Johnson has told this jury in no uncertain terms, in fact, in the clearest possible terms, that Edwards had no dealings with police other than a passing conversation with you in the street before 25 October. Now, that is plainly wrong, is it not?
Phillips: I have no idea, sir. I don't know what he is saying.
Judge Gibbon: It is plainly wrong, is it not, if he said it?
Phillips: Oh, yes, if he said it. But I can't understand why he would have said it because ...
Mr Topolski: You can't understand why he said it. He has said it more than once. You can't understand why because it is simply untrue, isn't it?
Phillips: I don't know.
Mr Topolski: Well, it is untrue. You have been telling us you had meetings with him in August?
Phillips: Yes, I saw him on 3 August.

I had instructed our defence to ask Phillips about visiting London with Edwards in the April, three months before the robbery took place.

To our amazement, Phillips admitted that it was true and gave a date – 15 April. He tried to rub salt in the wounds by claiming Edwards had gone to him frightened after being sent packing and told him that we were trying to acquire weapons.

Phillips, believing Edwards' bullshit, passed the information directly to the Metropolitan Police, resulting in a few people being turned over in the search for weapons. But, of course, they had no results, so the Metropolitan Police sent the pair of idiots packing. However, the people who had been turned over weren't happy, which left bad feeling between them and Lindsay and me. That was how Edwards took his revenge for being sent packing.

What I considered a breakthrough was Phillips admitting being in London in the April and, if what Edwards was saying about Lindsay and me having access to sawn-off shotguns was true, why were we never pulled, or at least put under surveillance?

Phillips showed that he had never had any notes taken, yet while I was being interviewed in the September, all the questions were based on what Edwards had been saying, or as Mr Topolski had put it, 'Quite a lot of information without any notes to go off.'

It looked very much as though Edwards and Chamberlain were the senior officers on our case!

Mr Topolski had finished with Phillips, leaving Mr Beck to finish off the cross-examination, and we knew he wasn't going to let anything go now he knew that Phillips had been to London with Edwards before the robbery had taken place.

As with Mr Topolski, Mr Beck was also confused on the point Edwards made when he claimed I had hit him with a Mossburg shotgun, and yet nothing had been done about it; I could have been arrested as early as April.

We knew Edwards had been running around London with Phillips in April, but didn't take any notice because we knew we were doing no wrong.

Mr Beck had had enough of Phillips.

Harrington furthered his questions, hoping, yet again, to salvage the damage done by the idiot Phillips. Lindsay and I weren't complaining, though. They were having a taste of what they had put us through.

Next up were Price and Sutton, and I had no doubt that they would all get their heads together. But Lindsay and I, as well as our barristers, felt there was still a chance they would make the same mistakes as Johnson and Phillips.

16

CUTTING EACH OTHER'S STRINGS

Price's evidence should prove to be very interesting as far as Chamberlain was concerned, mainly because during my interviews both he and Sutton claimed they didn't know who Chamberlain was on the photograph. Yet we had heard from Johnson and Phillips that they had been to the mountainside with Chamberlain, supposedly recovering cartridges, in the August before our arrest in September.

Of course, Sutton would have known about the find because he was the officer who signed the paperwork to go off to forensics.

Chamberlain had nothing to inform on us. We were actually in a position to inform on him as we knew he was bang at crooking here, there and everywhere, but Lindsay and I weren't grasses, a fact that Chamberlain knew. It was simply a case of Mr Topolski and Mr Beck hitting the right buttons.

Harrington finished his brief questioning with Price, and Mr Topolski took the floor to cross-examine him. Mr Topolski reminded Price about Chamberlain's two statements, one taken on 17 December and the second one after the mountainside visit on 21 December.

Mr Topolski: You go up the mountain at 12.15. Is that right?
Price: That's right, sir.
Mr Topolski: So you do that first, as it were, and then come back to sit down and take the witness statement from him?
Price: Yes, sir.

Mr Topolski: Had he come to the police station himself that morning, do you recall now?
Price: I can't honestly remember, sir, no.
Mr Topolski: Or had you met him somewhere? He wasn't in custody was he?
Price: No, sir, that's right.
Mr Topolski: Because he'd been in on 17 December and had an interview?
Price: That's right, sir.
Mr Topolski: A taped interview?
Price: That's right.
Mr Topolski: No doubt you were quite busy on this, and perhaps other matters, between the 17th and the 21st when you saw Chamberlain again. Would that be right?
Price: Yes, sir, I suppose so.
Mr Topolski: It wasn't necessary for you to listen to the tapes of these interviews, however, before sitting down and taking the witness statement from him?
Price: Well, we were only talking about a matter of days. I could remember ....
Mr Topolski: You could remember?
Price: From the interviews, what I believed to be relevant.
Mr Topolski: There is, and I think the jury have clearly in their minds, the difference between an interview under caution with a suspect and a witness statement. There is all the difference in the world between those two things?
Price: Quite correct, sir.
Mr Topolski: The interview, under caution, of course, the evidence that can be gained from that interview, that may lead to someone ultimately being charged with crime; the witness statement, quite the reverse, forms the basis of the witness's evidence for the prosecution, perhaps, in a trial of other people?
Price: Quite correct.
Mr Topolski: You wouldn't take a witness statement from someone who was still a suspect would you, Mr Price?
Price: It's not usual, no.
Mr Topolski: It's not usual. Have you ever done it in your entire career?
Price: Not that I can recollect, sir, no.
Mr Topolski: And how long is that career?
Price: Fourteen years, sir.
Mr Topolski: There had been a change of view about

Chamberlain, had there, in the four days between the 17th and the 21st December, therefore?

Price: Yes, sir.

Mr Topolski: Chamberlain ceased to be a suspect and was someone you wanted to call if he could help the prosecution case – I use help in a neutral sense, Mr Price – as a witness?

Price: Well, in the interim period we had sought advice on the matter via CPS (Crown Prosecution Service) and we had been instructed to deal with him as a witness. It was not a decision that we took alone.

Mr Topolski: I see. So it was in that four-day period between … So the jury have got the dates clearly in mind, between concluding the interviews with Chamberlain – and we know from the documents before us that that exercise was concluded at just after lunchtime in the afternoon on 17 of December – and by the time you sit down with him on the afternoon of 21 December, advice had been sought, advice had been taken, and Chamberlain's entire position changed?

Price: Yes, sir.

Mr Topolski: You would, of course, be no party to the arrest and interview of someone unless it was a genuine exercise, would you?

Price: Certainly not, sir.

Mr Topolski: You cannot just arrest someone for form sake to make it look good, or bad, can you?

Price: No, sir.

Mr Topolski: You can't play fast and loose with people's liberty in that way?

Price: Quite correct, we leave ourselves open to being sued for wrongful arrest.

Mr Topolski: 'Indeed, absolutely. What evidence did you have to justify the arrest of Andrew Chamberlain on the morning of 17 December, and I use the word evidence advisedly?

Price: We were in possession of certain information concerning activities that had occurred whilst he was having confidential dealings with DCI Johnson.

Mr Topolski: The fact that someone merely associates, that is to say is seen with and hangs about with, other people who may be committing crime doesn't necessarily make that person a criminal, does it?

Price: Not necessarily.

Mr Topolski: Mere association, like someone is in a car with someone else, doesn't necessarily mean that that person is in anyway associated with the driver's criminal business if the driver was going off to commit a crime?

Price: Not necessarily.

Mr Topolski: It gives rise to suspicion of that, but we've already drawn a distinction this morning, Mr Price, between information and evidence, and we can draw a further distinction – can't we? – between suspicion, information and evidence. They're different things.

Judge Gibbon: But you don't need evidence to arrest: reasonable grounds for ...

Mr Topolski: Reasonable suspicion. That's why I was adding the word suspicion into the equation, Mr Price?

Price: And that can differ from officer to officer on how he interprets the facts that are placed before him.

Mr Topolski: Indeed, absolutely. Let's have the classic law school example: the young man standing with a brick in his hand outside the jeweller's window, holding it back over his head. An odd policeman coming along may have a reasonable suspicion he is about to cause an act of criminal damage, at the very least, right?

Price: That's right.

Mr Topolski: A young man standing looking at the jeweller's shop with a brick at his foot, there may be some rather more interesting debate as to whether an officer arresting him in those circumstances genuinely had a reasonable suspicion that a crime was about to be committed, that's right?

Price: 'That again would differ from officer to officer.'

Mr Topolski: Indeed, that's why the law uses the word 'reasonable'.

Price: That's right.

Mr Topolski: And Chamberlain was suspicious, because Chamberlain had been hanging about in London with the Fraynes. That was your information?

Price: Correct.

Mr Topolski: But there was an extra, rather more important, dimension to all this, wasn't there, and that was to say his dealings with Detective Chief Inspector Johnson?

Price: Yes, sir.

Mr Topolski: Let's just look at your state of mind, your state of knowledge if we can, please, for a moment or two. When were you first made aware of Chamberlain and Mr Johnson having dealings? I will help you to this extent: they meet for the first time on 3 August.

Price: I can't be exact. As I've said from the outset I was on leave during August, but it would have been some time shortly after I returned to duty.

Mr Topolski: And as an officer actively engaged in this enquiry by then, you were informed, were you, that Johnson and Chamberlain had dealings?

Price: Had dealings, yes, sir.

Mr Topolski: Were you made aware of the nature of those dealings?

Price: I cannot recall, sir.

Mr Topolski: Well, was it not made clear to you that, as best you could, this investigation was to be conducted on the basis that the fact Chamberlain was an informant should not be revealed? Wasn't that made clear?

Price: I can't honestly remember.

Mr Topolski: You can't remember?

Price: I can't remember the context of the conversation, or what information exactly that was provided.

I couldn't really see where Mr Topolski was going with his questions. Price was proving a tough nut to crack, but I had some respect for him in a sense, for not being prepared to drop his colleagues in the shit, unlike Johnson and Phillips who blamed everyone but themselves. Mr Topolski pushed Price on why he had to go back to the mountainside in December when he knew that Johnson and Phillips had been up there in the August recovering cartridges under Chamberlain's guidance. Price could only answer that he wanted more, which I found very strange with it being five months after the supposed first find. I wondered whether Mr Beck could make any headway with him.

Mr Beck: A vicious robbery when a sawn-off shotgun was used?

Price: Yes, sir.

Mr Beck: When Andrew Chamberlain walked through the door and had been arrested, did you put your cards on the table with him and say, 'Forget all the meetings you've had. You are now a suspect. I want the truth.'?

Price: In respect of what, sir? I don't understand what you are saying.

Mr Beck: You've got a suspect for a vicious crime, correct?

Price: Yes, sir.

Mr Beck: Why didn't you simply say, 'Forget all about the confidence nonsense. I'm investigating a vicious crime. You are a suspect. Cards on the table.'?

Price: I was honouring a decision that had been made previously to protect Mr Chamberlain's identity at that time.

Mr Beck: Right. Now, you took a statement from Mr Chamberlain on 4 June, days into this trial, didn't you, this year?

Price: Yes, sir.

Mr Beck: And in that statement Mr Chamberlain said that he was acting from self-preservation?

Price: Quite correct, sir, yes.

Mr Beck: He was simply worrying about his fingerprints being on the gun and him being tied into the shooting?

Price: Yes, sir.

Mr Beck: And that had been dealt with, as it were, on the 3 August, because he'd met with you, Detective Chief Inspector, and disclosed his position, hadn't he?

Price: Yes, sir.

Mr Beck was having the same thoughts as I'd had when we received our committal papers in the December, some three months after our arrest. Chamberlain claimed in his statement, which was dated 21 December, that Lindsay told him in August that he did the robbery with a long lost friend.

Yet under the Judith Ward ruling, all paperwork had to be put forward to the defence. Chamberlain's statement on December 17 mentions Cook's name as the second robber, but, of course, the 17 December statement wasn't in our committal paperwork.

Mr Beck: So is it your evidence, officer, that those two things, the fact that he's not arrested by you until 17 December, four days after he's arrested for the burglary, that's pure coincidence?

Price: I don't see what your point is there, sir.

Judge Gibbon: Don't worry about the point. Put it again, Mr Beck.

Mr Beck: Your arrest of Mr Chamberlain on 17 December was totally independent of anything else that was happening to him in his life, just happened to be convenient to you, is that the situation?

Price: Yes, sir.

Mr Beck: And it's mere chance that he's been arrested and interviewed about a burglary four days before?

Price: That's right, sir, yes.
Mr Beck: I suggest to you that that is a nonsense, officer.
Price: No, that's as it happened. Although I cannot comment on his earlier arrest because I had no involvement in it.
Mr Beck: Did nobody mention this to you? Did Mr Johnson not tell you about the earlier arrest?
Price: I can't honestly remember when I was made aware of the fact that he had been arrested, to be honest with you.
Mr Beck: So it played no part in your calculations?
Price: That's right.

Mr Beck concluded his cross-examination and Price was then questioned by Harrington.

Mr Harrington: When you take a statement from a potential witness, do you have to have regard to the potential admissibility of the evidence in that statement?
Price: Yes, sir.
Mr Harrington: You have been asked about the statement that you took from Andrew Chamberlain and why it doesn't include references to something that Lindsay Frayne is meant to have said about another person.
Price: That's right.
Mr Harrington: If you had included anything in that statement said by Lindsay Frayne about himself, alleged to have been said by Lindsay Frayne about himself, obviously that could be evidence against Lindsay Frayne?
Price: That's right.
Mr Harrington: If you included in that statement something said to Andrew Chamberlain by Lindsay Frayne about another named person, would that have any evidential value against the other person?
Judge Gibbon: Well now, Mr Harrington, this was a statement being obtained with a view to the prosecution of the Fraynes.
Mr Harrington: Yes, that's precisely the point.
Judge Gibbon: Yes. I cannot think your point is a good one, with great respect.
Mr Harrington: Well, it's been referred to by my learned friend as a crucial piece of evidence. It would have been manifestly inadmissible, your Honour, in the submission of the prosecution against Cook.
Judge Gibbon: Yes, but it wasn't a statement being taken against

Cook, it was a statement being taken with a view to the prosecution of the Fraynes.
Mr Harrington: Yes, precisely my point, your Honour.
Judge Gibbon: In which case, which one of the Fraynes had said is fully admissible against him, even though it names a third party, and your point is a bad one.
Mr Harrington: Well, your Honour, it is not my position to disagree with your Honour about that.

After further legal talk, Mr Topolski asked a number of questions of no real significance and Price left the witness box.

Next to be called was Sutton and I thought that his evidence was going to be very interesting indeed. He was arrogant and thought himself the business, but he could be easily be drawn into an argument. If our defence gave him enough rope it was certain he would hang himself.

Johnson and Phillips had made too many mistakes. Price had dropped a few bollocks but not as badly as his superiors.

Harrington cross-examined Sutton first but Sutton seemed more interested in singing his own praises and saying how phenomenal the case had been. He seemed very proud of the fact that he was involved in such a big enquiry, which extended to London. He went on to say that he didn't know who Chamberlain was in the photograph when he interviewed us in September. Harrington swiftly handed him over to Mr Topolski.

Mr Topolski: In the statement, for his Honour's purpose it is on our page 287, and it is the second paragraph on that page, just for His Honour's reference. You can look at it if you want to, Mr Sutton, but perhaps in the interest of saving time, you'll take it from me this is what you say: 'At 9.30am, Thursday 8 August, I conveyed a Mossburg sawn-off pump-action shotgun to Her Majesty's Forensic Science Laboratory in Huntingdon. Upon my arrival there, I handed the shotgun over for examination, police reference number CC2. This shotgun I had earlier that morning removed from the lock-up store of the police station.'

You then go on: 'At 6.20am on 25 September I went to an address.' So you move on in your statement to deal with other matters, all right?
Sutton: Correct.
Mr Topolski: That statement, and that paragraph in that statement, is not actually, is it, an accurate reflection of all you

did that day in going to Huntingdon, Mr Sutton?
Sutton: No, it is not.
Mr Topolski: It omits, doesn't it, any reference to the cartridges?
Sutton: Yes, it does.
Mr Topolski: Why?
Sutton: I was instructed to do so.
Mr Topolski: By whom?
Sutton: Mr Johnson.
Mr Topolski: Right. Let's just look at that. When did you first know that Johnson and Phillips had gone up the mountainside on 3 August?
Sutton: I think you'll find it's 7 August, when I was instructed to take the cartridges and the gun to Huntingdon.
Mr Topolski: The effect of the conversation, we don't need the precise words, it is probably obvious: 'I want you to take the gun and the cartridges to the lab'?
Sutton: Yes, words to that effect, yes.
Mr Topolski: 'But what I don't want you to do is ever mention, if you can avoid it, taking the cartridges.' Is that the position?
Sutton: Not at that time, no.
Mr Topolski: Not at that time? When did the order come from Johnson not to make any mention; when you were sitting down to write your statement?
Sutton: No. When I came back from the forensic science laboratory and told Mr Johnson that we had a positive result verbally.
Mr Topolski: Yes?
Sutton: A couple of days later, Mr Johnson informed me of the information that he'd received.
Mr Topolski: And in telling you that, he also instructed you to make no mention of the cartridges, if it could be avoided. Is that what you are saying?
Sutton: Mr Topolski, Mr Johnson told me that the source of the information was a boy by the name of Andrew Chamberlain.
Mr Topolski: Very well. So, let's be quite clear and let's put it in simple English. Your superior officer told you to make no mention of the cartridges in order to protect the identity of the man Chamberlain, as someone who had been giving information. Is that a summary and an accurate summary of the position, Mr Sutton?
Sutton: Yes, he told me I was not to reveal the identity of his source.

Mr Topolski: And one of the ways you might have revealed the identity of his source was by making written reference to the taking of the 12 cartridges?

Sutton: Obviously.

Mr Topolski: Because a defence lawyer looking at that would say to himself, 'Hang on a moment. Where have these 12 cartridges come from?'

Sutton: I must stop you there, Mr Topolski, because obviously we sought advice from the Crown Prosecution Service.

Mr Topolski: Mr Sutton, I don't mind if you received advice from the Pope. I want to know what you were doing and what you were thinking. Do you understand?

Sutton: Yes.

Mr Topolski: You allowed yourself to be persuaded by a superior officer to deliberately omit reference to these cartridges, didn't you, for what I am sure you regard as very good reasons: the protection of the identity of an informant, is that right?

Sutton: It's not persuaded; it was instructed.

Mr Topolski: Right, you didn't need any persuading. He just told you?

Sutton: Exactly. He is a Detective Chief Inspector.

Mr Topolski: Very well. It is right, isn't it, that only after discussion between the lawyers and the learned judge in this trial, did that situation change. That's right, isn't it? Do you want me to develop that?

Sutton: If you would, please.

Mr Topolski: Normally, as learned judges have been good enough to tell the jury, normally if there is an informant in the case, that fact is normally not disclosed to a jury, or to the public for obvious reasons. This case has been abnormal. The learned judge has ruled, in the interest of justice, that information be revealed. Do you follow?

Judge Gibbon: The Crown conceded the point.

Mr Topolski: I was going to go on.

Mr Topolski (*To the witness*): Because Mr Harrington, counsel for the Crown, conceded, quite rightly and properly if I may say so, that it was right, in the interests of justice, that should be done and you now understand the position, Mr Sutton, if you didn't before?

Sutton: Yes.

Mr Harrington: Your Honour, this isn't really a true reflection

> of the history of this matter and I don't want to ... No, my learned friend is putting something which may suggest that the concession that there was an informer in this case came out only during the course of the trial. He knows that not to be the case.

Indeed. What Harrington explained was quite correct, as he would concede fuck all if it helped our defence. He was taking about the Judith Ward ruling which had been passed a few days into the trial. The ruling stated: Disclosure of Evidence – Duty of Prosecution to Disclose Scientific Evidence to Defence – Duty to Disclose Evidence Which Does Not Support Prosecution Case But May Support Defence Case.

However, I felt that Mr Topolski kept pushing the prosecution on finding the cartridges in the August, and somehow felt that this was what the prosecution wanted to happen!

Sutton claimed he didn't know that Phillips had any involvement with Chamberlain and that this was the first time he'd heard about Phillips paying Chamberlain expenses for his services. Of course, if what Sutton was saying was true, it gave a clear indication, again, that they didn't know their arse from their elbow.

Mr Topolski handed cross-examination to Mr Beck.

Sutton was being caught out from all angles and as much as he tried to dig himself out of the hole he was in, he just managed to dig himself deeper, and Mr Beck was like a terrier hanging onto a rat. Chamberlain hadn't mentioned that Lindsay had told him he did the robbery with Cook in his December statement. That was only mentioned when he made a statement a few days into the trial. Mr Beck spotted the error and Sutton could only answer that he was under instruction from Johnson . Of course, Judge Gibbon pointed out that, once the cartridges had been found and were proved to be cartridges fired from the Mossburg shotgun, there was no need to visit the mountainside again.

Mr Beck ended his questioning and Sutton was questioned briefly by Harrington as the day ended.

The next day, Sutton was called again. With help and guidance from Harrington, Sutton became the lovable little detective.

Mr Topolski and Mr Beck had another crack at him and he was soon over a barrel when he was asked why he hadn't followed up a witness who had seen Lindsay on the day of the robbery. He could only answer that they were too busy. He was looking pretty sad and Mr Topolski had only just started.

Mr Topolski told him he hadn't gone into the interviews with a fair and open mind to ask fair questions to see if a man was, or was not, involved in a crime. He also asked Sutton why he had dragged his heels when confirming Lindsay's alibi, and why was it so important to find a stripper in London. Sutton replied that they were both important.

> **Mr Topolski:** What was more difficult, do you think, as a piece of investigation: finding the man Bob; or finding the stripper who performed on 8 August at The King's Oak?
> **Sutton:** I think they were both important.
> **Judge Gibbon:** No, which was more difficult?
> **Sutton:** Which was more difficult?
> **Mr Topolski:** Let us have, just as a principle, two things to enquire about: find a man who might be called Bob who does dustbins and is an employee of the local council; or find a woman who did a private strip on 8 August at The King's Oak public house. Which is the more difficult?
> **Sutton:** I would have to accept the stripper.

Sutton fell right into Mr Topolski's trap.

Sutton had lost his temper when Lindsay had answered 'No comment' to his questions in the interviews, which Mr Topolski said is the fundamental right that still stands at the cornerstone of English criminal trails. Sutton agreed, but Mr Topolski asked, 'Why did Sutton tell Lindsay that a man who says, "No comment", is the sign of a guilty man?' To which Sutton replied that he merely wanted to get Lindsay to talk to him. Then Mr Topolski hit Sutton with the big bomb.

> **Mr Topolski:** But he talked. He gave his alibi. He had made his answers to you. He then exercised the right the law gave him.
> **Sutton** (*Standing there like a naughty schoolboy*): That's right.
> **Mr Topolski:** Can I just ask you about a question you asked Lindsay Frayne: 'You do realise that the forensic scientist says that you were one of the persons who entered the Halifax Building Society that day?' What is that question based on, Mr Sutton?
> **Sutton:** The saliva found in the balaclava mask.
> **Mr Topolski:** Had you read anything from the scientist about saliva in the balaclava mask?
> **Sutton:** No.
> **Mr Topolski:** Had you received some communication from the lab?
> **Sutton:** We had, yes.

Mr Topolski: The preliminary views, before he committed it to writing to the forensic scientist – who does not make a statement about anything, I don't think, until the very last day of the year, 31 December. But what you are telling us is, are you, that you received a communication from him as to his then view of the results of the test?

Sutton: That is correct.

Mr Topolski: What did that tell you?

Sutton: He didn't tell me. It was communicated obviously to other people in the office.

Mr Topolski: You put a very definite proposition to Lindsay Frayne: 'I can prove ... the scientist can prove you were in that building society.' I am asking you what you were told that formed the basis of that question?

Sutton: That the saliva found on the mask was of a particular blood group which was very rare, and that blood group is the same blood group as Lindsay Frayne.

Mr Topolski: Very rare. Do you know one in forty of the population are AB?

Sutton: Yes, I am aware of that. Yes.

Mr Topolski: Did you know that then?

Sutton: Yes, I did.

Judge Gibbon: But you are using ... The chances of the person who wore that mask was any one in forty members of the population who could secrete that?

Sutton: No, I wasn't aware of that, your Honour, no.

Mr Topolski: You were not?

Sutton: No.

Mr Topolski: Then why did you put the question, 'The scientists can prove you were there'? That is not an honest question, is it? Is it?

Sutton: That's forming part of my belief as well, together with the other evidence that we had.

Mr Topolski was showing the degree of questioning we had endured. Lindsay, like myself, gave them an account of our whereabouts on the day in question, but, of course, the arrogant Sutton didn't want to know the facts. As far as he was concerned he had found us guilty, which was why we decided to say 'No comment' to further questions. Mr Topolski asked Sutton why he felt it was important to spend so much time in London.

Mr Topolski asked Sutton why he had to take the shotgun personally to the ladies who had been held up. Everyone in the court, including Lindsay and me, thought it was madness that Sutton should be allowed to wander around with a weapon when a photograph of it would have been enough. To have the weapon brought into their homes must have been enough to give the ladies further nightmares.

Mr Topolski handed questioning over to Mr Beck, who wasted no time in driving in the point based on what the police termed an action book, which gives a day-to-day running of any enquiry. He pointed out to Sutton that the book did not run comprehensively, covering the enquiry as a whole. It was then pointed out that there was a £1,000 reward, which was denied by all the police when they were in the witness box. Not only did the book explain about the reward, but it was to be released to the press, which again was denied by the police.

Sutton wasted no time in shoving the blame onto Johnson.

Mr Beck pointed out to Sutton that they had been to the Double D Trekking Centre, something else Sutton denied! Then, to add insult to injury, so to speak, Mr Beck pointed out that the police station was just yards away from where the robbery had taken place!

Mr Beck asked why Edwards had been excluded from giving hair samples, but Sutton explained that forensics had told him that hair is not conclusive evidence.

Mr Beck had made his point admirably.

Sutton was then handed over to Harrington, who again tried to help the prat out of the mess he was in. Harrington finished his brief questioning and Sutton left the witness box. After some debate, our defence called Sutton back into the witness stand. No doubt they had things on their minds because evidence wasn't adding up.

Sutton left the box in preparation for other witnesses, some of whom were eye witnesses to the robbery, but Lindsay and I took no notice as it was nothing to do with us.

My father took the stand to confirm that Lindsay had been with him at the time of the robbery, but when Harrington started questioning him I couldn't believe what he came out with. He showed my father a photograph of the imitation gun from when he was our defence barrister. As annoyed as I felt, it endorsed the fact that Harrington was scraping the bottom of the barrel. After seeing the photograph, my father promptly told Harrington that he should know more about the case as he had represented me as my defence barrister.

Harrington brought his cross-examination of my father to an abrupt end, and Mr Beck and Mr Topolski had little to question my father on.

The trial was coming to an end. All that was left was the defence and prosecution closing speeches, and the judge's summing up. Then we were in the hands of the jury.

When the closing speeches were over, the judge gave Lindsay and me bail and said that if we wanted to do a runner now was the time to do it.

I was glad to see the end of it all. As far as we were concerned we had won the trial, but I knew from experience that I was sitting in Gwent, where we had never had justice before. But you never know ...

17

WEIGHED OFF

I woke that morning knowing it was our last day of freedom. I also knew that we were looking at more than just a couple of months.

Bruce had arrived early to film the final interview before we went to court, and the programme was to be broadcast that evening, regardless of the outcome. He asked me during the interview what I thought our chances were, and I replied that I didn't think there would be an acquittal.

As we were driven to the courts, I knew it was going to be some time before I would see the valleys again.

As usual, the media were out in force, ready to run their stories on the result of our trial, and Lindsay and I made the last, long walk up the steps of doom; a walk we had done so many times in almost a month of our trial.

We knocked on the door to be let through to the holding cells for prisoners, and sitting in one of the cells were Cook and Roger, who were also up for sentencing. The jury had been out for almost two days, which some of the screws said was maybe a good sign.

The morning came and went, with still no sign of the jury. Roger came back down and said he had copped 12 years but, Roger being Roger, just smiled and said he would appeal against the sentence.

The end of the day was drawing near and, just as I thought – I couldn't see the jury going into another day of deliberations – the phone rang in the office, to tell the screw that the jury was ready with the verdicts. All the screws walked with us up the steps to the dock.

The foreman read out the verdicts:

> Count 1, Conspiracy to deal in firearms. Guilty, both.
> Count 2, Shortening a shotgun. Not Guilty, both.
> Count 3, Possessing a prohibited weapon. Not Guilty, both.
> Count 4, Conspiracy to rob. Withdrawn.
> Count 5, Possessing a prohibited weapon. Not Guilty, majority 10–2, both.
> Count 6, Robbery. Guilty, majority 10–2, both.

All that was left was to be sentenced by Judge Gibbon. We were asked to stand and were sentenced to eight years imprisonment, with 18 months to run concurrently for conspiracy to deal in firearms.

There wasn't a lot that could be said at that point, so we went down the stairs where we were met by Cook, Roger and a few others, asking us about the result. After we'd told them, Cook had to take a seat. He felt he was looking at a 12-year sentence, maybe 10 if he was lucky.

We heard his name being called, and I turned to watch as he took each step as if he was going to the gallows. I had never liked him, but had some respect for him for coming forward, not wanting to see Lindsay and me get blamed for something we hadn't done – not that it made any difference.

One of the lads put a mug of tea in my hand as we waited in anticipation to see what Cook was going to be weighed-off with.

We didn't have to wait long before he came down the stairs, tapping his feet like Fred Astair. On reaching the bottom and with arms outstretched, he told us he had copped six and a half years. However, as he sat drinking a mug of tea, the six and a half years was sinking in fast and, with his head in his hands he kept repeating, 'Six and a half years.'

Our barristers were just as stunned as us. They knew as well as us that we had won the trial. Judge Gibbon said to our barristers that if we wanted to appeal, we should do so, but having just copped eight years, an appeal was the last thing on my mind. I just wanted to get to prison and get some sleep.

The screws were told to take us from the courts as late as possible as quite a few of the press were waiting to take photographs.

Being cuffed up ready for our ride to prison, I was thinking of ways to escape.

As we went through reception at the prison, most of the screws were telling us how sorry they were that we'd been found guilty. They had been following the case closely and had all the information from the screws who'd been in the dock with us.

Due to the publicity given to the trial, Lindsay and I were put in E cells. They were single cells with a bright green doors and a big E painted in white, which the screws checked every 15 minutes. The checks made no difference to me though, because after making up my bed I was out for the count.

The next morning I was woken by a few of the lads telling me we were on the front pages of the national newspapers. One lad slid the paper under my door and I saw a photograph of me with the headline: 'KRAY DOUBLES GO TO JAIL'. I turned a few pages and saw a photograph of Lindsay and me with Tony Lambrianou and Bullen. The paper was giving us a slating – with the help of Tony Lambrianou, who claimed we made his flesh creep. But what pissed me off more than anything was underneath the photo, although not mentioning his name, Bullen was classed as a mate.

A few other lads showed me another newspaper and I had to smile as that one was referring to us as Pinky and Perky and said that I was terrified of spiders. At the bottom of the page was a photograph of Roger with the headline: 'TV GUN SIEGE MAN JAILED'.

I was still smiling when Lindsay walked in asking how I was feeling, which was much better after a good night's sleep. He had with him a Welsh newspaper, which had printed a photograph of us putting flowers on Reggie and Ronnie's parents' grave. The photograph had been doctored by the newspaper, colouring Lindsay's hair black. What we found particularly disturbing was that the photograph had been stolen from our homes by someone. Then, as we turned to their main story, we saw personal photographs of Lindsay and me with our father; again photos which had been stolen from our family album!

The programme by HTV, *Wales This Week*, had been shown and, even though we hadn't seen it, we were given a very good account of it by the screws. It seems that Bruce had done a good job. After telling us about it, the screws walked away shaking their heads in disbelief; unable to understand how we were in prison.

After seeing the Governor – which is normal procedure when convicted – Lindsay and I were allowed to move out of the E cells and into a cell together.

We were assigned jobs in the sewing department, making prison jeans, but we would have preferred cleaning jobs, so we put our names on the waiting list. We were soon trained to sew and make the jeans, but, even though I hated the job, I had to play ball in the hope of getting our preferred jobs of landing cleaners.

We found we got on very well with Roger, and the three of us soon became friends. He was over on B wing, so when I had finished in the sewing department I would visit Roger's cell for a cup of tea. He had made an element out of metal mop pieces connected to the cell light, so boiling water in the prison-issue jug was no problem.

Cook was also on B wing, but on the next landing up from Roger. He was like a pig in swill, getting stoned all the time with his mates.

I checked to see if my hacksaw blades had been discovered, and on finding them untouched decided to make preparations for an escape. Lindsay wasn't too keen on the idea at first, but said that as soon as we had addresses to use as hideouts, he would probably have a different view.

We knew we would not be at Cardiff prison for long, as it was a local jail, and we were certain we would be moved to an English one. A lot of the Welsh lads were being sent to Dartmoor prison in Devon, which wouldn't be very convenient for visits. We were hoping to go to the same jail, as it would make it easier for our families.

I was getting really pissed off in the sewing department. So, to relieve the boredom, Lindsay and I would make some jeans with one leg longer than the other. We would also sew some with the zip on the wrong side, and would be doubled up thinking that some con somewhere would put on his new jeans, thinking he had the zip in the front, which of course was sewn up, with the zip on the arse side. If we knew the shipment of jeans was to be delivered to a nonce jail, we designed what we termed the bollock crushers, which we would sew so tight that they would have been painful to wear. But a lot of the time I skived off to Roger's cell, where we drank tea all morning and chatted about things in general.

Lindsay and I decided to make some alcoholic hooch to have a piss-up. Getting all the gear was no problem; the only problem was hiding the stuff when it was brewing. We knew that a screw with a good nose would soon find it, as the brewing process demanded that the hooch should breathe.

Roger could be quite an inventor, so between us we devised a top that allowed the hooch to breathe without stinking the place out.

The prison system was introducing telephones on each landing, which allowed prisoners to contact friends and family regularly when they bought a £2 telephone card. Another change that was being introduced was to do away with the traditional prison clothes, replacing them with red or blue tracksuits, and we were even allowed to wear our own trainers, which was a damn site better than the shitty slip-ons we'd previously had to wear.

Although some of the changes being introduced were good, some were a load of bollocks. Previously, if anyone was sick they could report sick in the morning and see the doctor the same day, but the new rule stated that an application had to be made the day before, so if prisoners were ill it was a bummer waiting until the next day to see a doctor. But we soon learned how to exploit their daft rules. Most lads, in order to dodge work, would make an application to see the doctor the following day, knowing they could spend the day in bed or get out of their cells to do a bit of business.

A cleaning job had come up, but the sewing department wasn't prepared to let Lindsay go for it, even though the screws in charge of cleaning duties were more than happy for him to have it. I'd had a gut-full of making jeans, so decided to see the doctor and tell him I was finding it hard to see my work in the sewing department, and that I was losing the sight in one eye. Arrangements were made for me to see the optician, who agreed that my left eye was causing problems. I then took my case to the Governor, explaining that if I lost my good eye, the prison would be liable for a massive damages claim, under the 1966 Factories Act. He could see my point and ordered that I either be on the sick or do some light duties with the cleaner.

Lindsay was still having problems getting released from the sewing department, so he simply decided he wasn't going to work there. The screw who'd promised him the cleaning job nicked him and put him on report to see the Governor the next day for disobeying an order. When he was up in front of the Governor (which is like a small court), Lindsay was asked why he had refused a direct order by refusing to go to the sewing department. He explained that he was on the list to work as a cleaner and felt it was unfair that they wouldn't let him go. The Governor asked whether there was anyone he wanted to call and he replied that he did. When the Governor asked who, Lindsay pointed to the screw who had nicked him. With them all laughing, Lindsay was granted the cleaning job on A3, which meant that he had to move into the cleaning cell with another cleaner, so I decided to move into an E cell until the other cleaner had moved on.

Being in a single cell suited me. Staying in a two-man cell would have meant that someone was put in with me, and it can be difficult being two'd up with someone who is on a short sentence.

While I was on the sick, the Governor had kept to his word and allowed my door to stay open, the same as the cleaners, and as I had plenty of free time I decided to concentrate on escaping.

I began making arrangements for addresses where I could hide out when I was back in London. I knew I had to move to a cell halfway down the landing so that I could cut through the bars and use the education block as our cover. The wall wouldn't prove a problem: the hacksaw would cut through a metal chair leg and I could shape it into a grappling iron.

Some of the lads we knew were being shipped out: some to Dartmoor and some to Long Lartin, Worcestershire. I knew time was running out, so I moved the hacksaw blades (which had been hidden for a few years) and decided to split them, thinking it would be just my luck if they were all found. I had everything arranged for when we were over the wall, I just needed to get the cell to escape from and pick the day when we felt it was right to go.

A letter had come in from Reggie saying that Campbell wanted him and Ron to write bad things about us in return for money, and to put the letter from Ted Hynds into effect. What Reggie was explaining through Ronnie was, we could tell, the truth of the matter regarding the letter. It proved that Campbell was still being a rat as he was still leaking stories, as well as asking Reggie and Ronnie to be disloyal to us. But what Campbell failed to realise was that Reggie and Ronnie were not rats and certainly weren't daft enough to fall for his tricks, especially as he'd proved himself to be a grass at our trial. As far as the letter from Ted Hynds went, that was something going on within the Krays and what I had termed The Inner Sanctum, and although I had other things on my mind, such as going over the wall, I had to respect the loyalty and trust given to Lindsay and me by Reg and Ron.

One day, I woke up with earache, and as the day went on it got worse. By the time the door banged shut in the night the pain was unbearable, so I pressed the buzzer. A night screw came to the door, but, due to the change in rules, he couldn't give me any medication. I was walking the cell floor, pacing back and forth in agony, when I felt something running down my neck. When I put my hand to the side of my face it was soon covered in blood, with green, slimy stuff mixed in. I knew it had to be more than just earache, so I pressed the buzzer again, but when I showed the night screw he still said there was nothing he could do.

I thought, 'Bollocks to it. I am not whingeing to him any more, fucking slag.'

I couldn't lie down, so I carried on pacing the cell. By then I couldn't hear anything and the muck was running out of me, dripping onto the floor. I grabbed a pillow and wrapped it around my head, and spent the rest of the night pacing and watching the clock, waiting for the door to open in the morning.

After the longest night I have ever known, the door finally opened and I was heading for the doctor. I knew it was pretty bad when I passed Lindsay's cell and could only see his mouth move. There was no sound.

When I saw the doctor, I pointed to my ears and asked for painkillers but he shook his head and told me I couldn't have any. I didn't mind too much because, reading his lips as he spoke, I realised he was saying, 'Hospital'. But for some reason, a screw had to take me back to my cell and take my card off the door before taking me to the hospital block. I was told to wait in a hospital cell until the doctor arrived, but by then I was hoping I would pass out, just to have some relief from the pain. The door would open and someone would come to look at me, then it would shut, open again, shut again ... I was getting really pissed off. The morning was going into the afternoon and I still had blood and muck pissing out of my ears but didn't have the energy to ask what was going on.

Finally, the door opened and I was taken to a taxi. I could hardly stand, but knew I was on my way to the hospital so I forced myself to walk. Double-cuffed to screws, I was taken through corridor after corridor then into a room where I waited to see someone.

As I sat waiting, I decided I'd had enough, and, with what little energy I had, I told the screws that if I didn't get something for the pain, I was going through the window and would take one of them with me. That did the trick as the next thing I knew a doctor was looking at my ears and, with a look of panic on his face, I was being injected in my legs and operated on there and then.

Even though the pain had eased a little, I was still in considerable discomfort, but I was given some more injections and I settled enough for the doctor to treat me. I was then moved into a room where a number of screws sat around me. They knew I still couldn't hear, so they told me, by writing on notepaper, that the Governor wanted me back on the hospital wing in prison, but that the doctor had said I couldn't be moved.

The pain came back after an hour or so, so different painkillers were used to try to stabilise me, but none seemed to work. A nurse came in and also by writing a note told me that they had a new painkiller which had just come out, but it had to be put up the back passage. 'Fuck that!' I thought. I didn't want anything going up my arse, that was one way traffic. She must have seen the worry on my face as the screws let her out. I suffered as the pain got worse and worse until, out of desperation, I asked for the new painkiller and felt the pain fade away within a few minutes.

The days passed, but most of the time I was sleeping. I had a number of screws with me throughout the day and two covering the night shift. One screw in particular gave me cakes, which his wife had sent in, and at times like that I was able to look beyond the uniform and see a decent man.

The weeks rolled by and I gradually got stronger. Some of the screws would encourage me to take a walk with them through the corridors, and it crossed my mind to do a runner; with no bolts, bars or a big wall to go over I could have been gone. But I'd got to know the screws fairly well over the weeks and if I did go I knew I would have left them right in the shit. My principles had got the better of me and I was thankful I was on the mend.

The packing was taken out of my ears and to my relief I could hear a little. I was getting bored, so I knew I was feeling well enough to go back to prison. I didn't want to go back to the hospital wing – that was enough to depress anyone – so I asked to go back to my cell on the wing and catch up with what Lindsay had been doing since I'd been gone. When I arrived back on the wing, everyone commented on the weight I had lost; more than likely I'd left half my weight on my pillow before I went to the hospital.

I must have sounded like a sad case, glad to be back in jail. Lindsay said that he had gathered up the hacksaw blades and put them back where I had first hidden them. I had forgotten about my escape plot, but could see Lindsay was well up for it by then, so I told him to put the plan on hold until I was back to full health.

Lindsay told me that while I'd been away, he and Roger had got a strike party together because they were prohibiting smoking on visits. They were due to see the Governor, so I decided to go along to help put the point across but, of course, the Governor wasn't prepared to listen.

Roger had arranged for a sit-in during exercise break the next day in protest of the smoking ban, even though he didn't smoke. The next thing we heard was that Roger had been shanghaied out of Cardiff jail and sent to Long Lartin.

All the lads who were geared up for the sit-in looked towards Lindsay and me for advice, but we decided that a sit-in would have been a foolish mistake. Instead, we decided that we would light up as usual on visits, and smoke until a screw pulled us. Some of the lads were afraid they would get nicked, but I told them they would get nicked having a sit-in, which was far more serious than having a fag on a visit.

I wasn't there long enough to know the outcome of their action, as a day or two later, on the Sunday morning, screws came to tell Lindsay and me to get our kit together as we were being taken to Long Lartin.

Some of the lads who had already moved there had written to me saying that it wasn't a bad jail, so I didn't mind moving there. One of the lads came to shake my hand and I gave him the details of where the blades were hidden and a telephone number in case he managed get over the wall. There was no point in taking the blades with us, as we knew Long Lartin was a top security prison, and it was very doubtful that we would get anything past them.

We were soon cuffed up and on our way, taking the scenic route – Monmouth to Ross on Wye – onto the M50. I was quite looking forward to the change but, as I saw the 'Welcome to England' sign, I turned to Lindsay and told him I would never return to Wales. Although I was leaving Wales behind, my homeland, I felt a sense of relief.

We left the M5 in the county of Worcestershire and headed towards a little village called Evesham, then went on to a smaller village called South Littleton. After travelling through a few lanes leading to a wider road, I could see the great big walls with rounded tops and cameras at every point.

We pulled up at the gatehouse and were let through. The reception area wasn't very big, which told me that prisoners weren't released as often as in local jails. We went through the usual procedure of a strip search, and the screws went through our gear meticulously.

When the procedures were over, we were told to place our gear on a trolley, before stepping out into the compound. We walked to gates which separated the great big metal fence topped with coiled razor wire from the wall. Between the wall and fence stood dog handlers with their well-brushed Alsatians.

As we pulled our trolleys through the gates, a screw pointed to the wing that we had been allocated. The building didn't look like a traditional prison building; it was more modern and I could see the gardens were kept to a professional standard.

The screw opened another gate and, as we were sandwiched between that gate and another, the screw spoke into a speaker asking for the door to be opened. A voice came back immediately indicating all was clear, then with a click the door opened and we were on the centre, with cameras pointing at all angles.

As we walked towards a corridor, a screw pointed out that the trolley could go down the goods passage, which ran parallel to the corridor with a number of steps. We reached a big wooden door displaying the sign 'F wing', and a screw talked into a speaker again. We heard a voice reply, 'Okay then.' With another click, the door to F wing swung open.

Two screws sitting at a table with a board in front of them asked us to leave our trolley, and as we walked through to the office, the hustle and bustle of prisoners going back and forth was going on around us.

A number of screws were sitting in the office with an SO, who took our details from the screws who had brought us over from reception. He began writing our names, sentence and numbers on a board that was hanging on the wall. Each name was in a box, which showed which cell the prisoners were housed in.

I looked at the board, which held about 80 to 90 names with sentences ranging from 8 years to 40, and I noticed that some had 'recommended' next to them, which generally meant they were never getting out.

Lindsay and I were handed a brass key each and told that we could lock our doors when we weren't in our cells. Smiling at Lindsay, I said, 'That's alright. Our own fucking door key in jail.'

The SO told us he would take us to our cells on landing 3 so, after grabbing our gear from the trolley, we walked up two fights of stairs to where two screws sat on the landing. The SO spoke into a speaker on the wall to release the doors of two empty cells. I heard two clicks, then we were walking down the corridor, where a few lads nodded and smiled. The SO opened the door, and as I walked in, I couldn't believe the size of it. I asked the SO if he was taking the piss by showing me the broom cupboard instead of the cell, but when he shook his head I knew he was serious.

I put my gear on the floor and sat on the bed, trying to adjust to the size of the cell. It must have been a little under a seven cube. With the bed, an old chair and a cupboard, there wasn't much else that could be fitted in there, only myself. Lindsay walked in laughing but it was no laughing matter. The windows weren't too bad though. They were at the right level for a person to look through, unlike Cardiff prison where you needed a chair to stand on, to look out.

We heard our names being called over the loudspeaker, telling us to go the ground floor. When we got there we were met by Danny, who we had known at Cardiff. He gave me a pillowcase and said that there was some hooch in it for Lindsay and me to have a drink in the evening. He told us to meet him out on the pitch after the dinner bang-up as all the Welsh lads would be there, including some we knew from Cardiff jail.

As I made up my bed, some of the lads came to the door to introduce themselves and tell us about the jail and its routine. Two Asian brothers also came along and offered us some weed, but I refused, telling them I never touched the stuff. Laughing, they said together, 'You will.'

A screw shouted, 'Bang-up in five minutes,' and everyone returned to their cells, still chatting. More shouts came from screws: 'Behind your doors,' and I could hear click, click, click as each door was locked by the electrics.

Over the dinner period I unpacked my belongings and slowly came to terms with the tiny conditions I had to consider home for the next few years.

The hour and a half dinner bang-up soon passed, but there were no screws opening the doors; the click on the door indicated that it was open. I walked onto the corridor, which I learned was called a spur , and I couldn't get over how quiet it was compared with Cardiff prison. Lindsay and I locked our doors and made our way to the exercise yard.

Danny met us at the bottom of the stairs, but before we could leave F wing, the two screws at the table asked where we were going, so they could write it on the board. 'Exercise yard, Guv,' I replied to the one, who smiled as we went.

Danny was soon showing us the way, as we walked off F wing. He also showed us the canteen, which was right at the end of our corridor. We followed him down a long corridor, which branched off to E wing and D wing, and he pointed out the stores where we could get prison gear later on. We went through more corridors, which led the way to A wing, B wing and C wing.

We then followed Danny through a gate onto a great big field, and I understood why the screws were smiling when I said we were off to the exercise yard. The space was unbelievable compared with the small field at Cardiff. As we walked towards what looked like a big bus shelter, Danny told us that the big field was used on weekends and the basketball yard was for exercise throughout the week.

As I got closer to the shelter, I recognised quite a few lads from Cardiff prison and, after shaking hands with them, Danny introduced us to other lads who were from Wales but had been at Long Lartin for some time. One of them pointed out that the security cameras were all aimed at us as we were chatting, so we began to walk around the huge field. Even then all the cameras followed us.

I asked Danny about Roger, and was told he was on D wing, and although it was allowed to visit lads on other wings, it was limited to the ground floor.

It was nice that my fellow Welshmen shared a unity. Knowing that we all stood together helped me feel more settled.

We found our own way back to F wing to check out the small TV room and large video room and, to our surprise, there was also a pool room. I then went to the office and asked the SO about getting prison kit. He told me he would ring through to the stores then call us on the wing speakers.

Just before we went up to our landing, we were offered a cup of tea by a chap called Salam who told us he was from Iraq, and a few of the lads who were passing joked that we shouldn't talk to him as he was a terrorist. We chatted with Salam for a while and he told us what the food was like, what times meals were served, etc., and, as we left him, he gave us a bag of prison-issue tea bags. We thanked him for his hospitality as we went back to our cell.

Everyone was really friendly, and an Asian lad next door down to me introduced himself as Stan, and told me he had followed our case in the newspaper. He also told me he was from Newport.

Stan also told us that as there were no toilets in the cells. Each cell had a box with different coloured buttons in, which allowed the men to come out at night if they needed to use the toilet, or night-san, as they called it. He explained that we were to press the green button if we needed the toilet, but if the amber light came on, it indicated that there was a queue and when the door clicked open we each had 10 to 15 minutes to use the toilet. But he added that most of the lads still had piss-pots in their cells, which were emptied in the big sluice in the recess. We learned that there was another button in the box, which enabled the men to talk to the screws on the control board if they were having any problems.

I went to have a look at the recess area. There were the hand basins, six each end, with toilets which had low doors, allowing screws to see over if they were doing a count or roll check. Just off from there was a small room, which had showers and a bathroom.

As I was sitting down having a cup of tea with Stan, I was surprised when he pulled out money from his pocket. It was unusual to see money in prison but he explained that prison wages were paid in 50 pence pieces and other small change. My brain instantly went into overdrive, thinking of ways I could smuggle in 50ps, but Stan must have read my mind and told me that all money had to be left behind or put in a box before going in to a visit, so if any money was found when we were coming back from a visit it was confiscated.

Our names were called to go up to the stores to get our prison-issue kit, and even though we were allowed to wear our own clothes, Lindsay and I knew some of the prison gear would come in handy. Stan had a friend who worked in the stores, so he came along and introduced us to his mate, who gave us a big bag of prison gear. A number was stamped on each item, so that when it was sent to the laundry we could be sure that the same clothes were returned to us. Everything was brand new, from towels to underwear, slippers to donkey jackets and boots. All the gear was made by prisoners at various jails throughout the country, so when we were asked what size jeans we wanted and saw they were made at

Cardiff prison, Lindsay and I smiled at each other and told the stores lad, 'No thank you.'

As we were heading back to F wing with the bags on our shoulders, we saw lads coming from the hotplate with their tea. We had missed our dinner, so we dumped the bags in our cells and went to the ground floor to get our tea. The food wasn't too bad compared with the slop they gave out at Cardiff, and I sat on my bed eating while Lindsay ate his sitting at the table.

After the hour bang-up, Lindsay and I decided to open the bottles of hooch that Danny had so kindly given us. As we took our first drink we could taste the strength, and although a bottle wasn't enough to get drunk on, it was enough to enjoy.

We went down to the pool room to have a couple of games and, as bang-up wasn't until nine o'clock, we still had three hours with the door open. The room was empty, so Lindsay and I played pool and drank our hooch, happy as sandboys. However, three blokes soon came in and asked for the pool cue. Lindsay and I looked at each other and were a bit confused, so I asked one of them what they wanted the cue for. He replied arrogantly, 'To play pool, you daft fucker.'

I wasn't going to give him the cue when I was playing, so I told him to put his name on the board to book the next game. Lindsay knew that the worst thing they could do was insult me when I had a stick in my hand. I told the bloke he could have a game of sleeper with me first and then, if he felt up to it, I would gladly give him the cue to play pool. Looking rather puzzled, he asked what a game of sleeper was, so I told him that if I wrapped the cue around his head, when he woke up he could have it, if it was still in one piece. He stood looking at me, no doubt sizing me up. Then, so he was left in no doubt that I was serious, I told him I was going to ram it straight through his head, and then see if his two mates' mouths could take a whole pool ball when it was rammed down their throats.

They looked rather surprised by my outburst, so I told them we were new in the prison, and that all the people we had met so far had been very kind indeed, and because I was in a good mood they could walk out of the room. I finished by telling them that I wasn't prepared to have my day messed up by some bully-boy fuckheads, and that if he carried on, I had no doubt I would be adding another 20 years to my sentence. They looked at each other, turned around, and left. I seemed to have made my point. The last thing we wanted – or needed – was a punch-up on our first day. I was quite happy with the place as jails went.

Lindsay and I had a few more games, and when we'd had enough I went to the blackboard, where names were chalked up for order of play, and wrote 'Wanker' on it three times. Then, taking the cue with me, I looked around for the three blokes who had pissed me off. I didn't have to look far. All three were standing with some of their mates, no doubt telling them what I'd said in the hope of getting a posse together. I walked towards them and held out the cue to the gobby bastard and told him I had put their names on the blackboard. As I walked away one said, 'But you don't know our names.'

'No,' I replied, 'but Wanker seems to fit the bill.'

As I walked away, all the lads with them burst out laughing and shouted after me, 'Nice one.'

Our first day was soon over. Lindsay and I had spent most of the evening on the ground floor chatting with friends we had known on the outside, and some we had missed when out on exercise.

A screw shouted that there was five minutes to go, so I poured hot water into my cup for tea, then the screw shouted, 'Running,' as the clicks could be heard running in order of cell numbers. I said goodnight to Lindsay and shut the door. My first day at Long Lartin prison was over.

As I settled down to write letters to friends and family, I pressed the night-san and, lo and behold, the door opened. I didn't really want to go out, I was only testing it for the first time, but decided to make another cup of tea and get some fresh water. As I passed Lindsay's door, I smiled through the hatch and he smiled back, saying, 'All right here, isn't it?'

The next morning, at about 8.15, I woke to the sound of the door clicking open. Unlike Cardiff prison, with all the noise, idiots shouting, and doors opening and shutting, it was so quiet I almost forgot I was in prison. Everyone emptied their piss-pots in silence, until they were in the recess, and then all that could be heard was, 'Good morning.'

The doors were open until 12 o'clock midday. We had been told we had a week to settle in before we were offered jobs.

Lindsay went down to the hotplate to get breakfast for us both, while I made us a cup of tea. Many of the lads had jobs to go to after breakfast, so the wing was relatively empty.

We went to the video room, where some of the boys had put on a film, so we watched the film and TV until dinner time.

One of the lads came to my cell offering to wire my music system to the lights in my cell. I watched him as he worked and took in all he was doing. Then, after paying him a few packs of tobacco, I went down to Lindsay's cell and wired in his system.

After settling in throughout the week, Friday was payday and each wing was paid and given canteen on a rota basis. Stan showed us how to get our wages – we had been told we were to receive induction money – and waiting in a small queue to be handed about £3 or £4 in 50 pence pieces was a novelty in itself. We could then queue to buy items from the canteen.

Lads throughout the prison ran their own little shops from their cells, and when I asked if there were any betting shops, I was told that there were people who took bets. I was also told we could buy Chinese and Indian meals, and just about any other meals that were made throughout the world, as there were cooking facilities on the ground floor for the prisoners' use, so it wasn't unknown for a Chinese chap to cook extra and then sell it.

The place was running like clockwork, and the screws were happy as long as the prisoners were happy, and as long as everyone was in their cell when the electric doors were running, we hardly ever saw a screw – only when they checked the numbers after each bang-up. It was the way a prison should be run. After all, we didn't come to prison to be punished, the punishment was being deprived of freedom.

Our induction period was soon over and I stayed on the sick after having an eye test and putting my case to the Governors. Lindsay started a course learning draughtsmanship on computers.

We heard the good news that Ian and Phil had been acquitted at their London trial, and that Gwent police had been laughed out of court with their ridiculous accusations against them.

Throughout the day, when Lindsay was at his classes, I passed the time by writing fiction books, reading and learning different languages. If I wanted a break, I would go and watch a film. Then, when Lindsay was due back from his class, I would have cup of tea waiting and we chatted until it was time to go for dinner.

In all jails there is a vicar, or Devil Dodger, as we called them. Long Lartin had two churches for the different faiths and could also cater for any religion from around the world. The vicar asked Lindsay and me if we would like people to come in to give us a visit and chat about anything. I initially told him I wasn't interested, as I didn't want to get roped into religion, but when he said that cups of tea and coffee would be laid on and that the visitors were allowed to bring in fags for us, I changed my mind. Laughing, I said to Lindsay, 'This religion thing isn't so bad after all.'

'Maybe the Archbishop is looking after you,' he replied.

Having visits from friends and family was good. We were allowed to smoke on visits and were also allowed fruit. When I saw we were allowed melon, my eyes lit up, and I soon had some of the lads visiting us, filling a melon with 50 pence pieces. I would get back to my cell, break open the melon, and get out £20. It was easier to smuggle in £10 or £20 in notes, but they lost their value in prison: £10 was worth £5 and £20 was worth £15, so with my melon idea, what was brought in was what I could spend. However, the prison would give out, for example, £6,000 in wages in 50ps on Friday and by the Monday the accounts had taken in well over £20,000 in 50ps.

Refurbishment began on the wings, and on completion of A wing, the first to be done, the cells were fitted with electricity points. Therefore, the other five wings had temporary transformers installed until the work was done on those.

Lindsay and I decided to brew some hooch with yeast we'd bought off one of the kitchen boys, a carton of orange juice and a bag of sugar. We soon had a couple of gallons brewing nicely. We devised a way of dodging the screws as we knew the security screws could pounce on a wing in the hunt for illegal contraband.

We often visited Roger on D wing and, as he was on the ground floor, he too was in on the brewing. It was a nice break to have a few glasses of hooch and a chat. Our drinking vessels were ordinary jam jars but they served the purpose very well.

When the brew was ready, we invited a few friends from our wing. Stan came up and Brian, who was a few doors down from Lindsay. Through using the gym, we'd become friendly with a Jamaican called Presser, who had dreadlocks down to his arse and was one hell of a powerful bloke on the weights, so he was happy to join us as well. Having chilled the hooch under the cold tap in the bathroom, we all set about drinking. Having a free drink of alcohol was a real treat for the lads and there was no stopping them.

After an hour we all felt quite merry, but as we chatted our stomachs began to swell like pregnant women and were getting quite painful. Luckily, after a few visits to the toilet, we were all okay, but we realised we'd taken the hooch off too soon, so Lindsay and I had to make sure we got it right the next time.

Time seemed to fly by, and with Christmas fast approaching, we arranged to see our barristers to discuss an appeal.

When we met Mr Topolski and Mr Beck, we decided that a police investigation was called for. We knew it could take some time, as opposed to an early appeal date, but Mr Beck advised us that it would be better in the long run, so we instructed them to get on with it.

It wasn't long before Gwent police found out about us asking for a police investigation. One of the lads on another wing came over with a local paper, which described Lindsay and me as Gazza Nappers, referring to the kidnap of Paul Gascoigne, but the reporters couldn't even get it right when it had been dictated by the police. As I read further down, I laughed as the newspaper referred to the Freddy Mercury letter and the cure for AIDS. I thanked the lad for the newspaper and showed the article to Lindsay. We laughed like hell – the newspaper had certainly made my day a lot brighter!

To satisfy myself that Gwent police were dictating to the local press, I wrote a letter to the journalist inviting her to come to Long Lartin, so I could clear up a number of matters she'd reported. She sent a letter back asking what I wanted to talk about, so in reply I told her that we had a police officer who'd been involved in our case and whose conscience was getting the better of him about stitching us up, and that he was prepared to tell all to her with an exclusive story.

Of course, I didn't have any copper ready to tell all, but if the newspaper was fair and just, the reporter would have thought she had a big scoop, and would no doubt have been at the prison as soon as possible. But it wasn't to be: I heard no more from her.

That was the cherry on the cake as far as I was concerned. It proved that the local newspapers were just as biased as the officers involved in our case.

We were having regular visits at the church. My visitor was a chap called Steve, while Lindsay chatted with a lady called Helen. Over a cup of tea and a fag provided by Steve, it was nice to chat about things other than prison.

Two new lads came onto the wing, and I later learned that one of them, Dai Matthews, was from the same village as Lindsay and me. He told us how he had a coffee shop in Amsterdam but had been caught up with the scumbag grasses from Newbridge, which had resulted in him getting involved with heroin. When he let me read his paperwork, I saw the names of the grasses and knew most of them.

Dai introduced me to his co-defendant, Paul Revell. They'd had a lucrative business in Amsterdam and they were quick to point out that everything was going well for them until they met their scumbag friends. I had to agree with them. The grasses they named were real scumbags – I knew them.

The feeling of being in jail for Christmas was the same in Long Lartin as it had been in Cardiff, and the quicker it was out of the way the better. We were 18 months into the sentence (including remand) and I knew that once we were into the New Year, that was another year out of the way.

We made sure we had plenty of hooch brewed for over Christmas. A few of the lads had arranged parties and Lindsay had his guitar sent in so he could play while we all sang along. With the New Year just days away, a big party was planned, but some of the lads decided they weren't going to bang-up at nine o'clock. They wanted to stay out to see the New Year in. I knew it was a recipe for disaster and advised against it, but everyone kept saying that the worst that could happen was a day or two down the block, so I agreed.

On New Year's Eve the drink was flowing and everything was going great until the screws shouted, 'Bang-up.'

This moment had been on our minds for days and the time had come to refuse bang up until we'd seen the New Year in. But we found that the ones who suggested we all stay out were the ones who now wanted to bang up. I thought, 'Okay, I'll go along with that, and banged my door shut, quite content after having a good day. But as the click went on my door, I heard Lindsay call one of them a wanker, for calling off the stopover. The next thing I heard was fighting outside as Lindsay tried to strangle Brian and almost had another man's eye out. I was locked in my cell with it all going on outside, but for some reason one of the women screws had asked at the control desk for my door to be unlocked. As it opened, I could see that Lindsay was well into one, with a table leg in each hand and cupboards and tables smashed up.

I was told that if I could calm Lindsay down and get him to his cell, the matter would be forgotten, so I took the chair leg off him and started to walk him to his cell. But as I did, another lad pounced on Lindsay who, even with six screws hanging onto him, pasted hell into the lad. His face looked as though it had been slashed open, but in the scuffle, and with the weight of six screws behind him, Lindsay's thumbnail, which he kept fairly long to play his guitar, had ripped the lad's face.

When it had all calmed down, a number of screws wanted Lindsay down the block, but had the problem that they'd let me out, so we all ended up in our cells. Throughout the night, each was telling the other that it wasn't finished. However, as the drink wore off, we all calmed down and ended up laughing about the matter.

The next day I could see that Lindsay had dished out some injuries to three others, but it was finished. Another case of drink in; senses out.

Reggie and Ronnie were still in touch, either by normal mail or through lads on transfer. Reggie wanted us to try and get down with him, but we were settled at Long Lartin. Apart from that, our brewing skills were getting better and one two-litre bottle of hooch was enough to get pissed on.

Another chap I'd become friendly with was Mickey O'Brien from Cardiff.

Mickey had been in prison almost ten years and had been charged, with two other blokes, for the murder of a man in a newsagent's.

Sometimes, when I was having a break from the cell, I would visit Mickey on the ground floor of B wing where we would chat about each other's trials in court. I thought it was bad enough getting eight years, but he'd got life. He told me that he had been offered parole, as long as he signed paperwork confessing to the crime. Of course, he'd told them to fuck right off and I couldn't blame him. I couldn't help wondering how many more were in the same position, rotting in jail because they wouldn't confess. If it was a nonce, the story would have been much different: the system always looks after those slags.

As the weeks passed, Lindsay was well into his education, while I was busy writing and keeping watch over our brews. Lindsay would still play his guitar, and some nights we would have a singsong while having a drink with a few friends.

Somehow I began to feel down. I didn't know why, it just crept up on me. Some of the lads told me it was normal and could creep up on a prisoner at any stage of their sentence, so I decided to see the doctor. That's what he was there for. The doctor was Welsh and well into his rugby but as it wasn't my sport I told him so, and said that my sport was boxing. He seemed to take offence at me not showing an interest in rugby, and from that time on I didn't like the Welsh bastard.

He sent me to see the psychologists, who were nice enough women but they fired daft questions at me, such as whether I knew Ronnie Kray.

'Of course I know him,' I answered.

Then they asked whether the TV talked to me. A few days previously I'd had a visit from Bruce Kennedy of HTV, and he had advised me not to talk to them. So, in answering their question, I said that the producer of HTV had told me not to talk to them. Not realising that what I had said could compromise me in any way, I was told I was going to be packed off to a top security hospital for the criminally insane in Liverpool. There were only three top security hospitals in the country: Broadmoor, which Ronnie was in; Rampton; and Ashworth in Liverpool, where they wanted to send me.

I told the SO in the office that the only way I would be taken to Ashworth was in a body-bag, and went back to my cell in one hell of a mood. The locks were running, so I shut my door and was just about to eat a pie when my door clicked again and I saw the SO open the door and step back. He told me I could either have it the easy way or the hard way, then he stepped back out of the door. All along the corridor and down the stairs were muftis with their shields, sticks and helmets.

I looked at the SO, smiled and said, 'I think I'll have the easy way.'

I wasn't allowed to pack anything, and was taken straight to the hospital unit, where I was put in a cell in preparation for my trip to Liverpool's nuthouse.

18

CRIMINALLY INSANE

I wasn't long in the cell at the hospital block and was soon leaving the gates of Long Lartin on my way to Winston Green prison for an overnight stay. I sat in silence while the screws chatted amongst themselves; I was trying to come to terms with being nutted off to a top security nuthouse in Liverpool.

When we arrived at Winston Green, I was handed over to the hospital screws and told to put on a pair of canvas shorts, which I named the sparkly shorts. With just a mattress on the floor and a thick, rough canvas blanket in the cell, I realised that by telling the screws at Long Lartin they could take me in a body-bag, I had said the wrong thing and had brought on the shitty conditions that I was faced with. The only thing I could do was sleep and hope the conditions at Ashworth would be a little better.

The morning soon came and I was given my clothes back in preparation for the journey to Liverpool. Long Lartin screws were to take me, and had brought all my gear from my cell. We were soon on our way, and I knew that once I was caught up in the system of nuthouses, it was very unlikely I would get back out again.

We arrived at Ashworth in the early afternoon and the screws were waiting at the door. I'd had images of the old buildings at Broadmoor, but was surprised at how modern the place was, with the same style walls, separate buildings and well-kept grounds as Long Lartin.

The Ashworth screws were soon demanding that Long Lartin

screws take off my cuffs, which had been biting into my wrists. There were more surprises when I was taken into the building: I could see a full-size snooker table with a number of screws and prisoners cleaning the cloth. I was told that someone had been hit around the head with a snooker cue, smashing out his eye, so the cloth wasn't being cleaned to keep the table at its best, they were cleaning off some chap's eye.

I was taken into a room, told to strip off and given a medical there and then by a number of doctors, some of them female, but my dignity was way down the ladder. I had other things on my mind.

I was then taken into the office where they went through my gear a piece at a time, and was told that at Ashworth they were not screws but nurses. But even though they had keys on leather straps and not chains, they were still my keepers, regardless of what they preferred to be called.

I was then shown around, and saw that the snooker room was central to all rooms. I was shown the library, which was used for visits, the TV room – in which about a dozen blokes sat – then the eating area.

Walking back through the corridor, I was shown two corridors which diverged off in a V shape. Between them was the bath and shower room.

I was shown my room, which had all the modernism of any hospital, and behind a sliding door was a toilet and hand basin. After my tour of the building, I was asked if I needed anything, so I said I needed tobacco. To my surprise, they said they would get me toothpaste, shampoo and other toiletries as well.

After the rules were explained to me, one in particular being that I couldn't go to my room until the end of the day at eight o'clock, I went into the TV room. I was allowed to mix with the other prisoners, or patients, as they called them. They were friendly enough, but I could sense some weren't the full ten shillings. I began chatting with a bloke in his fifties: a Londoner by the name of Danny. He advised me on the ones I should give a wide berth.

As the day wore on I was still in the habit of calling the nurses Guv, as most of them were men, but they asked me to call them by their first names, just as they called me by my Christian name.

The day was at an end and we asked to go to our rooms to be banged up for the night, and as the door shut behind me I saw a letter on the table. On opening it, I realised I was held under a section. 'Oh God, that's me fucked,' I thought, and I knew I had to get out of the place and back to jail as soon as possible.

When the door opened, I knew, under Ashworth rules, that I had to get up and be out of my room within half an hour, so I made my way to the TV room with the others. Some of the lads told me we were going to the library and shops.

After breakfast we were on our way to the shops, and as we walked out of our complex, it was like walking down the road of a holiday village. The shops were like sort of in-shops, with a barbers, library and even a cafe area. I saw signs giving directions to the swimming pool and gym, so I asked one of the screws to give me a tour, which he kindly did. It was like a leisure complex. They even had their own radio station. That wasn't it all: the screw told me they had a big cinema, which we visited every Sunday to socialise with the other inmates.

I bought what I needed from the shop, and the library allowed me a number of books and videos. They even had a selection of music tapes, but we weren't allowed those as we were on induction. I thought, 'I could get used to this,' as I found that back at our complex the day was more or less our own.

I was called to the office to meet my psychiatrist, a little Asian woman who appeared very understanding about the way that I had been sent there. I then met my psychologist; she too was understanding. Towards the end of the day I met my probation officer who was also very nice. I knew I had to be on my best behaviour. I had been told that I was being assessed for eight weeks, but I also had to be on my guard with some of the nutters, and I found that I was exhausted by the end of the evening.

I began to get into the routine of the place and found they still had the same system as prison, with the metal razorblades in a slot with the cell numbers, so I decided not to shave. One screw asked me if I was growing a beard, so I gave him the same explanation I had given five years previously about blades going in the wrong slot and the risk of infection. I was then allowed the disposable razors, but they were kept in the office in a box.

The psychiatrist called me to a room, as paperwork had been sent up from the psychologists at Long Lartin. As I looked at it on her desk, I could see it was the full report on why I had been sent to Ashworth.

She asked me whether the TV still talked to me, so I asked her to explain in what context. She asked whether I heard voices on the TV telling me to do things, but I could only smile, which I found was the wrong thing to do when sitting in front of a shrink. She asked me why I was smiling, so I explained what I had told them at Long Lartin, that I actually had been talking to a TV producer on a visit, and that he had run a programme on our case. She looked rather confused and asked if she could view the programme.

I told her she was more than welcome, and that she could also telephone Bruce Kennedy at HTV Wales to validate my story. She then went on to ask whether I was also in talks with Ronnie Kray and what I had to say about that. Just then, a nurse came to the door asking me to sign a cheque which had been sent in by Ronnie, and the look of shock and horror on the psychiatrist's face was priceless. I could only smile, and I silently thanked Ronnie for his precise timing.

I was asked to leave the office and watched as the senior nurses and my psychologist started a debate with the psychiatrist. They realised that the staff at Long Lartin had made a terrible mistake in having me sent there. After the others had left, I was called back in, with the psychiatrist telling me she had telephoned Broadmoor and they had confirmed that I knew Ronnie and had visited him on many occasions, and that my correspondence was validated.

However, covering themselves, I still had to go through assessments for eight weeks, just in case I was a clever nutter. The bottom line was, Long Lartin had dropped a bollock.

I pointed out that, due to the mistake at Long Lartin and psychologists not verifying my story, I should be sent back there with my brother as the law states that brothers should be kept together to make family visits easier. The psychiatrist agreed with me, but asked me to go through their procedure to ensure they did their jobs properly, and they promised they would help me get back to Long Lartin.

I passed the time by analysing some of the patients, or nutters, as we referred to ourselves. One day, we were all sitting in the TV room, when one lad went right off on one, smashing up chairs and tables. Everyone ran out, including the nurses, but I just sat there as chairs and tables were being smashed around me. Then, when the bloke took a breather, I told him that if anything hit me I would batter the fuck out of him. The nurses were telling me to make a run for it, but I just sat there watching TV.

The bloke was very powerful, so bending and smashing up chairs and tables was no problem for him. Then he went into the snooker room and, grabbing hold of the pocket on the corner of the table, ripped it off with such ease that the whole table lifted. He eventually calmed down and was taken to the cooling-down cell, and was no doubt given a few injections to bring him back down to earth.

An hour our two later, he was brought into the room where we ate our meals, and we could see that he was well out of it as he sat at a table, dribbling away.

Some of the lads had blagged their way into hospitals after finding the regime tough in the prison system. But they didn't realise that after eight weeks they could be held under a permanent section, which stayed with them for most of their lives.

I got friendly with a chap named Lee, who was diagnosed as a psychopath, and he was more than happy for me to probe into his mind. As he wasn't a bloke of great strength, his mind was always busy plotting ways to hurt someone, and it seemed that the worse they were hurt the bigger the buzz he got. We found out there were a number of nonces in amongst us, and we decided to play them off against each other, with the result of them bashing out each other's teeth and kicking the shit out of each other, which seemed to give Lee great excitement.

Every weekend we were allowed to watch a film and socialise with other patients, and one day, as our group was entering, another one was leaving. We noticed Ian Brady was with those leaving, and Lee looked at me and said we could have some fun with him.

Inside was the same layout as any workmen's club, with chairs and tables and, as in Broadmoor, we were allowed to drink alcohol-free lager. It didn't seem so long before that I was drinking it with Ron; now here I was, nutted off myself, the same side of the fence, drinking on a social night out with other nutcases. The films were played on a big screen just like a cinema, and as we were on induction, we were allowed to mix with other complexes, or wards, as they called them. Our ward was called Tennyson ward: they were named after poets.

In the evenings, most of the lads played football, but with boxing being my sport I trained on the bags which were provided in the gym, and worked out on the weights. After a good workout, we were allowed into the swimming pool, which was a far cry from prison. It was more like freedom.

I knew I was constantly being assessed, so I had to be careful about what I said, just in case it was taken the wrong way. I was nearing my assessment date and hoping to get back to Long Lartin. I was constantly being called into rooms to chat with my psychiatrist and psychologist, as were the other patients, and I was reassured that I had their full support to go back to prison, and that a dreadful mistake had been made.

Of course, like any person, free or locked up, the down days would creep up and, not being able to hide it from the nurses and the team designated to watch over me, I was promptly called to the office and asked what was troubling me. Trying to keep sane in a nuthouse was enough to bring anyone to their knees, let alone being in their system on other people's bullshit.

The hospital, along with Long Lartin prison, had arranged for

Lindsay and me to have contact on the office telephone, and Lindsay told me that he had been moved to D wing after I had been shipped out. He also had the good news that the police investigation was under way: they had been to see him and were due to come and see me. I thought, 'That's all I need. Explaining to investigating coppers my complaints against a bunch of nutters in the Gwent police force.' Lindsay went on to tell me that it was South Wales police that were investigating Gwent police. That really made my fucking day.

I was sitting in the library, having a bit peace and quiet, when I spotted a way to get over the wall. What was strange was that it was so easy. Of course, I would have to cut through the bars, and with no blades I knew I had no chance, but even though Ashworth had the same sort of wall as Long Lartin, they didn't have the high fence with razor wire and dogs patrolling inside it.

Ronnie sent a letter asking me to try and get down with him, but I thought, 'Bollocks to that.' Broadmoor was even more depressing and I wasn't planning on becoming a permanent resident of British nuthouses. Reg also sent a letter asking me to get down with him at Blundeston prison, Suffolk.

I soon got into a routine, and time began to move at a steady pace. The coppers came up from South Wales and, of course, Nan Mousley had to be with me as she did with Lindsay on his interview.

There wasn't a lot I could tell as far as the interview was concerned. If the investigation was fair and just, they would see the discrepancies. However, what pissed me off, which I explained to them, was how the local newspaper got our personal photos.

My psychiatrist called me to the office and said that Long Lartin wouldn't take me back, and asked whether there was another jail I would like to go to. It seems that the doctor wouldn't allow me back directly from a top security mental hospital.

That was all I needed. I was getting really pissed off, so I asked to see the psychologist, who offered me a relaxation tape, but I explained that, as I was on induction, I didn't have a tape machine. The solution was that I could have my system, with headphones provided by them, as long as I kept it quiet. Although I knew from experience that nothing can be kept from a con, I still agreed to having the system. By the end of the week, everyone on our ward was swinging away to music in their cells.

We weren't allowed in our cells during the day, so I requested that we be allowed to lie down over the dinner period, rather than sleep in the TV room or the library, especially as the library was used for visits. After lengthy negotiations with senior nurses, my request was granted for everyone. I was beginning to feel like Jack Nicholson in *One Flew Over the Cuckoo's Nest.*

The date for my review soon came and was held in the library. It consisted of my psychiatrist, psychologist, senior nurse, hospital probation officer and several others who seemed to have invited themselves. I knew that if this went wrong, I would be lost in the system for years. Halfway through the review, they called me in and fired questions at me from all angles. If I really was a nutter, there would have been no escape for me.

After a wait which seemed an age, the whole panel agreed that I wasn't a fruitcake, which gave me a sense of relief. It was now just a case of getting back to Long Lartin. I had the best assessment in the country, proving I was not mentally ill, so I sent a message back to Long Lartin saying that I was going to sue the psychologists for nutting me off and not knowing their jobs.

But, of course, I told them that if I was allowed back to Long Lartin, I wouldn't take the matter any further, and after a lot of wrangling between Ashworth and prison, I was allowed back to Long Lartin after ten weeks of being assessed.

I was soon on the phone to Lindsay, telling him to sort a cell out for me on the same wing. He had been moved to the same wing as Roger and, pleased with the news that I would soon be on my way, Lindsay told me that a big party would be waiting for me when I arrived. There I was again, eager to get back to jail.

It was decided that Ashworth nurses should take me back, not Long Lartin screws come to pick me up. I didn't care if the Queen was coming to get me, I wanted out of the nuthouse. I was soon on my way, and knew Lindsay would have the hooch chilling for when I got there.

After I had been dropped off by the nurses and handed over to Long Lartin screws, I got onto the wing where Lindsay was waiting with Roger. It was good to see them again, and Lindsay took me to my cell, which he had arranged opposite his cell on landing 3. We could only have a brief chat, as it was time for the lunchtime bang-up, but the hour soon passed and I was in his cell with a nice cold bottle of hootch.

While I'd been away, Lindsay had got himself a little budgie and, as Roger was in charge of the aviary, Lindsay suggested I have a bird as they were good therapy. But I'd had enough therapy at Ashworth to last me a lifetime.

Roger dropped in but didn't stay long, knowing Lindsay and I had a lot to catch up on. Lindsay introduced to me to a number of lads he had met since being on D wing. One of them was Gary, in whose cell the party was to be held in.

The party was soon under way and I was introduced to many more people, including a chap called Wozy or The Woz. He was a big bloke with the red beard of a Viking. We were soon drinking, laughing and eating food which had been arranged for the party, and with music blasting and all of us singing, the night ended well. I was taken back to my cell legless through drink.

Stan, who Lindsay and I knew from F wing, had moved over to B wing and invited us over for a meal and a drink to celebrate my return. We were allowed onto other wings, but only the ground floor, and had to leave at eight o'clock to return to our own wing. Stan had set up a table covered with a white sheet. A music system was playing on the table, and along with Stan's friend we sat down to a meal, which they arranged for another friend to serve. Stan had got the bug for brewing hooch and had a couple of bottles chilled ready. It was as though I was in a restaurant on the outside.

The next day, Lindsay introduced me to a few lads who were musicians. Dave played guitar with Lindsay, and Malcolm was their singer. I was doubled up laughing when Malcolm gave me an example of his singing abilities, as when he burst into song he sang into a hairbrush.

With Lindsay still on his course, his computer graphics became quite impressive, and it was at the classes that Lindsay and Dave decided to form a band, through the music department. I was a drummer in my early days, so they asked me to play drums for them, but I declined their offer, as I was busy preparing for our appeal, should it come. The police investigation was still ongoing and it had been indicated to us, through our solicitors and family, that South Wales police were doing a thorough job.

A new rule, which had been brought in while I was away, was taking random piss tests, to check if anyone was smoking weed. It was the most stupid thing they could have done in a top security prison. Most of the lads knew that by smoking weed it was in their system for 28 days so, rather than lose days off their release date, most began changing over to smack, which was only in the system for three days. I could see that the new ruling would be a recipe for disaster at a future date.

We would often visit Roger for a drink and a chat, and he had a cockatiel which he had named Magic. It seemed birds were the 'in thing' on D wing, so I asked for a budgerigar when Roger had one available.

Roger was brewing quite a large amount of hooch and selling it on to different wings, so having a drink at any time was no problem. Some afternoons I would have a drink with The Woz and when Lindsay came back from his class he would find us both legless and, more often than not, pick up my tea from the hotplate.

Lindsay and I decided to get brewing ourselves, and with Gary working in the kitchen getting the fresh yeast wasn't a problem.

We moved to two cells further down the landing where we were opposite each other and had the corridor window, beneath which were two chairs. We had two more chairs outside our cells, which proved useful to our group as our drinking could be done at the end of the corridor rather than in our cells, which gave us more room, and we could see what was going on down the corridor.

After reading books from the library, we took a keen interest in how to build a still, burning off the hooch to make pure alcohol. The Woz was on a welding course, so we decided to build a still on a small scale, to see how it worked, and to see if pure alcohol could be made. With two plastic buckets top-to-top and rammed together, Roger had made up an element out of metal mop pieces and, with pipes coming off the main bucket, running to the different stages of distilling, we decided to have a test-run in my cell.

After switching on the element, which was wired up to the light, it was a case of waiting to see if the process would work. After a few minutes, the table on which the bucket sat began to shake. One of the lads asked who was shaking the table, but we all had a dumb look on our faces and headed for the door, fighting to get out. The bucket exploded, with hot hooch saturating my cell. Luckily, none of us suffered any injuries, and we set about making a different design.

We soon had the still mastered and the pure alcohol was like gold dust. When we mixed it with Coca Cola, it proved to be very popular with most of the lads, but was too pricey to sell on the wings, although there were a few who could afford it.

The cash wages had stopped, and wages were paid by way of a statement each week. The currency soon became tobacco, phone cards and weed. But very soon the hooch was climbing the ladder as currency. The screws were constantly trying to find the stuff, and we allowed ourselves to lose 40 per cent of it. But usually what the screws found and tipped away was the decoy hooch and wasn't our top-of-the-range drinking material.

When we sent bottles for sale to other wings, we would send lads with pillowcases containing bottles of water, so that when they were pulled by security screws, the lads with bottles of hooch would sneak past. The game of cat and mouse went on for most of the day, and in the evenings we found the screws left us alone: banging up at nine o'clock was most important to them.

Lindsay had acquired an electric guitar and amp, and was still having jamming sessions with Dave and Malcolm. He also jammed with Colin Richards on the ground floor. Colin was in a wheelchair, after being shot by some coppers, but it didn't interfere with his guitar-playing ability. Like Lindsay he was a very good player and they turned out some cracking sounds. With makeshift microphones and by wiring the amps, we would have little shows put on, with us all drinking and ending the night with a singalong.

Christmas was soon on us again and, with Lindsay and me in the two end cells, we built a sort of Santa's grotto. It made it more Christmassy but it also disguised hiding places for hooch, brewed in preparation for parties.

A screw came to Lindsay and me, telling us to tune into the Welsh radio. We found the channel and heard that the police investigation on our case was well under way, with questions being raised about the honesty of four police officers. This was good news from our point of view, as it gave us an indication that the investigation was proving to be fair.

Of course, an appeal date was far from my thoughts. Even though I had been preparing for the appeal, there wasn't a lot I could do at that point.

Christmas passed – not that I could remember much of it, due to abuse of hooch – and a big party was arranged for New Year's Eve, but with the memories of the previous year still fresh in my mind, I was a bit hesitant. After discussions about how the party was to be conducted, I was voted party-stopper, ensuring that everyone went behind their doors at nine o'clock.

We also arranged to set up all the amps for the guitars, and Malcolm agreed to sing his set, which he had practiced. Everyone on the wing was invited but with a clause: everyone had to turn up dressed in a toga. This, of course, was easy to do. All we had to do was wrap a sheet around ourselves. But, as the day wore on, it was also decided that no one was allowed to wear clothes underneath: only prison-issue pants or shorts, and that was it.

Throughout the day, preparations were under way: the hooch had to be chilled; meals prepared; and soundchecks made. Anyone would have thought we were at the Ritz. Even the blue prison-issue underwear was used to dim the lights on the corridor.

Other landings arranged their own parties, but everyone knew that landing 3's was the business. We decided to have the party down Pete and Paul's end – two lads we got on very well with through business deals. Also at their end were a few Geordies and Johnny. When they'd been at our parties in the past they were a good laugh.

Everything was in place: tea time bang-up came, and when the doors were opened, the party was to begin. As the clicks started running for the doors to open, we all popped our heads out first to see if the toga idea was a serious one. Of course it was serious, and as each of us emerged from our cells, we saw that some had cut their sheets down in the Gladiator theme, while others were more reserved. When Roger came walking around the corner, we saw that he had gone the full hog and looked like Caesar, with robes wrapped around his arms.

The party was on, with us all laughing at each other, drinks flowing, Lindsay and the band playing, and Malcolm singing as though he was at the London Palladium. Screws who came off other landings to see everyone in their togas showed a bit of concern, wondering if the lads would bang up, but, being fair to them, they had every right to stop the party as the place smelled strongly of booze and weed. An incident occurred when one lad was playing the bowls and then went into the office telling them it was the best party of his life and that he wanted it to go on. He threatened the screws so he was taken down the block to sober up.

Apart from that the night went well, with us all waking in the New Year with hangovers and bumping headaches.

With Christmas and New Year out of the way, our solicitor told us that Chamberlain had been arrested with a friend for doing an armed robbery around the Bristol area, and I wasn't surprised when she said that Chief Inspector Johnson had given him an alibi. But what Johnson didn't realise was that Chamberlain had been followed down to Wales by the police from the Bristol area after he'd done the robbery. Chamberlain was remanded at Belmarsh, a London prison, for his own protection, and was later sentenced with an accomplice to five years for armed robbery.

One evening, we were having a party and celebrating after the Welsh rugby game, when one of the screws told us that the jail had been locked down due to someone being killed on another wing. Lindsay and I didn't give the matter much thought, until the screw asked us to go to the ground floor with him. We were well into the party, so told him where to go, but realised it was something serious when he stayed there with a grim look on his face.

He took us to one side and told us that Dai Mathews had been killed and that his mate Paul was in a terrible state and needed to talk to us. We went to Paul straight away and, as gently as I could, I asked him who had done it, knowing that Lindsay and I would retaliate. He mentioned the bloke's name but said that it had been an accident. We then made arrangements for Paul to move onto our wing so that we could keep and eye on him.

We arranged to have a meeting with Mr Topolski and Nan Mousley. For some unknown reason, Mr Jimmy Beck was taken off as my representative, which pissed me right off. I had nothing against Mr Topolski, but as more evidence began to emerge in our favour, I felt that taking Mr Beck off the case weakened our defence. The good news was that, even though Michael Mansfield couldn't represent us at our appeal, our shared QC (Queens Counsel) was to be Mr Paddy O'Connor, a perjury specialist from the same chambers as Michael Mansfield.

A preliminary hearing was set up at the Court of Appeal in London in front of three judges. The centre judge was Judge Brown and a side judge was Judge Auld. At the hearing they agreed that all four police officers should be called to the appeal to be cross-examined, and it was stressed that it should be as soon as possible, as he felt we had been in jail long enough.

Long Lartin had been shutting down a wing at a time for gutting and refurbishment, to bring it up to date. A number of other wings had gone through the process, and D wing was to be next, moving over to F wing. Everyone on the wing was quite looking forward to it, as D wing was the dirtiest wing in the jail.

Each person had to move to the same cell on the other landing. When Lindsay and I were on F wing, we knew our seating area in the corridor had a much better view than D wing, which was more or less set at the back of the jail.

The move took all day, with everything new from furniture in the cells to new chairs in the TV rooms and electricity in the cells. But what everyone appreciated more than anything was the full-length doors on the toilet cubicles.

Yet again, parties were arranged for the evening, and with our new view we could see all the comings and goings, from the visiting area to new lads coming in. After a busy day, the evening was at an end so we finished off our drinking in our cells after the nine o'clock bang-up.

Everyone could see the change when new lads were brought in, as most of them were on heroin, and fights seemed to break out more frequently. I would often be called to the recess and asked to stitch up some of the lads who had been striped (slashed with a knife or makeshift blade). Some of the lads would end up in debt for smack, and they knew that if the screws found out they had been slashed, they would be taken to the hospital and sent to the block for their own protection.

The method used in slashing was by melting three razorblades into the head of a toothbrush, which made it virtually impossible for me to repair a wound. I usually had to suggest that they went to the hospital.

It was through this change with smack that the place began to gradually change. It wasn't unusual to see someone have a hammer smashed through their head for a debt as small as £10. The drug testing for weed was not only changing Long Lartin, it was changing the whole of the prison system, and certainly not for the better.

When everything was being renewed, all the cells were fitted with new doors. The old cell doors could only open into the cell, which meant that when some of the lads had barricaded themselves in, the screws could only jack the doors open. But the new doors could be opened either way. The old spyholes in the doors were a one inch by twelve inch piece of strengthened glass fitted approximately four feet from the floor, in the middle of the door. The new versions of the spyholes were made of two inch by twelve inch strengthened glass, again four feet from floor level. Both versions had a metal flap covering the glass.

When we were on D wing, most of us had curtains hanging over the door. This was to give a little dignity when using the bucket, as there were women officers on the landings. Of course, on the new wing, some of us still put up the curtain, and most of the screws would just shout though, checking that the person was still in their cell. But security screws checked each one from the outside, just in case anyone was digging through their cell.

The new screws saw the curtains as breaking the rules, and asked on many occasions for them to be taken down, but it was to no avail, and a number of us were nicked by one particular new screw and sent down the block on adjudication, where it was pointed out to us that the curtains had to be removed. The screw felt it was a victory, and assumed he was now disliked, showing his dislike of everyone on his wing. One day, he began taking the piss out of Lindsay and me and a few others, and our Welsh accents, and spoke to us trying to sound like us. We all found it very amusing at first, but, because we didn't retaliate, the power soon went to his head.

On going down to the hotplate one day to get my meal, he was serving and, trying to put on a Welsh accent, asked me what I wanted.

I answered him in Welsh and he didn't have a clue what I had said. Lindsay was right behind me and the screw, looking embarrassed, as everyone was laughing, asked Lindsay what I had said to him, to which Lindsay replied, 'You are nothing but a stupid English pig, and if you don't know the language, don't take the piss.' The whole place erupted with laughter.

The next day he'd moved on, taking the piss out of some other person, but they weren't so polite and threw a whole container of spaghetti over him. As I walked past, I told him that he was supposed to eat it, not wear it. The next day he was wearing beans, then peas. He had got the message; and the curtains went back up.

Lindsay had the band up and running but sometimes Steve, who became their drummer, wasn't available and I would fill in for him. They were doing so well that they were invited to put on a show in front of the church people. Of course, we saw it as a night out, and arranged to smuggle in the booze a few days before the event.

A selected number of prisoners were invited to watch the show with the church people and we all took our seats, with our bottles hidden under the chairs. Two little old biddies became curious about what we were drinking, so the Woz asked if they would like a tot of prison hooch. By the end of the night they liked our hooch so much that they had to be helped from there, pissed out of their heads and legless. The prison band put on a good show and one of the screws videoed it and allowed the lads to have copies.

The smack was rapidly sweeping the prison, and the smackheads were stealing from cells, so our doors had to be locked at all times. When they were on the smack, they were no problem at all. The problems started when they needed their next fix. Blokes were getting bashed all over the place, and we became so used to it, we hardly ever took any notice.

One chap owed a debt, and while he was in the TV room, two blokes began beating hell out of him with a metal bar. When he asked for a break, they began breaking his arms. We were all watching TV, but turned our chairs around to get a better look. He was swiftly dragged outside for a further hiding so, shunting our chairs back around, we carried on watching the television. A screw came in five minutes later and asked whether anyone had seen anything, but we all shook our heads and off he went. Even when we were getting our canteen, someone would be smashed around the head with a jam jar in a sock. It seemed a full jam jar in a sock was the preferred weapon of the month.

The biggest mistake that the psychology department made was

when they wanted armed robbers to help them do a survey, based on their thoughts about their crimes. Many nonces told other prisoners that they were in for armed robbery. That way, they could be filtered in with the normal prison population. But the psychologists came around and handed out letters to those who really were in for armed robbery, and left out the nonces. The mistake left them trying to explain why they didn't have a letter. It didn't take long for some of the lads to put two and two together and nonces were getting stabbed up and beaten to a pulp.

One nonce, under the guise of an armed robber, was killed on another wing. It was soon broadcast by the local radio that the nonce had done some terrible things to children, and on hearing of his death, the whole prison could be heard cheering at true justice for the dirty, stinking slag.

It wasn't unusual to see someone being taken away in a body-bag after topping himself, we could have been chatting with them the night before, and then they would pass you on the stairs in a body-bag.

When that door shuts at night, there is no telling what goes through a man's mind, even to the point of, 'Enough is enough'. I could well understand why people turned to drugs, and I was thankful I had the good old prison hooch to help ease lonely nights. I would have my music blasting away and, singing like a good 'un, I never felt I was in jail. I was well happy, putting on Elvis and singing to that.

Poor Tony below me must have been really pissed off, and all the lads invested in headphones so I could listen to my music without disturbing them. Then all that could be heard was me singing away, without any music.

Our hooch was becoming renowned throughout the jail, with Roger's and ours selling well. New lads arriving in the jail would be sent to us, asking to buy a two-litre bottle. We had three strengths: the strong one for the regular drinkers; the next one for weekly drinkers; and the third for the weekend drinkers, which wasn't as strong as what we drank, but enough to make them relaxed and have a good night's sleep. One lad came up once asking for a bottle and, by mistake, he was given the strong drinkers' hooch. Off he went, happy as a sandboy, but we heard that halfway though his bottle he was so pissed that he wanted to stab all the screws and was taken off to the block.

With Lindsay having access to computers and printers, he designed labels for our bottles of hooch, indicating three different strengths: S for strong; M for medium; and W. One of the lads asked if the W stood for weak, but we replied, 'W is for "Wanker's drink"'.

Lindsay went on to design tote tickets, which we ran every week. We also had, in preparation, our own money, which we planned to use as currency.

Lindsay and I had a problem when it came to hiding excess containers of hooch, as we knew the screws were doing spins (cell searches).

While I was looking out of my cell window and wondering how to hide the hooch, I noticed that wasps were attracted to a jar of jam on the windowsill, which stopped them coming into the cell. I was still watching them when Don dropped in to see me and I put a smear of jam on his finger. He watched as the wasps took the jam and made no attempt to sting him, and he was so fascinated that he began giving them names.

Lindsay and I looked at each other as the same thought occurred to both of us. We told Don, who knew about the problem with the hooch, to put a few gallons of the booze, along with a cannabis plant which needed hiding, in his cell. We then spread jam at various points around his cell and what seemed like thousands of wasps settled on the jam. Don was like a pig in swill with his newfound friends.

As we expected, the screws were soon on our spur, spinning for contraband, and Don's cell was to be turned over next. I lifted his door flap, but couldn't see him for wasps. Then, when his head emerged, I couldn't see his face because wasps were crawling all over it. It was a hell of a sight.

Two screws opened his door to tell him he was about to be spun, but jumped back as hundreds of wasps flew through the open door. They both shouted, 'Bollocks to that!' and gave his cell a miss.

Don had saved the day, and for many days after he thought of the wasps as his friends.

Everything was running smoothly, considering we were living in a war zone.

It was summer and the football season was well under way, but as football wasn't our sport, Lindsay and I never bothered to follow the games on TV. A big game was to be played one evening, so the screws allowed the doors to stay open for the extra hour, which meant we didn't need to be banged up until ten o'clock that night. Of course, the game went into extra time, so Roger went on a mission, asking everyone not to bang-up until the game was over.

Because so many had stayed out, the screws locked it all off, no doubt ready to bring in the muftis. When it was going on for 11.30pm, everyone went peacefully into their cells, but next morning the doors didn't click open for breakfast. The screws had arranged to lock down

F wing, and began shipping out at random those who they thought were the instigators of the night before. Roger was the first to go.

Lindsay decided to have a drink. All the hooch was in his cell as we had drunk all that was in my cell during the night, so I had fuck all to drink. It wasn't long before Lindsay was taken down to the office, pissed out of his head, and promptly shipped out to another jail. I watched from my window as they took The Woz away too, and many more who we had become close to during our time on D wing and F wing.

19

OUR LADY OF LONDON – THE SCALES OF JUSTICE

The cell doors opened around tea time and I found they had shipped out almost thirty from our wing. It was like a ghost town and they had even emptied Lindsay's cell. Gary was the only one remaining out of our group, so we got a couple of bottles of hooch and had a drink. I was left with Roger's bird, Magic, and Lindsay's budgie.

I found out that they had taken Lindsay to Lincoln prison; Roger had gone to Whitemoor, Cambridge; and The Woz had gone to Swaleside, Isle of Sheppy.

I walked up the landing and saw Fahad, a Palestinian I had got to know, with all his friends – Iraqis and other Arab chaps. He told me he understood that with Lindsay being shipped out I was on my own, and if I wanted any help they were all there for me. It was a nice thought. I smiled and told him that I would get Lindsay back, just as I had got myself back from the nuthouse. They all smiled.

The next day they brought in other prisoners to fill the wing, and with most of them being smackheads, the screws knew they had made a terrible mistake by shipping out all the lads. Some screws admitted it was a bit harsh, and said that docking wages was enough, but it was too late. Each jail had sent their worse cases in the transfer, and the wing was like a powder keg waiting to explode.

Smack was openly being dealt amongst the smackheads and I felt it was a shame to see blokes who had been potheads all their lives changing over to smack just because weed was in their system longer. After a week or two, they were selling all their belongings in order to get more deals, and their cells were emptied of their music systems and even their curtains; anything of any value. They would get their smack on credit, which usually resulted in them getting slashed-up or battered to a pulp, then going down the block on the numbers.

As I didn't smoke weed, or take any other drug for that matter, I had a good little business going, by selling my piss. How they got it into the pots I don't know, because when we were taken away to do a piss test, a screw was watching at all times, but I wasn't complaining; a cup of my piss was worth more than half an ounce of tobacco.

As the drummer had been shipped out, I was asked to fill in, playing in the band. I accepted their offer and would play all sorts of music when I'd had my bottle of hooch. A chap called Charlie was very talented on the trumpet and composed his own songs, which he then arranged for all us musicians to play along with him.

I worked on getting Lindsay back to Long Lartin, and the indications were that it was going to be allowed. Of course, Lindsay had lost his cell, but the lad who'd moved in was quite happy to move out when Lindsay did eventually come back.

With Roger gone, I began brewing on a greater scale – filling in the gap that Roger had left with his customers – and employed three young lads in their early twenties to help me. In view of Don's help in the past, I employed him, with Cassey, Mick and Stretch – another lad given the name because of his size. I taught them how to get the bottles of hooch to different wings.

The kitchen screws began mixing the yeast in with the bread dough, trying to stop the brewing, but that didn't deter us. With a bucket of warm water and half a pound of sugar, when we were breaking up the dough, we found that the yeast separated by attacking the sugar, so it was business as usual.

Friday was always selling day, after sheet change and getting canteen. I would have, on average, 120 x two-litre bottles under my bed, and within half an hour they'd all be sold.

After spending eight to ten weeks in Lincoln, Lindsay was allowed to come back and, as he had done for me, a party was arranged in Gary's cell. Gary had taken his bed apart, thrown it out and named his cell 'Ye Olde Cider Bar', and with beer towels and beer mats sent in, it was as if we were in the small back room of a pub.

With hooch chilled, and meals ready for the evening, I met Lindsay down the corridor as he came onto the wing, and just like me when I came back, he was happy to be back at Long Lartin.

The party was soon under way and, with drinks flowing and food being brought to the cell, everyone was having a good time. One of the lads pulled me, asking what we were doing by having Jeremy Bamber at Lindsay's party. I didn't have a clue who he was, but it was explained to me that he had committed a terrible crime, shooting his whole family, including twin children.

I pulled Bamber and asked him about what I had been told, but he told me that he hadn't done it and that, like myself, he, too, was going through the appeal system. Who was I to play judge and jury? Bamber invited me to read his case papers, and although what I read was very sad, there were irregularities in his paperwork which could give him grounds for appeal, so I wasn't about to run around pointing a finger.

Summer was coming to an end, and so was the police investigation, after a long year. We knew that our appeal date wouldn't be very far off.

The jail, because of the smack, was like a madhouse, and we felt it was time to tool ourselves up, as people were being mugged just walking through the corridors, and fights were breaking out all over the place.

A bloke on another wing was killed, and the whole jail was locked down while different blokes were pulled in as suspects. Smack had got a grip on the jail, but our hooch trade seemed to pick up, with some of the smackheads buying bottles to help them through their cold turkey.

I arranged to have a computer sent in – which was allowed as long as it didn't have a modem – and began preparing my case. With the police investigation over, we were waiting for the paperwork of their findings about Gwent police. Nan Mousley had received it and was due up to go through the investigation with us.

She turned up at a visit with folder upon folder of paperwork. I thought she had brought them up for us to read in our cells, but she said that we had to read what we could on the visit. There were hundreds of pages and I knew we couldn't possibly read it all in the hour and a half visiting time. But she wasn't prepared to let us have even part of it, so I called a screw over and asked him to put my paperwork through reception.

Nan told me I couldn't have it, so I sacked her in front of the screw and off he went with my paperwork, ready for me to pick up after our visit. She explained that it was the only copy she had and, as she was still representing Lindsay, she asked what she was meant to do, but I told her not to worry as I would see that Lindsay had copies after I had read them. Obviously she wasn't very happy, but we had waited a year for the investigation, and a week or two for her to wait while we went through the paperwork, I felt, was not too much to ask.

When I got back to my cell, I could see why she didn't want us to have it. The South Wales police had done their jobs well and there were letters from Johnson telling judges to go easy on Chamberlain.

It became more clear after reading the investigation into Chamberlain's statement made at HMP Horfield, and gave me an idea of what Johnson was up to. I called Lindsay in and, showing him page 1508, we read, 'Chamberlain said he went back on a later date and was offered £2,000 to say it was the Fraynes' gun. This was the day he made a tape-recorded interview. He said that he accepted that offer, and was told by them that if he did not accept it, they would charge him with conspiracy. He said that he had, in fact, been charged with conspiracy but never went to court, the charges being dropped two weeks later.

We also read that, when being interviewed by South Wales police, Johnson and Phillips, along with Sutton and Price, were saying, 'No comment'. Yet in our interviews, when we were doing the same, they told us it was a sign of a guilty man. Superintendent Rees of the South Wales police had proved me wrong, and did a thorough investigation. Lindsay and I spent the next couple of weeks reading the paperwork and taking notes.

Lindsay picked up with the band again, so when the music department bought a new kit of drums ready for another concert, the music teacher, Alan, allowed me to have the old kit. I swiftly took the drums back to the wing. The screws on the desk asked what I was doing with them, so I explained that I was taking them to my cell, and as I struggled with them, the screws helped me. I pointed out that they let people have guitars, trumpets and organs, so why couldn't I have a kit of drums?

I must have been the only prisoner in Britain with a full drum kit in my cell. I had to smile when I saw Tony's face as he watched me taking the drums in. He must have thought, 'Oh, God, no.' But I played out on the landing and it wasn't long before we had a full band playing, and we were turning out some good tunes while jamming.

At around the same time, I also became friendly with an Asian lad by the name of Arge. He was a big, powerful bloke and well into his weights. He would often visit me for a drink, and with brown and red sauce bottles chilling in the window, we would sit and chat over a bottle.

Lindsay and I decided to have a mellow Christmas, having a drink instead of the wild parties of the past. We had our own currency up and running with the select few, and it worked quite well. And it excluded smack.

I could put up with people smoking their weed, but would have nothing to do with anyone involved in heroin. We could have earned a lot of money in that field of business, but out of principle I couldn't. It was a dirty drug which brought a lot of pain and heartache.

We knew the New Year had to be the year of our appeal. We had been in Long Lartin for our third Christmas, and hoped it was the last. If we won the appeal, we would be out. If not, we would apply to go to a Category C prison in the hope of having home leave.

One of the lads came out of his cell and told us that Ronnie Kray was dead, and tuning into the radio we found it was true. I couldn't believe it; I had received a letter from him just a few days before. It was announced that he'd had a heart attack.

Ronnie knew he wasn't going to get out of there, but our thoughts were with Reg, knowing he must be devastated at losing his brother. We sent a letter of condolence to him, and on the day of the funeral everyone jammed into the TV room. There we all watched the news in silence, as Ron was taken through the streets by horse-drawn carriage, with crowds and crowds of people seeing him off.

Ronnie would have been well happy with that.

We were visited by Nan Mousley and Mr Topolski, who introduced us to Mr Patrick O'Connor QC, or Paddy O'Connor, as he was known. I was still very unhappy that Jimmy Beck had been taken off the case, and felt I was losing interest in the case altogether. The prison authorities indicated that if we admitted our guilt, we would be seriously considered for parole, on the basis that we address and recognise our guilt, but I couldn't admit to something I hadn't done.

Lindsay and I had a date to get out, but the likes of Mickey O'Brien, and others, who had been sentenced to life and still fought to prove their innocence, had no chance.

Bruce Kennedy visited and said that he wanted to make a second programme as a follow-on from the first, and we agreed. They were going to pursue Edwards, as they had spoken to his girlfriend, who gave evidence in court.

Bruce Kennedy wanted me to do a telephone interview, in preparation for the programme, *Wales This Week*, but I knew a phone card wouldn't last very long, so I asked in the office if I could have a phone call from them. I was asked if it was a legal call, and I said it was, not mentioning it was from HTV. I was allowed the call with one of the screws standing by monitoring it and, with Bruce asking me questions for the programme, all the screw would have heard was me talking on legal matters to do with my case.

Cook also gave a detailed account of how he did the robbery with

Edwards and, being on home leave, he was filmed giving his account, as opposed to giving a telephone admission from prison.

HTV arranged to send the video of the programme to us but, of course, it had to be vetted before we could watch it. When we went to the office to pick it up, the screws were laughing and asked about the phone call which was on the programme. But I could only point out that they approved the call.

We had a date for our appeal and the case was expected to last for three days. Lindsay and I decided to hand over our hooch business to Don and his mates. We just didn't have the time; we had to prepare for our case.

We assumed we would be taken to a London jail for a week, giving us easier access to the appeal courts. But the authorities decided against it, as being in the centre of London there was the possibility of someone busting us out, due to the number of contacts we had in London, and the route to the High Courts would have given us a discernable, fixed travel pattern. So we had to travel from Long Lartin each day. In my opinion, hijacking the prison van would have been much easier.

The door clicked open in the early hours, allowing Lindsay and me to shower in preparation for our journey to London. We were soon on our way, and some of the screws travelling with us were from our wing. Heading into the City of London, there were camera crews in the road a mile before we got to the appeal courts, and armed coppers were at different points all the way to the courts. When we pulled up at the gates, we were surrounded by camera crews and flashes of photographers' cameras. Lindsay and I were cuffed together, on top of the cuffs we had for our journey. Being double-cuffed proved to be awkward when walking into the court. We could hear reporters shouting our names in the hope we would turn around for them to get a snap.

When we were taken into the cell area, we asked for a room to change into our suits, and were told to change in one of the barristers' conference rooms. After the change, we sat down waiting for someone to take us to the cells and watched the court screws running around shouting that they had lost us.

We soon realised what had happened: they thought Lindsay and I were barristers in conference, so we took advantage of the situation, and when one screw popped his head in, I asked him, 'Do you mind? We are in conference.' He went away, with panic on his face, apologising as he went. The other screws thought that, somehow, we had got out. The screws from Long Lartin must have gone straight to the cafe for refreshments after handing us over, so the court screws had to find them.

When they were brought back to the cell area, they could clearly see us in the barristers' room, but we just carried on talking. We were soon taken to a cell with the door slammed shut. Another five minutes and I was going to tell the court screw I had finished with my client, and ask him to let me back up to the courts. I am confident that, if I'd done that, I could have got out.

We had a brief meeting with Mr O'Connor and Mr Topolski, before being led through the maze of corridors, taking steps which were like those of an ancient castle. As I sat on an old wooden bench, I thought what a depressing place it was, with its dingy lighting and plain walls.

We were soon called to sit in the dock, where we were on the same level as the three judges, looking down onto the courtroom. With the three judges sitting, the centre judge was Judge Auld and beside him was Judge Dyson. It was Judge Auld who was at our preliminary hearing back last year and was the one who insisted the four police officers be called as soon as possible. Unfortunately, I can't remember the name of the third judge.

The appeal started with the usual legal talk, after which the first to be called in was Chief Inspector Johnson. After Harrington – by then a QC – had gone through all the bollocks, which I've no doubt he'd rehearsed for many months, he was then in the hands of Mr O'Connor, who wasted no time in steaming into him.

Johnson was a bag of nerves, but he had obviously been primed as his answers to all the questions were, 'I can't remember.' But Paddy O'Connor wasn't letting him off the hook so easily, and although Harrington tried to object to some of Mr O'Connor's questions, the judges told him to sit back down.

Johnson kept dropping his notes and he still babbled on when he bent down to pick them up. I didn't have a clue what he was on about and said to Lindsay, 'Do you think we should bring out the floppy shoes and funny noses?'

I had seen blokes in better condition in Ashworth. I despised the pathetic little man. He was embarrassing me by being Welsh.

The next person to be called was the one and only Inspector Phillips, and I remembered the words he used when talking to the local press at our trial: 'They couldn't organise a beaver league.' We had arranged everything, from our defence to TV programmes, right down to the appearance of the dribbling little idiot in court, who had to endure being questioned by one of the top QCs in the country. It wasn't about winning. We had beaten them hands down at our trial; Mr Topolski and Mr Beck had seen to that. No, the appeal was about how far was the system was prepared to go with their stupidity. After Harrington had finished with him, Phillips was questioned about the threats made to

Edwards' girlfriend when forcing an alibi out of her. He was fucked from the start. No doubt seeing Johnson leaving the witness box a shaking wreck had worried him. The questions were too overwhelming for him and the judges told Mr O'Connor to back off a little, but after giving Phillips a few minutes, he steamed into him again. The three judges looked at each other rather perplexed and the whole court went silent.

I was biting my lip to such a degree that it bled.

After the judges whispered amongst themselves, no doubt convinced by Phillips' outburst, Mr O'Connor was instructed to carry on, but I could see that Phillips was on the ropes and Mr O'Connor was in a prime position to finish him off with a flurry of questions. But he didn't – he kept to the same pace. As Johnson had done with Phillips, Phillips began by blaming Johnson, claiming he was acting on his instructions. They were grassing each other up as the shit hit the fan.

Next up was Price, and Mr O'Connor put him in such a position that he perjured again in court, an allegation he denied. But Mr O'Connor questioned him about his evidence. His response to Mr O'Connor was, 'I didn't mean it.' He knew what had been done to us was wrong. He knew he was fucked. I felt that if Mr O'Connor went up a gear with them, he would have slaughtered them with their bullshit. As Price left the witness box looking dishevelled, I leaned over to Lindsay and said, 'And another one bites the dust.'

Next up was Sutton, or the Jaw as we called him: little Mr Confident, daft as a brush! He was hitting problems from the start, a far cry from his arrogance when interviewing Lindsay and me in our early interviews. As he did during the trial, he blamed everyone but himself, insisting he was acting under orders from his superiors. He seemed to have decided that if he was sinking, he would take them all down with him. His superiors were thick and dangerous, whereas Sutton was just plain thick.

Even though it was me in the dock and my liberty depending on the appeal, they embarrassed themselves to such a degree that I felt a kind of pity for them. They were simply given too much rope and began hanging themselves, and everyone around them.

Sutton was boxed into a corner regarding the letter which the CPS had instructed him to write to them, and when Mr O'Connor asked who had told him to write the letter in the December after our arrest, he leaned over the witness box and pointed to Harrington, who swiftly hid behind his books as he sat on the bench.

Not surprisingly, an early lunch break was called, no doubt to try to put right what bigmouth Sutton had revealed.

After lunch, it was resolved when Sutton suddenly remembered it was another person who had told him, not Harrington.

My mind went back to our trial, when Harrington had told Mr Topolski that if we didn't have London barristers, he, Harrington, would have been representing one of us. Of course he would, and we would more than likely have been in jail doing the same sentence as Reggie and Ronnie!

The three judges ordered that the – now named – man be called into the appeal court the next day.

The two days at the appeal courts had taken their toll, and as soon as we got back to Long Lartin, I was glad when the door banged shut and I could have a glass or two of hooch to send me to sleep.

We were back up again at 5am for the journey back to London, and were told that our case was getting favourable reporting in the local press along with HTV Wales and BBC Wales.

As we headed towards London on the last day of the appeal, the weather was beautiful, and as we listened to the radio in the prison van, we heard that a heatwave was forecast. I thought that it would be a nice day to be released; yet somehow I knew that we would be travelling back to prison cuffed up.

Paddy O'Connor held a conference with us in the cells and showed his concern about the calling of the CPS man who Sutton had named instead of Harrington. Mr O'Connor decided that he would just ask him about the function of the CPS, and wait for his answer.

When the CPS man was called, Lindsay and I could see he was a scapegoat. He was looking more than nervous. Mr O'Connor began by asking him about how the CPS functions and how his job was conducted. Then, after about five minutes, Mr O'Connor asked him to explain the CPS job description and, just as we'd predicted, the CPS man replied that he couldn't remember.

The appeal was coming to an end, and Lindsay and I were satisfied that we had won, but when we were called up after lunch, the three judges announced that they were reserving their judgement. I knew from that point that we had lost our case.

Back to Long Lartin we went, and many of the lads waiting for appeals themselves met us on the ground floor. Mickey O'Brien, one of the Cardiff Three, and Michael Hickey of the Bridgewater case asked us how it had gone, but as we weren't jumping for joy and had been returned to jail, it showed it hadn't gone too well.

I didn't let it get to me too much. I was satisfied that Paddy O'Connor had shown the police for what they were. Sutton and Price had received commendations for our arrests, and no doubt the awards took pride of place on their walls at home.

We soon got back into the swing of things in prison. We set our sights on being moved to a Category C prison, in the hope of applying for home leave. We were made to wait almost six weeks before we went back up for judgement, and as we pulled up to the gates, we were met again by TV reporters and the blinding flashes of cameras. No time was wasted, and we were soon sitting in the main court where the Lord Chief Justice sat.

Lord Justice Auld then announced that we were knocked back. Lindsay got up and walked out as he was still explaining his judgement, and then Lord Auld went on to say that he couldn't understand how the appeal had got as far as it did.

I thought, 'You fucking hypocrite!' It was he, along with the other two judges, who had asked for a speedy appeal. As Auld looked at me, closing his dribble of a so-called speech, I got to my feet and said under my breath, 'I hope you and the other two so-called judges rot in hell.'

Lindsay had already been taken back to the cells. It was over; there was nowhere else to go as far an appeal was concerned.

Back in the cells, Paddy O'Connor expressed his sympathy and then advised us both never to return to Wales. I could see his point. We shook his hand and asked him to arrange a copy of the judges' Judgement and, yet again, I was saying I couldn't wait to get back to jail.

The same lads were waiting to hear about why we'd had a knock back, and when we told them, they lost all hope and must have drowned their sorrows the same as we did that night.

The next day, Lindsay and I both decided there was no point in moping over losing the appeal. We had under two years left, and both knew we had no chance of parole, but it was the home leave we wanted, and were going to apply as soon as we got to a C Cat jail.

Lindsay suggested we apply for the only Category C prison in South Wales, which was in Usk, but our application was promptly refused, as they weren't taking prisoners from top securities, let alone two brothers together.

The only other C Cat which was close to Wales was Channings Wood, but they wouldn't accept us both together either. So we tried a number of other C Cat prisons, only to be told we were outside their catchment areas, but being in the English prison system was outside our catchment area.

It seemed no Cat C prison would take us, which pissed us right off. It appeared the Welsh were getting a tough deal and we expected to stay at Long Lartin with no prospect of home leave. I then decided to apply for any jail in Northern Ireland, pointing out that we had family there, but we were then told at Governor level that we couldn't go there because we weren't Irish. I told them that I wasn't English either, yet I was in the English prison system.

Long Lartin had changed dramatically over the time we were there. Most of the potheads had changed to smack due to the piss tests and, due to the fights, most people were tooled up. We even had to attend the prison shop tooled up, just in case some smackhead was out on the rob.

We had a mop stick cut in half and drilled inside, and a round, pointed piece of metal pushed onto one piece which was the handle, with the other piece of the stick acting as the casing, which hid the pointed metal rod. With the two pieces put together, they were placed inside the bird cages, so that they looked like perches.

When it was taken out of the cage, it was easy to walk around with what appeared to be a piece of mop stick, until the one piece was slid off exposing the pointed piece of metal, which was known as a shiv, not known for cutting, more known for plunging!

It was those weapons that had to be carried when going to get our canteen as it was there that the bullies would rob other prisoners, or recover debts. If I saw anyone who I knew was tooled up get in close to Lindsay, I showed I had every intention of ramming the shiv straight into them if I felt they were a threat. Most of the bullies knew this and gave us a wide berth, knowing we weren't playing games.

Don and his mates decided to hand the hooch trade back to us, as the bullies were taking advantage of them. A number of people owed for quite a few bottles and when they found out that Lindsay and I had taken it back over, most of them promptly paid for what they owed. There were a few exceptions, but they obviously didn't know us very well.

One bully, who had been sent from Dartmoor Prison because he raped another prisoner there, owed for a number of bottles and ended up having a nasty accident in the shower room, and his injuries were so severe that the side of his head caved in and had to be rebuilt. When he walked into the office, he was in such a state that the SO thought he'd been in a car accident and whipped him off to an outside hospital. A few others, through clumsiness, walked into doors, resulting in quite a few black eyes and thick lips.

The bloke who had to have his face rebuilt, put up mine and Lindsay's names, which resulted in the outside police paying a visit. After a number of arguments with the screws, and Lindsay and I telling them we had nothing to say to the police, we were asked whether we had attacked him because we knew he was in for raping a woman in Cardiff. He was another one running around making out he was in for robbery, when it turned out he was really a nonce.

No charges were brought against us and he was sent back to normal location on another wing. He was a heroin dealer and he paid his merry men to come over with quite a big gang, but we were soon down the stairs to confront them. Lindsay fought like fuck and one bloke came at me with a blade, but he lost his footing and fell right by me, so I pulled out the shiv, and, placing it against his heart, told him to fuck off. He scurried back on all fours and disappeared into the crowd on the spur.

Lindsay had a few screws on him, but he threw them off and ran at the bloke whose head had just been rebuilt. One of the screws had been slashed across the arm and called for me. I went after the slasher, knowing it was the bloke I had warned earlier, but he ran into a cell and locked himself inside. The bloke whose head was rebuilt had his head caved in again, and his mates dragged him into a cell and locked the door to stop us getting at him. Lindsay was taken to the block and I went back up to the landing to clean up, but the screws came for me and took me to the block as well.

They had taken quite a few of the blokes we had been fighting with to the block, and one of them came to my window when he was on exercise and asked the score. As far as I was concerned, it was just a misunderstanding, but I told him that if I saw the main instigator on the landing, I was going to do him pretty bad. We all agreed that we wouldn't say anything when in front of the Governor, but the main shit-stirrer decided to stay down the block for his own protection. Lindsay had to be charged as he had been caught fighting on camera.

The next day, the door opened and a number of screws were there, telling me I wasn't being nicked and saying that I could go back up on the wing. It seems that the screw who had been slashed would have been slashed further if I hadn't run after his attacker, but I refused to leave the block without Lindsay. The screw asked me why I wouldn't go without my brother, so I told him that my mother said I mustn't. There wasn't much he could say to that, so he just laughed and closed the door.

I was soon up in front of the Governor for refusing a direct order. He had a trainee Governor sitting in on the adjudication and two screws stood behind me as I was given my charge. When the screw got to the point where I had said what my mother said, the Governor put his newspaper in front of his face and was laughing like hell. The two screws began laughing too, along with the screw who read out the charge.

The poor trainee Governor sat with a straight face, wondering what was going on, which made everyone laugh even louder.

The Governor assured me that Lindsay would be following me up to the wing as soon as he was charged. Still laughing, he said that if he was in the same position as Lindsay and me, his mother would probably say the same thing regarding his brother.

Our parties began to quieten down to a more reserved drink in the evenings, but one evening I drank so much after the door shut I must have passed out. Lindsay, being a little concerned, asked the screws to come and check me out, but when I didn't respond to them they, too, became concerned and strapped me onto a stretcher and took me off to the hospital wing. An outside doctor came in and told the screws that I was pissed and asked what nightclub had I been to. They looked at each other, rather hacked off, and asked the doctor what they should do with me. She told them to put me to bed on the ward and keep an eye on me.

The next morning, I woke up in the block with one hell of a hangover, and when the door opened, the screws stood there laughing and asked me about my good night out. When I got back to the wing, everyone on the landing said they thought I'd been taken off for dead. A day or two later, the two screws who had taken me to the prison hospital told me that they had been just about to eat their curry, and when they were taking me to the hospital, they turned the stretcher upside down so that my hair was sweeping the floor, in revenge for missing their hot curry. Of course, it was all in jest: they could have nicked me if they'd wanted, so we all ended up laughing over the incident.

After a few days, Lindsay and I were called to the office and told that they had found a Category C prison that would take us both together.

However, there was a slight problem: HMP Littlehey was known to take in a number of nonces. After having a long talk, Lindsay and I decided that the only way to get home leave was to give it a go. We knew we didn't need to talk to the people there and it would only be a matter of time before we got to a Category D, which was a much easier jail again, so we told the screws we would go for it. The paperwork was put in motion and it was just a case of waiting for a date to be moved.

Lindsay and I knew we were on our way to a Cat C prison.

20

UNFINISHED BUSINESS

Lindsay and I were packed ready for our move to Littlehey prison and hadn't realised the amount of gear we had accumulated during our time at Long Lartin. We had eight prison travelling boxes each, and the stores lads had given us two dozen prison tracksuits, just in case we couldn't wear our own clothes.

We were overwhelmed by how many of the lads came in asking us to stay. Even the PO, Minty, off our wing asked us to stay, using the offer of him trying for home leave for us as an incentive. But we both knew we needed a change and as we loaded up our trolleys ready to be taken to reception, all the lads shook our hands and bade us farewell.

Then we were off, with Lindsay pulling the trolley as he'd done years previously when we had walked onto that very same wing. As we walked through the grounds to the reception area, we took one last look at F wing, and saw many hands waving and heard shouts of, 'Take care, both.'

We were taken to a holding prison, HMP Onley, Warwickshire,
Littlehey screws were waiting to pick us up for our journey to
When we arrived there, we were put in a big cell with
prisoners. Some were just starting their
was one big-headed bastard who thought
saying, 'Shut up, you prat. Save your
banged up for the night.' I
mouth shut, knowing
and that would be

After a few hours, the Littlehey screws turned up, but when they saw how many boxes we had, they refused to take them. They were right horrible fuckers and I could see myself heading back to Long Lartin.

The screws from the holding jail told Littlehey screws that they couldn't leave our gear, so reluctantly they allowed it onto the bus. We had to stop at two other jails on the way to drop off other prisoners, and as the bus pulled into the first stop, one young lad wanted a piss, but when he asked the screw, he was told to fuck off and sit down. I could see the lad was desperate and in pain, and if it was me I would have pissed on the bus, so I got to my feet and asked the same screw if I could have a piss. He could see by looking at me that I wasn't going to take any of his shit, so he allowed me, and the young lad, to go by the side of the bus.

After dropping everyone off, Lindsay and I, and a number of others, were on our way to Littlehey, and I was hoping we would go through reception fairly quickly as it had been a long day.

When we arrived at the gatehouse, Lindsay and I could see the prison had recently been built and there were no big walls, just a fence with razor wire around the top. We were asked a few questions in reception, then one of the screws began going on about Lindsay and me being Welsh, and started muttering something about sheep. That was it, my back was up, so I went right up to his face and said, 'We fuck them; you fucking eat them; and if you talk to me like you talk to these nonce fuckers here, I will take your fucking eye out.' Without giving me any more bollocks, he walked off.

Another screw asked us to strip down and put on a boiler suit, which set me off again, and I told him that I was a prisoner, not a fucking … Then I told him that we had prison-issue tracksuits and … ned it he told us that they were not … t. I put my own clothes back on … eir fucking block or send me …

… y had between them, they … e were put in a cell, and … d up, glad to get our …

… t about canteen … d association. … ged up until … ore bang- … osed to … hoice other than to put up with it in order to try and get home leave and then move to a D Cat.

I looked upon all the prisoners as nonces, so didn't talk to any of the fuckers.

I took advantage of the shower facilities on association, but one day, while I was running the shower, I'd hung my towel on the door when three blokes came in.

One said he wanted my shampoo, but I knew what it was about. I had been in the system long enough to know what I had in front of me, so I started laughing like hell. They looked a touch bemused, obviously not used to the reaction I was giving them, and one asked, 'What's so fucking funny?' I pointed to the main one and said, 'Your mates are going to be wearing you now, so take your little nonce arses and fuck off.' He answered, a little too quickly, I thought, 'I am not a nonce,' to which I replied, 'You will be with your head up your mate's arse.'

They were soon gone, and when I got back to the cell, Lindsay asked what I had been doing, talking to the three blokes in the shower.

'Educating them, Linds,' I told him.

'Oh right,' he replied.

When we'd arrived we'd left biggest part of our belongings in reception, so I went to the office to see if I could be taken to get my music system in order to listen to the radio in the cell. The SO refused and told me it wasn't allowed, but he added that I could buy one out of his catalogue. I stood there thinking he was having me on, but he wasn't, he was quite serious. Out of curiosity I asked him about the commission and he was more than happy to tell me that he made a nice profit. If it wasn't for the HMP on his shoulders, I'd have thought I was in one of those jails they have in America – the ones you see on TV.

The screws had taken our belts off us at reception, so Lindsay used a pair of white laces as braces. I would laugh, seeing him with his makeshift braces, and everyone else must have thought he was the hillbilly from Wales.

Lindsay and I would sometimes lean on the rails outside our cell, and watch as bullies got bullied by bullies. It looked like everyone was getting slapped while the screws looked on. We passed many an hour watching the fights, and saw the bullies taking things from the weaker ones. If it had been a normal jail, I probably would have sorted a few of them ou
but knowing they were all nonces I kept out of it. In fact, I rather en
the entertainment.

We decided to use the phone, but one bloke was on it fo
a load of bollocks to someone. So I went onto the next
the same thing, as well as a long queue. It was pissi

back to my cell to calm down. After an hour, I went back and, on seeing the queue had gone, I thought I would soon be making my call, but when I got to the phone the same bloke was on it. I just grabbed him, wrapped the phone cable around his neck and began strangling the little shit. I could hear whoever he was talking to saying, 'Hello, hello,' but I took no notice and rammed his head against the wall then beat him with the phone.

I'd had it with the jail, so I went down to the office and asked them to get me out of there. They told me that once I was off induction, things would get better and even more so once we had a job.

Lindsay and I applied to the education department and I signed up for one of the Law classes while Lindsay chose another class. But one day when I was in the class I couldn't believe what I was hearing: nonces were passing their case papers around and talking about what they had done. That was it! I got up, walked to the classroom where Lindsay was and told him, 'Come on, we re off.'

Then I asked the screw to let me off the education block, but he refused. I told him that he could either let me off, or I would take my pick of any nonce and cave his fucking head in, then he would have to open the door. Without any hesitation, he opened the door and told us to go back to our wing.

The place was getting me down. The screws were all nonce lovers, which I found difficult to understand. They seemed to have more of a problem with Lindsay and me being Welsh than being surrounded by nonces.

When we were out on exercise, we walked around the opposite way to all the others. We hated them so much we didn't even want to be seen walking the same way as them. Back on the wing, I noticed an empty cell. I asked a screw to open the door, so that I could get a chair, but he told me it wasn't allowed. Then, as I was walking away, a nonce came along and asked him the same thing, and the screw immediately opened the door and let him take the chair.

While I was waiting for my canteen, one nonce told me to be careful with the screws as they had already killed someone who was giving them grief, but I just told the nonce never to talk to me again. We had learned to use our fear to keep us on our guard and in some ways we even ...rned to enjoy our fear.

work... knocking back the classes, we were taken on a tour of the building ...which had all the modern facilities, from paint shops to facilities, an... ...stering. A screw was showing everyone around the of the offices. ...dered away from the group I found myself in one

The screws knew the nonces wouldn't answer them back for fear of being sent to prisons where they weren't looked on so favourably, so when a screw said, 'Jump', the nonce asked, 'How high?'

Lindsay and I decided to have a game on the snooker table, but every time we went to the office to book it we were told it was booked for the day. So, first thing in the morning, as soon as the cell door opened, I went down to the office and managed to book the snooker table for a morning game.

Lindsay and I were chatting in the cell when a bloke came to the door and told us that we had upset a few men who were regulars on the tables. Lindsay got off his bed and slammed the head into the cheeky bastard, breaking his nose. Lindsay then walked onto the landing and told everyone on the ground floor that if they had a problem, they were to meet us in the recess and we would sort it out, but they all bowed their heads and slunk off to their cells.

I went to the office and asked to be returned to Long Lartin, but was told that, due to a shortage of places, we could not transfer back.

We found that some screws were beginning to busy themselves with petty issues, and on things we were entitled to. They were still refusing to let us have our radio from the stores, so Lindsay decided to put in a Request and Complaint form, which was standard practice in prison if a prisoner felt he wasn't getting anywhere with the screws on his wing. If they couldn't resolve the problem, it went to Governor level.

We had the right to write the form in Welsh or English, so Lindsay wrote it in Welsh, knowing that it would have to go out of the office to be translated and would reach a Governor before the SO on the wing. When he handed in the form, the SO looked at it and asked Lindsay what it was, so Lindsay explained his right to write in Welsh. The SO crumpled it up and threw it in the bin, telling Lindsay he didn't recognise the country, its language or its people.

Lindsay walked out and came up to the cell to tell me what had happened and I was soon up off my bed, telling Lindsay to watch my back as I went straight to the office and asked the SO what he thought he was playing at. He started giving me lip. He really thought he was someone, but the screws with him walked out, leaving him on his own. They knew what he had done was wrong. I was ready to do him there and then, but as he realised he was on his own, I could see he'd lost his bottle and he started dribbling and pleading with me not to hit him, so I left the tosser and decided to go from another angle.

I wrote a letter to the leader of Plaid Cymru, Mr Daffydd Wigley, and when I took it to the office, I told them that the letter was sealed under rule 37a. The SO knew I was going to take it further, and as I pointed my finger close to his face, I told him that if he pissed me off any more I would do him over bad.

I was called into the PO's office. He knew what the SO had said and decided to let Lindsay and me move off the induction wing. But, of course, there was a catch, which was that we had to work in one of their factories. We agreed, hoping things would pick up on the other wing, and we could have single cells.

The next day we were allocated a job making shoes, and we learned that they were not for prison-issue but for Marks and Spencer.

Lindsay and I decided to get on with the job, hoping things would get better.

We were still hearing rumours that a number of screws had topped someone and, in view of their arrogance, I knew we had to be on our guard.

One of the civilian screws came to us asking why we didn't have steel toe cap boots on, as we were employed under the 1966 Factories Act. He also said that if we didn't have any he would nick us. I took him to one side and told him that I didn't like him or his fucking jail and, if he nicked me, I would break his fucking back. He said he would let us go and get boots from the stores, so off we went, glad to get out of the shithole.

As we were nearing the stores, we could see nonces walking out with boxes of brand new boots, so we told them we wanted boots to work in the factory. To my disbelief, they put out two pairs of the mankiest boots they could find. I asked them if they were taking the piss, but the slags knew what they were doing, so I threw the boots at them, making them run to the back of the stores.

That was it. I was done and I wasn't taking any more.

After dinner, Lindsay and I were called to the office and asked to go back to work, but we both refused. Then, from somewhere, they dug out a screw who claimed to be Welsh – obviously a traitor to the nation. He told us that if we didn't go back to work we would be nicked, so I told him that we would also be nicked without safety boots. When he said that the boots weren't that bad, I offered to swap them for his but, of course, he wasn't prepared to do that, so I told him where to go and went back to my cell.

I packed everything in preparation to go down the block, but that afternoon we were left alone. For some reason, I was getting a buzz out of the screws showing their dislike of our Welsh background and, strangely, one screw in particular – the main instigator – was of mixed race, so I thought he would have known better. I knew we were walking on dodgy ground, especially with the rumours flying around about them topping someone, but if I were to retaliate I knew I would take one of the slags with me and Lindsay had the same view.

The next morning, Lindsay and I were called into the office by a PO assistant Governor who began talking to us like they talked to the nonces. Lindsay started blowing a gasket and told the PO that if he carried on talking down to him, he was going to knock him through the plate-glass window, and I am sure I heard Lindsay say that he was going to chop his fucking head off. The PO started shouting at Lindsay that he was nicked, but Lindsay was shouting back at him telling him to put us down the block. I just sat laughing at them having a right go, but none of the other screws came to his aid, so the PO began to lose his bottle. Lindsay told him again to fuck right off and arrange for us to go down the block, before storming off to his cell.

I was still laughing and could see the PO shaking with rage, so I said that Lindsay was having a bad day. But then he started talking down to me. I grabbed him by the throat and told him we knew about what they had done to another prisoner and, that unlike Lindsay, I wouldn't be giving him an idle threat, and if he sent his bully boys after us, it would be arranged for someone to have him on the outside.

That shut him right up, so I went back to my cell before we both headed to the block, rang the bell and asked to be let in. But the block screws looked confused and told us to fuck off. Then a number of our wing screws turned up and asked us to return to the wing or they would nick us. We told them to go ahead; they could either nick us for refusing a direct order, or for battering them. In the end they nicked us for refusing to go back to the wing and we were promptly let into the block.

For the first few days in the block, the screws showed their hostility to us, but after realising we were not nonces, and that we hated being around the dirty, stinking fuckers, they began to have a bit more sympathy. We soon had a number of Governors paying us visits, not for anything in particular, just asking us if we had wellies, which of course was a reference to the sheep in Wales, but I found it quite amusing, especially as it was coming from as high as a Governor.

I knew that if they were going to do us it would have been done by then, but I had every makeshift weapon that I could possibly construct and knew Lindsay had the same. If anything was to go off, I would make sure it would be fatal for as many as I could.

They also decided to have us nicked for refusing to wear boots in the factory, so in our defence I wrote our case, stating that under the Factories Act, wearing second hand boots, which could be defective from wear and tear, could cost thousands in damages if toes or feet were lost in an accident. Also, from a dermatological point, they were unsatisfactory and could spread disease.

Our adjudication came up, with Lindsay going in first to state his case, but he wasn't long and I was called up in front of a woman Governor by the name of McAllister. From the beginning I could see she was a horrible bastard, and after I had stated my case she had to have a think, no doubt hoping to produce another brain cell.

She asked whether, if she gave Lindsay and me new boots, we would be prepared to go up on the wing. If it had been a decent prison I would have agreed, but I pointed out that if she had decided to give us new boots, then we had been right from the start and the adjudication was a farce. Also, nicking us for refusing to go back to the wing was a load of bollocks, as it was our right as prisoners to go to the block. There was a strange twist to the situation, as usually nonces are down the block to keep away from the normal prisoners. Here, we wanted to stay down the block away from a jail full of stinkers.

The Governor sat thinking for a moment, obviously mulling over what I'd said, then suddenly she went into a rage. She was like a raving banshee, and I thought, 'Keep your hair on, love, or you'll end up bursting a blood vessel.' Even the screws seemed shocked by her outburst.

Shouting and screaming, she told me that she was going to send Lindsay and me as far away from Wales as she possibly could. Then, spitting bolts, she told the screws to take me back to my cell. I heard them going for Lindsay then heard her tell him the same as she had told me.

In a way I was relieved to be getting out of the shithole, and as prison rules stood, we should have been moved to another Category C prison. I knew Long Lartin wasn't going to happen, so I could only wait and wonder which prison would be as far away from Wales as possible. The block screws allowed me to talk to Lindsay from the shower room while he was on exercise, and we agreed to ring our parents as soon as we reached another jail. We both knew that some screws up to Governor level weren't to be trusted and there was no telling what they may try to do. We had to keep our wits about us and never let our guard down for a second.

I was first to leave, and as soon as I was cuffed up, I was in the van and on my way, with my belongings to follow at a later date. As soon as we were on the road, I could see we were heading towards London and I thought they were taking me to Wandsworth prison. I knew from the prison grapevine that Wandsworth was where many prisoners would have the shit kicked out of them and be left for dead down the block. It had also been rumoured that Winston Green prison in Birmingham was the same, and that in those two jails, prisoners would be bumped off and it was made to look like an accident.

How true the rumours were I didn't know, but I knew that if I was in for a booting I would clock each and every face, so that if I survived I would hunt them down and dish out my natural law.

My concern soon evaporated when we reached the M25 as, even though the screws weren't saying anything, the further we travelled the more I was convinced I wasn't going to a London prison.

As we came off the M25 and headed towards Kent, we were joined by a police escort, although why it was needed I don't know. I had very close friends in the Dartford area and, with my thoughts running away with me yet again, I wondered if I might be going to the same prison as Reggie in Maidstone. However, we passed Maidstone and I watched as the police escort took another route and we headed towards the Isle of Sheppy. It was then that I remembered Swaleside prison.

We crossed a small bridge to the Isle of Sheppy and I knew it was unlikely I would be on normal location after coming from the block at Littlehey. I knew I could still be due a kicking, but decided to play it by ear. When the prison came into sight, I looked at the signpost and noticed that there were three prisons on the island: Swaleside was a B Cat; another one was a C Cat; and the last one was a D Cat.

'Just my luck,' I thought, as we turned into the gatehouse of HMP Swaleside.

As I had arrived without my belongings, I was given a bed pack and taken to the block, but, due to overcrowding, what they termed the block was the ground floor landing of a normal wing, but with paper furniture. The cell was no different from the block.

I was allowed to make a phone call and found out that Lindsay hadn't rung anyone, so I assumed he was still at Littlehey.

The cons were rushing around in preparation for the night-time bang-up, and as I looked around, it appeared that I was the only honky there. The only prisoners I could see were black blokes, sorting out their last deals of the night.

The next morning I was greeted with hostility from the screws, and I've no doubt they had received a little message from Littlehey. I was told that I was one of only two white blokes on the wing, but I didn't really give a fuck what colour people were, I was just relieved to be around proper criminals instead of dirty, stinking nonces.

I made a phone call and found out that Lindsay had telephoned our family to tell them he was on the move, destination unknown.

The other white bloke came to my cell for a chat and a cup of tea, and we both laughed as he,too, was Welsh and lived only a few miles from my hometown.

As with every race, colour or creed, there is always a bully lurking in the midst waiting for his next victim, and I had one opposite my cell. I found it strange that he was kept banged up while my door was opened for a shower, but he kept giving me the big one and demanding this and that, so I got two metal mirrors and smashed the spyhole glass, and told him that if he put his fucking face by it again while gobbing me, I would ram a pencil straight through his fucking eye.

After making another phone call to our family back in Wales, I was told that Lindsay had been taken to HMP Albany, on the Isle of Wight. The Governor at Littlehey had kept her word and had sent Lindsay and me as far away from Wales as she possibly could. However, being out of Littlehey was a Godsend.

A couple of prisoners who had just been sentenced, named Ray and Trevor, were brought in one evening and put in cells near me.

Even though I was in for what was termed a temporary block, my door was opened in the evening, along with the rest of the wing, while we were on association. However, I still had the same paper furniture as those in the block, so after making a few enquiries I was moved to a cell with the normal cell cupboards and table. It was like moving to a state-of-the-art flat. It's still strange how the little things mattered.

Just as I was settling into my new cell, I was moved over to another spur, and, after washing the cell out, I sat on my bed relaxing with a mug of tea. Then the door opened, no knock first, and in walked a black bloke who demanded that I give him tobacco and belongings out of my cell. He was a typical bully boy, and as I got to my feet I told him to slam the door shut and that only one of us would be walking out through it. As I walked towards him, he ran like the wind through the door and, in temper, I shouted down the spur, 'Come back again and I will cut your fucking throat, you black bastard.'

Every door on the spur opened and heads started popping out to see what the shouting was about. And as I looked at them I saw that not one head was white.

New rules were coming in every year, and one rule at Swaleside was that every prisoner had to do a week's study with a test on health and safety, which Ray and I passed with distinction, getting top marks.

The piss tests were taken quite seriously, and being marched to the block, then made to stand and piss in front of a screw, was humiliating. It was beginning to annoy those who didn't bother with any drugs. Our praise for having a negative result was a certificate which was signed by the Governor, but most of them were photocopies.

Heroin was so widespread throughout the system that those who smoked weed were considered old fashioned. They were also taking one hell of a risk with the drug testing being so frequent.

Prisons had changed dramatically over the years, and heroin addicts were being sent straight from prison onto the streets. This bumped up the crime rate to such an extent that ex-prisoners with no jobs turned to crime more frequently in order to fund their habits. The increase in the number of prisoners going back to jail could be clearly seen, and it was obvious that the system had failed them.

I applied for a cleaning job in the servery hall, mainly to get out of my cell and, due to more rules, I had to take a course for a week on the use of the buffers which were used to polish the floors. Although I had used buffers many years previously at Cardiff prison, I was amazed to learn quite a lot about the use of different cleaning fluids.

Ray and Trevor were moved to different wings, so I would meet up with them on the big field where we would share a flask of tea and a chat.

With 18 months left to serve on the whole of my sentence, I was asked to apply for parole and, of course, parole is for those who are guilty of their crimes, but I was told that if I said I was guilty and addressed my offending behaviour, I stood a very good chance of getting parole and being released on licence. So that was the end of that. I resigned myself to doing the full term, and expected nothing from the system. I was then told I couldn't get home leave due to the same rule of not recognising my guilt. I knew that if the rule was correct, there was no need to have gone to a Category C prison.

I eventually heard from Daffydd Wigley of Plaid Cymru. He had passed my letter on to his colleague, Ilfydd Lloyd, who was another waste of time. So much for their 'Free Wales' slogan, when they allowed Welsh prisoners to be sent to jails at the far end of the country. I knew it was a case of getting my head down and finishing the sentence.

Lindsay was in touch regularly, and different lads coming to Swaleside would tell me that he was causing quite a stir in Albany, so I thought I would try and work on getting him up with me. He had tried other jails which were off the Island, but it appeared that Littlehey had put a black mark on our paperwork.

After all the drinking at Long Lartin, I decided to take advantage of the gym and was pleased that the prison catered for boxers and had equipment such as bags and skipping ropes.

After a few rounds on the bags, some of the lads considered themselves boxers, although they'd never been in a ring in their lives. I watched as they hit the bags and hurt their hands, so I started correcting them, and teaching them what I had learned in my boxing days, and could see an improvement from the first day.

There was one set of sparring gloves, so they asked if they could try a touch of sparring and I agreed. I wore the sparring gloves, as the first lad sparred with me wearing bag gloves, an idea which would never have been contemplated in any gym.

As soon as we started, the young lad, in his early twenties, thought he was in a bout, and, just as I had experienced with some of the lads in my own boxing gym, the more experienced boxers are able to see the venom within the person they spar with. I didn't realise how out of condition I was, and the young chap was soon over me like a rash. So, not wanting to hurt him, I drove a massive blow to his stomach which took the wind right out of him.

After I brought him round, I taught him to spar in the proper fashion, and found I had quite a few lads taking an interest, with many telling me they wanted to take up the sport when they were released.

I slowly began to get in shape and trained hard in my cell.

The time was moving at such a rapid pace, I was beginning to see the end of the sentence, something I'd never been able to do in the past. I made enquiries about moving Lindsay to Swaleside, and found that the black mark which Littlehey had put by our names was a load of bollocks and a number of screws at Swaleside agreed.

I had taken my complaint to the prison ombudsman, pointing out that we should not have been sent to Category B prisons, and putting Lindsay and me on different islands proved how vindictive that particular Governor was.

It was finally agreed that Lindsay could come to Swaleside, so I moved up two landings to the 3s where there were a number of empty cells, and I washed one out in preparation, so that Lindsay would have little to do on his arrival apart from making up his bed. We hadn't seen each other for almost a year and I knew most of the lads on our wing, many who became good friends, were looking forward to meeting him.

Lindsay soon arrived and after introducing him to Shaun and Steve, we spent the evening catching up, chatting and laughing about past incidents.

Lindsay was given my job, so he, too, had to do the week's training course, while I was asked to do a job in the officers' mess, giving me enhanced status.

We decided to move over onto the drug-free wing, where Lindsay was given the job of cleaning the prisoners' kitchen and I had the job of keeping the stairs clean.

We were on the same wing as Ray, and we would spend our spare time passing legal chat back and forth, in preparation for further appeals.

I spent a lot of time reading and Lindsay became friendly with a

Turkish chap named Rick, as they both had the same interest, playing the guitar.

Rick, like many of the other nationalities in prison, asked what we were doing in a prison so far away from Wales, as he thought we should have been in a Welsh prison. Many found our answers hard to understand, and thought it was disgusting that Welsh women prisoners have no prison facilities in Wales, leaving them with no choice about going to prisons in the English system. After my experience at Littlehey and their prejudice towards the Welsh, I could see their point.

With under a year left of our sentence, we were coming up to another Christmas and I was fighting our case in the High Court by way of judicial review. I had been knocked back on my parole because I wouldn't recognise my guilt, and refused go on courses to deal with my offending behaviour. I wanted the prison system to recognise that those who are innocent in prison need not apply for parole, and should be told that they have to do their full term.

In a way I was lucky, as I had a date for my release, but prisoners who were sentenced to life and protested their innocence were in a worse predicament, which I felt was wrong. It felt strange that I had a judicial review taking Michael Howard, the Home Secretary, to the High Court, and I passed him on the stairs when he was visiting the drug rehab, which was a closed spur on our wing.

With the last of the Christmases out of the way, we were months away from release. We hadn't seen our families since being in Long Lartin, and the prison had no system to prepare us for our release.

I woke one morning with a big lump on the side of my head. It wasn't a boil or anything like that, so I promptly went to see the doctor who said that he would remove it in a number of weeks. I thought, 'Bollocks to that. I'm not walking out of the gates looking as if I'm growing another head.' I told Lindsay what the doctor had said and that I wasn't happy with the time it would take to remove it, so I decided to remove it myself over the dinner period. I broke open a number of new razorblades, and put them in a bowl of hot water to sterilise them. Then I began my operation. I made one cut downwards and the other left to right and, with blood everywhere, I peeled open my incisions to reveal the lump. Then, using another blade, I began cutting underneath the lump, removed it and placed it in the sink for further inspection.

With the dinner bang-up over, Lindsay walked through the door and saw me looking like a surgeon with a difference, operating on myself. With blood all over the place, I smiled and told Lindsay my operation had been successful. After taping up the wound and covering it with a small dressing, I began to examine the lump and was satisfied that it was like a gristle globule, so I was more than happy with my self-operation. After a few days, my wound was healing nicely and looked as though I wouldn't have a scar.

We discovered that we had a number of weeks back, which we had lost throughout our sentence, so our release date was 14 February – Valentine's Day.

As we sat in our cells for the last night, it didn't really sink in that the next day we would be free men. We had finally reached the light at the end of the tunnel and began giving away many of our items to those friends who had become like family over the months.

We had spent almost five and a half years locked up, on the bullshit of police officers and people we'd considered friends.

As Lindsay and I went through the same old ritual at reception, being given money and a train ticket to anywhere in the country, we silently walked to those great big doors, which are the prisoner's enemy when starting a sentence, but now were the beautiful, pearly gates to our freedom.

I heard a screw shout, 'Release the door,' and listened as the electric clicked in, putting the door in motion. As it slowly slid open, Lindsay and I took one step forward. We were the only ones being released that day and, as we stepped into freedom, the door clicked into reverse, closing behind us as we stood taking in the fresh air. Lindsay looked at me and smiled.

'Where are we going then?' he asked, with a big grin on his face.

I shrugged my shoulders.

'Wales?' he asked, his smile turning to a laugh.

'Why not?' I said, patting him on the back.

'We have some unfinished business,' we both said, smiling.